Architectural Britain:

The Saxon Period to the Present Day

Architectural Britain:

The Saxon Period to the Present Day

Hubert Pragnell

 THE NATIONAL TRUST

Dedication

To Dorothea, who accepts that for me architecture is more important than a hot meal but who likes the Gherkin; Charlotte, who sympathizes with her mother when I rush off to look at a building, and Christian, who likes Canary Wharf and anything taller.

First published in the United Kingdom in 2007 by
National Trust Books
10 Southcombe Street
London W14 0RA

An imprint of Anova Books Company Ltd

Designed by Mark Holt and Lee-May Lim

ISBN-13 9781905400492

A CIP catalogue record for this book is available from the British Library.

10 9 8 7 6 5 4 3 2 1

Reproduction by Spectrum Colour Ltd
Printed and bound by SNP Leefung Printers Limited, China

www.anovabooks.com

Page 2: Greenwich; view from Observatory Hill with Queen's House in foreground, Inigo Jones, c 1616–37; former Royal Naval Hospital beyond, c.1694–1750; and the Canary Wharf development in the distance started in 1988.

Contents

Foreword by Ptolemy Dean

One of the greatest pleasures of life is the 'reading' of historic buildings. By 'reading' one might mean the recognition of a particular building's age and development from its physical appearance. This might be the form of the structure, its construction, or the shape and size of the window and door openings. There are many qualities to be spotted, but even at first glance much is apparent and can begin to explain a building's age and development. They are the visible clues as to how it was designed and why, and from which we can begin to assess a building's historic and architectural significance. It is an undeniably satisfying process passing through places and understanding, through the unfolding sequence of buildings, how they evolved, and at what periods this development appears at its most intense. In a way our built inheritance is the best visual diary that our forebears have passed down to us.

This is the true language of architecture, with all the different local and regional traditions, which like our linguistic dialects, provide a flavour that is specific to any particular place. The only real way to learn any language is through reading, and in the case of a visual language such as architecture, this means looking. It is appropriate therefore that the author of this book has spent time looking and drawing historic buildings of all ages. The process of drawing provides a way of distilling and refining what gives them their essential and character defining qualities. The finished drawings can also express more succinctly than photographs the important visual signals that we need to look out for in the buildings that surround us.

The more people who can read and enjoy historic architecture, the more importance architecture will be given in our society. We live in an increasingly fast and distracted age when people have less and less time to look and see, and consequently to understand the rich heritage of the past that surrounds us. It is very easy to be blinded by the value of change and progress often justified in terms of economics and pragmatism. This is why books such as this are not only physically appealing but of such importance.

Introduction

We can learn much about a period of history from the study of architecture, especially in the case where little in the way of written evidence or other visual artefacts survives. A church represents the spiritual aspirations of a local community; a cathedral may show the results of endowments by clergy, nobility and even pilgrims who came to pray at the shrine of a saint. The ruins of an abbey such as Fountains, Jedburgh or Tintern speak of the strength of medieval monasticism. Westminster Abbey, which fortunately survived the Reformation, was both monastic and coronation church, as well as the destination for pilgrims to the shrine of Saint Edmund the Confessor. Its lavish royal tombs and chantry chapels display medieval dynastic connections as well as being remarkable works of medieval sculpture and decoration. Others, such as Tewkesbury and Malmesbury, were handed to the townsfolk to become a parish church although the conventual buildings of both were destroyed.

Domestic houses come in many forms, from the humble cottage to the nobleman's mansion. For obvious reasons the former is likely to be insubstantial and easily destroyed by man or nature. The latter might have played a part in the diplomatic and social power struggle between families aspiring to royal or political favour, or asserting the simple maxim that wealth demands size. Such grandiose buildings as those built during the Tudor period were often a royal reward for support during the royal struggles with the Church, and were even constructed from material sacked from a monastery—Burghley house is one example.

This book cannot claim to be comprehensive in coverage, but presents nevertheless a broad outline of the main phases of architectural development from the Saxon period to the present day.

Styles overlap in period and, like fashions, often seem to go round in circles, returning in revived forms. So we have medieval Gothic and 19th-century Gothic; or 18th-century Queen Anne and early 20th-century revival. Building materials also vary from region to region: flint churches are common in eastern England but not in the north, granite is used in Cornwall, and yellow limestone in the Cotswolds. Half-timbered cottages are common in Kent, Sussex, Cheshire and Shropshire, but not in Derbyshire where stone is more common. Streets of London-clay brick terraced houses are found in London and south-east England, but in Lancashire the terraces are of limestone, or millstone grit. Stone-clad warehouses of the 19th century are a feature of large ports and industrial centres, but not of English south coast resorts.

Frequently the history of architecture features only the finest examples of architectural development, especially so in the field of domestic building. Oxburgh Hall, Norfolk, is romantic, constructed in pinkish brick and adorned with battlemented turrets and ornamented chimneys; however, the near contemporary cruck cottage in Didbrook, Gloucestershire, also has a place in the story of architecture. The formal grandeur of Bath or Edinburgh new town or the Gothic villas of north Oxford have immediate appeal, but there is much to be observed in the variety of terraced house from a later 19th-century suburb such as London's Islington or Fulham.

An architectural history of Britain would not be complete without reference to Canterbury Cathedral or King's College Chapel, Cambridge, or indeed Strawberry Hill. Because of their significance in the development of architecture in the 17th century I have devoted separate chapters to Jones and Wren. In the case of the latter, whose contribution to the rebuilding of post-fire London was considerable, my choice of examples must be limited and the selection of drawings even more so. As the story arrives at the present century so the movements and examples become so numerous that it is often impossible to make more than a brief mention or passing reference, and my choice of examples must by necessity be selective.

It is often necessary to represent a building from several angles in order to convey a true impression. Occasionally a drawing may have an advantage over a photograph in that detail can be emphasized, or the drawing may comprise several different viewpoints. On the other hand, an aerial photograph may give us an immediate understanding of a complex plan such as that of Hampton Court, or the former Royal Naval Hospital at Greenwich. I am very conscious that certain areas receive only a brief mention; our industrial heritage deserves far more space, after all who can fail to be moved by the Ironbridge in Shropshire, or Templeton's Carpet Factory in Glasgow. It is to the credit of local authorities that former warehouses and mills are now thought to be worthy of conservation.

As with a study of the history of painting, the best experience is to study in front of the actual example. A good reproduction of Monet's *Thames at Westminster* (1870) may look impressive, but seeing the original offers a totally fresh light—the paintwork is alive. Similarly, to visit Barry and Pugin's Houses of Parliament gives one a feel of size and drama unobtainable from pictures. Standing before the giant Romanesque west front of Lincoln Cathedral at dusk on a winter's day is a magical experience and well repays any exhaustion from the climb up the hill.

We must also remember that a building, whether it be a cathedral, parish church or country house may have only assumed its present appearance over several decades, or even several centuries. A cathedral or parish church may have grown over the years to accommodate an increasing population, or increasing numbers of pilgrims, or may have been expanded through endowments to accommodate a family burial. A great house might have gone through several major reconstructions or expansions in its history, perhaps now appearing Jacobean on the outside but with Adam, or even Gothic, interiors. It might have a medieval core, 18th-century living rooms and a 19th-century library— all set within 17th-century walls.

This poses the sometimes vexing question: in which period do we place a building? Restorers faced by this dilemma include those working for English Heritage at the Queen's House, Greenwich or for the National Trust at Chastleton, Oxfordshire, or those who restored the apartments damaged by fire at Windsor Castle in 1992. The study of a specific building can be a challenge and the exact sequence of development is often difficult to follow, not least when the building incorporates the various stylistic revivals. A fire, as in the case of that which damaged Uppark in 1989, poses a particular challenge to restoration and conservation teams, but one from which much can be learned and likely applied on future occasions.

Britons are fortunate in having an architectural heritage which dates back through many centuries and spreads the length and breadth of Great Britain. In more recent decades television has brought British heritage much more into the public eye. In the 1970s series *Spirit of the Age* eight distinguished architectural historians took viewers on a journey from the Normans to the present, calling at Lincoln Cathedral and St Pancras Station on the way. In 1985 the late Alec Clifton Taylor accompanied viewers on walks around *Six English Towns*, introducing the great variety of building materials as well as providing a personal critique of some examples of urban planning. The Open University has also produced some excellent programmes on British heritage. Various adaptations of classic novels, for both film and television, have given viewers glimpses of great British houses such as Belton House, Lyme Park, Sudbury Hall and the streets of Lacock village, which featured in *Pride and Prejudice*. Also the splendid *Buildings of England* series of books, started by Nikolaus Pevsner in the early 1950s, has encouraged many a weekend explorer on foot, and more recently the series has been extended to cover the whole of Britain and Northern Ireland.

This book is also written as an invitation to go out and explore. What we may have for long accepted as familiar and part of our daily 'visual furniture' may take on a new dimension as we try to unravel the phases of building: sometimes the back of the building may be totally different from the front, as an examination of the streets of York will show. Perhaps not all parish churches are as complex as St John's, Burford, Oxfordshire but many repay time spent on a visit, and even a simple Norman church such as St Mary at Brook in Kent may surprise us with its wall paintings. If on the other hand you want to encompass the breadth of architectural development from the Norman to the present day without walking more than a mile, the City of London is the place. Starting at Temple Bar and ending at Aldgate, it may come as a surprise to find how many older buildings still survive.

I would like to thank the National Trust for having faith in this venture and for giving me the opportunity to indulge my passion for exploring buildings; Ian Fisher for his helpful comments, especially about aspects of Scottish architecture and for casting a critical eye over the text; Edward Holland for discussing aspects of Welsh architecture with me; Tim Jennings for suggesting improvements to the illustrations; Annie Lee for casting a very critical eye over the manuscript; Karen Dolan and Tina Persaud at Batsford for their encouragement and advice, and my wife Dorothea, who allowed me to rush off to look at buildings and become a semi-recluse when at home writing.

London: Nine hundred years and nine hundred yards apart, the White Tower, c.1080, with the Swiss Re Building beyond, c. 2000

1

Saxon and Norman Architecture

While most general histories of Britain begin with the coming of the
Romans in AD 43 and the first permanent settlement, it is not possible
to trace a continuous architectural story. True our knowledge of
everyday life increases with archaeological excavation, and we have
considerable knowledge of the layout of major settlements, military
sites, and villas such as Fishbourne. However there are no substantial
remains above ground level of buildings as such, apart from Hadrian's
Wall and the northern gateway at Lincoln. We know that the Romans
built temples, amphitheatres and markets, but we do not have their
complete structural appearance, as do some continental cities, such as
the basilica and Porta Nigra in Trier, Germany, for example.
Christianity also flourished in Britain for a short period after the
Constantine decree of about AD 312 that forbade persecution of
believers; in 314 bishops from both London and York attended the
first Council of Arles. With the withdrawal of the legions between
about 370 and 410 Britain lay open to invasion and destruction by
Angles, Saxons and Jutes. Civilisation as we know it came to a halt
and the settlements of the invaders may indeed have been outside the
former Roman towns. Even London is thought to have been
uninhabited for a period. Britain's architectural history essentially
begins with the Christian mission sent by Pope Gregory in 597,
culminating in Augustine's installation as archbishop of Canterbury,
though the Christian site of Iona in the Inner Hebrides predates this
by some 34 years.

Why did Canterbury become the base for the Latin mission?
According to the Venerable Bede, when Augustine arrived there were
at least two Roman churches in the vicinity of Canterbury that could
be restored for worship. One of these was St Martin's, which was used

Opposite: Iffley, Oxford. West
front of Norman church,
c. 1161.

by Bertha, the French-born Christian Queen of Kent, married to King Ethelbert. It was through Bertha that Augustine was given refuge, and allowed to build a monastery dedicated to Saints Peter and Paul outside the city walls. Within the walls, he was permitted to patch up a building for purposes of worship, which became the site of the later cathedrals. Eadmer the Singer, a chronicler writing in the 1060s, described this building as 'arranged in some parts in imitation of the Church of the blessed Prince of the Apostles' (that is, St. Peter's, Rome). What Eadmer saw was in fact a later church, which was much later excavated, in 1993, under the nave of the present cathedral. This church, destroyed to make way for the Norman Cathedral of Lanfranc in 1070, was about 46 metres (150 feet) in length with an apse at both ends. Tall westwork (the west-facing monumental entrance) with flanking towers divided the western apse from the nave, while a square tower divided the monks' choir from the presbytery and an eastern apse and aisles flanked the nave—so creating a basilican plan. The church had features in common with surviving German Romanesque churches, such as that at Gernrode.

The churches built in the immediate decades after Augustine's arrival cannot have been as grand. Indeed architecture was no rival to the minor arts in Dark Age Britain if we take as evidence the illumination in the Book of Kells, produced at Iona, the Lindisfarne Gospels, or such treasures of jewellery and gold and silver metal-work as those found at Kingston Down, in Kent, and Sutton Hoo, in Suffolk. We might also remember that the Anglo-Saxon kingdoms that eventually emerged from several centuries of pillage and destruction also produced great literature, such as *Beowulf* and the first record of historical events in the Anglo Saxon Chronicle. We also owe the foundations of the British legal system to laws promulgated during the Saxon period.

We know that Augustine's other church at Canterbury, which became his Benedictine abbey, was at first a small affair in the form of a rectangle with smaller chambers, or 'porticus', arranged around it. These chambers were intended for the burial of St Augustine, on the north side, and the Kentish royal family, on the south. The inner rectangle was divided by a wall between the nave and chancel; a narthex, or porch, was later added to the west front, and buildings, probably at first in wood, were set out around a cloister to the north. A short distance to the east was another smaller church, dedicated to St Mary. In 1049, inspired by a circular structure at Saint Benigne, at Dijon, Abbot Wulfric connected this smaller church to Augustine's by means of a rotunda. But in the 1070s all of this was swept away to make room for the large Norman abbey.

Apart from the wood-constructed nave of Greensted church in Essex our knowledge of Saxon church building is confined to stone structures. Yet large tracts of England were under forest, so wood must have been the preferred material where stone was not readily available. Certainly the general population lived in wooden houses or

Greensted-Justa-Ongar, Essex: 10th-century original nave of split timbers incorporated within later reconstruction. The chancel is built of brick.

huts, and literature of the time records feasting in large wooden halls: traces of a large royal building have been uncovered at Cheddar in Somerset. Many of the stone churches that do survive are from the 7th century rather than the later period after the Danish invasions of the 9th century when St Dunstan, Abbot of Glastonbury, set about reforming the English Church.

It appears that church building types differed between the south and north of the country. At Reculver, on the coast about eight miles north of Canterbury, there are the remains of another very early church referred to in the Anglo Saxon Chronicle in AD 669 as 'given by King Egbert of Kent to Bassa his Mass priest, to build a minster'. The original church was in the form of a rectangular body, or nave, about 11 metres (37 feet) long and 7 metres (24 feet) wide, surrounded on the north, south and west by chambers, or porticus. At the east of the building was an apsidal chancel, divided from the nave by three arches supported on columns. The size of these columns may be gauged by examining the comparable examples in Canterbury Cathedral crypt. In front of the central arch stood a carved standing cross embedded in concrete, fragments of which are also preserved in Canterbury Cathedral.

Another exposed early church is that of St Peter, Bradwell-on-Sea, Essex, which dates from about 653. Built of rubble stone, perhaps from a Roman camp, it looks from a distance like a large shed. On closer examination there is evidence of north and south chapels or porticus having once existed, as well as a western porch covering the door. The eastern apsidal projection has disappeared, but evidence survives in the blocked up wall of triple arches, similar to those that would have divided the nave and chancel at Reculver. Also in Kent, there is evidence of an eastern arch division at the church of St Mary and St Ethelburga, Lyminge.

The most impressive surviving pre-conquest church is that at Brixworth, Northamptonshire, which was built largely from reused Roman brick by monks of Peterborough, in about 675. The nave consists of four large blocked arches that originally opened into porticus. Above the beautifully gauged brickwork surrounding the

arches are clerestory windows. At the east end are traces of piers supporting a triple arcade leading to a square presbytery, acting as a choir or sanctuary, in front of a polygonal apse. At the west end is a two-storey porch which led to an upper gallery. This porch was later extended into a tower (perhaps in the 10th century, although the present structure is later) and a circular turret stair was added to the west facade to provide access.

At Earls Barton, also in Northamptonshire, there remains a remarkable tower dating from about 1000; the rest of the church was subsequently rebuilt. The tower is square and built in four stages;

Sompting, Sussex:
Early 11th-century so-called
Rhenish helm tower.

it is probably constructed from rubble stone covered with mortar, while the corners are clasped with so-called long and short work of vertical stone blocks divided by horizontal stone insertions. Each face of the tower is divided by vertical strips and short diagonals, and one wonders if perhaps the builders knew of the much more sophisticated decoration of diagonal strips on the 9th century entrance gatehouse to the abbey of Lorsch, in the Rhineland. At intervals the tower is pierced with semi-circular headed openings, supported on short bulbous columns. A similar strip decoration can be found on the tower at Barton-on-Humber, Lincolnshire, while the tower of St Michael in the Cornmarket, Oxford has comparable treatment of openings in its upper stage, although the surface is rubble stone. In Sussex, at Sompting, a tall Rhenish helm tower, also dating from about 1000, provides a convincing link with continental trends in the Rhineland.

In the West Country the most interesting Saxon church is the little chapel of St Lawrence, Bradford-on-Avon, probably dating from the 8th century. It is of a cruciform plan in that the short rectangular nave and chancel originally had a short north and south porch, but the latter has since disappeared. Here there seems to be the influence of antique remains from nearby Bath, with an attempt at semi-circular arched blind arcading on the nave and chancel. Inside, the arch leading into the chancel is moulded, and there is an attempt at crude fluting in the jamb pier of the north porch, leading to the nave. The building only survived because it was absorbed into a cottage until its rediscovery in 1856.

Although the pre-conquest cathedral at Canterbury is supposed to have had a crypt, surviving examples are rare. The three extant examples are at Hexham and Ripon, both built by Bishop Wilfred of York from about 700 in the form of rectangular chambers, and at Repton, Derbyshire. The vault at Repton is held up by columns that look as if they have been bound tightly with rope to create spiral bulges; at first sight the capitals look as if the craftsman had seen Classical Doric examples, although these are crude by comparison.

If Kent was the springboard for the Latin mission to re-Christianize Britain, it was in northern England, after the Synod of

Whitby in 663 and the supremacy of the Latin over the Celtic church, that the monasteries of Jarrow and Monkwearmouth became centres of scholarship under the Venerable Bede. Surviving examples of early churches in the north indicate they were often built to simple two-cell plans with a rectangular east end, and there is only rare evidence of porticus or inside chambers. At Jarrow the church, St Paul's, dedicated by Benedict Biscop in 685, comprised a rectangular nave with apsidal east end, later extended into a rectangle. The wall still contains primitive round-headed windows. At both Jarrow and the associated monastic church of St Peter's, at Monkwearmouth, the plans were simple two-cell structures, with the Monkwearmouth church incorporating a tall tower at the west end. A virtually unaltered example of a northern Saxon church remains at Escomb, the only later addition being the insertion of several narrow windows. Here, the entrance is through a porch at the south west corner, while

Bradford-on-Avon, Wiltshire: Chapel of St Lawrence c. 8th century, complete apart from southern porch.

inside the chancel arch is flanked with long and short blocks, with the arch springing from a projecting block that cannot in any way be classed as a capital.

There are numerous other examples of Saxon features incorporated into substantial later reconstruction, almost to the point of being hidden. At Breamore, Hampshire, for example, a Saxon central tower with short transept arms is flanked by later medieval nave and chancel. As we have already seen, enclosed chambers called 'porticus', probably used for distinguished burials, ran along the sides of the nave in early churches. Being enclosed, these chambers could not be classed as an aisle. The aisle, a continuous passage divided from a central vessel by piers or columns, was introduced into Christian church planning from pagan basilicas from the fourth century; however, it does not appear to have been developed in Britain until the eleventh century. A surviving example of a Saxon aisled church is Great Paxton, Cambridgeshire, which has splendid wall piers dressed with long, thin pillars.

By the time the Normans arrived the Church was firmly established with a system of diocese, which survived until the Reformation, and a pattern of country parishes that has lasted to the present day. Probably there were large buildings, especially monasteries, that were damaged by successive Danish invasions, although there was nothing to compare in terms of size, grandeur of craftsmanship or decoration with the Romanesque churches of the Rhineland. For example, the court at Winchester could not compare in architectural terms with that at Aachen or Mainz. However, while history books mark 1066 as the time of the Norman arrival, they had in some senses arrived some time earlier, and this date simply marks the beginning of their permanent occupation: there had been trade and cultural influence before 1066, and Westminster Abbey, founded in 1050, was virtually a Norman building by its completion in 1065.

The Anglo-Norman Romanesque style is not only distinctive but seemingly almost impervious to destruction by the normal passage of time. Often only deliberate demolition has rendered a building less than complete. These buildings were built to last and were often

Cardiff: Castle with remains of
Shell keep on 11th-century
motte.

London: White Tower, c 1080. Although heavily restored in the 18th century it remains the finest example of a Norman keep in England. It is also the earliest in stone and was supervised by Gundulf, Bishop of Rochester. He used Kentish ragstone for most of the exterior wall surface although harder limestone from Caen was shipped across the Channel for dressing buttresses and surrounds to windows.

extremely substantial with walls of cut-stone blocks filled with rubble over one metre (three feet) thick. The style can be said to have been evolved in Normandy over the previous one hundred years, with a strong influence from regions as diverse as Lombardy, Burgundy and the Rhineland, and brought to maturity in Great Britain. Examples can be seen from Cornwall in the south-west to Dunfermline Abbey in Scotland and Kirkwall Cathedral in the Orkney Islands.

Following their arrival by force, the Normans spent the first few decades of their occupation securing the defensive needs of the country, as well as reforming the Church. This involved the dismissal of the Saxon clergy, including Stigand, Archbishop of Canterbury, and the rebuilding of major cathedrals and monastic foundations. As in many periods of history, piety seemed to go hand-in-hand with a firm military rule, and this fact can be demonstrated no better than by examining Norman castles.

The most famous castles are the Tower of London and those at Rochester and Dover, which are all, as is typical, situated at major strategic points in order to guard against invasion or civil unrest. Some castles may have been constructed on the sites of earlier wooden Saxon fortifications, such as that at Pevensey, depicted on the Bayeaux Tapestry, and were initially rebuilt in wood. The castle at Porchester, Hampshire, consists of a rectangular enclosure within the original Roman camp, while Old Sarum, in Wiltshire, was raised within the Iron Age hill fort and was later to be a source of friction with the nearby cathedral. By about 1100 the stronghold at the centre of the fortified enclosure known as the keep or donjon was being rebuilt in stone. The White Tower at the heart of the Tower of London may date from the 1080s, but the stone curtain walls with rectangular and semi-circular mural towers were built during the 13th century, and are pre-dated by those at Dover castle, which are among the earliest.

Norman keeps were often raised on an artificial hill known as a motte and enclosed by walls to form a bailey or precinct. Beyond the walls there would have been a wet moat, as for example at the Tower of London, although in many examples, such as Rochester, Dover, Durham and Goodrich, there would instead have been a deep ditch cut into the subsoil or rock, providing a hurdle for any would-be assailant. Keeps were of three basic types: rectangular, circular or shell (as at Windsor) and angular (as at Orford, Suffolk, and Conisborough, Yorkshire). The rectangular type might be up to 27 metres (90 feet) high and would have contained accommodation for the retainer and his family as well as quarters for the garrison. The White Tower at the Tower of London still retains its hall and impressive chapel, the latter being responsible for the apsidal projection at the south-east corner, rising to the full height of the keep. The chapel also created an apsidal projection at one corner of Colchester castle, where the keep is constructed of re-used Roman brick. Contrary to popular belief, a dungeon may simply have been a strong-room or cell in an ancillary building rather than the cellars of a keep, which may have been used for storage and might also have contained a well.

Walls were generally very thick and filled with a rubble core. The White Tower was faced with rough Kentish ragstone, with its buttresses, battlements and windows dressed with smoothly-cut Caen stone. At the south-east corner of the tower the wall bulges into a semicircular apse in order to accommodate the eastern termination of the chapel. The base of the Tower, as in other Norman keeps, is splayed to give additional stability as well as extra defence. Those keeps that survive in a good condition are generally preserved at the core of extensive enlargements. With the decline of the castle, others were frequently used for building material.

The Norman contribution to church building was immense; standing in the nave of Durham Cathedral gives one the feeling that it was built to last for all time. The building is massive and austere and, with the exception of the addition of the eastern 'Chapel of the Nine Altars', in about 1230, there has been little internal alteration since completion in about 1135. The cathedral, which was part of a Benedictine abbey, is cruciform in plan with two western towers and

Durham Cathedral: the nave from the south aisle c.1100.

a central tower over the crossing, which was subsequently rebuilt. As in many Norman churches, the external walls are divided by strip buttresses and pierced by small semi-circular arched windows. Entry to the nave is through a deeply recessed arched doorway on the north side. The interior is divided into bays by piers with vertical shafts rising from the pavement to the springing of the vault. Each bay is divided into three stages, a feature common to all Norman greater churches that evolved from the abbey at Jumièges and the churches of Caen. The lowest bay is the nave arcade, above which is the cruciform, and then the clerestory within the curve of the vault. Sometimes, as for example at Ely, these divisions were almost equal in height. At Durham the lowest bay is divided by immense circular drum pillars incised with chevron, spiral and diamond patterns. Similar features can be seen at Dunfermline, Selby and Waltham abbeys.

Canterbury Cathedral, c.1100: capitals in the western crypt.

Unlike other Norman greater churches, Durham was rib-vaulted and we can see the introduction of pointed transverse arches, probably the earliest in Europe, perhaps a decade earlier than St Ambrogio in Milan and Speyer in Germany. Peterborough Cathedral retains its original wooden nave ceiling, more typical of a Norman interior. Side aisles were often groin-vaulted on a quadripartite plan (each bay divided into four sections by the vaulted ribs). Durham also has the earliest example of flying buttressing in Britain, although in this case it is hidden beneath the side aisle roofs.

Although the Norman style appears austere by later standards, it is renowned for the high quality of its decoration and incised carving. Popular decoration includes chevron, beak-head, cable and billet. Capitals were of the unmoulded cushion variety beneath a projected abacus (the slab forming the top of the capital), or deeply incised with foliated patterns or strange creatures that were a mixture of bird, animal and monster. Sometimes these creatures, as in the crypt at Canterbury Cathedral, play musical instruments, while the curving designs of leaves and intersecting strap patterns are probably derived from contemporary goldsmiths' work. A popular form of wall decoration was blind arcading, made up of continuous single arches or intersecting arches.

There are hundreds of existing parish churches with substantial Norman work and some, for example Barfreston, in Kent, and Kilpeck, in Herefordshire, remain virtually unchanged. These churches are built to simple two-cell plans consisting of an aisle-less nave and chancel, increasingly entered through a south porch rather than the west front. At the east end Barfreston, for example, is square, whereas Kilpeck has an apse. Some of these churches preserve an original single-cell plan and one of the most unchanged is that at Winterborne Tomson, Dorset, which dates from c. 1090 and is built of local rubble stone. Here even the apsidal chancel is without a window. The only external alteration is the piercing of the south wall with three larger windows, undertaken in the fifteenth century. Crypts are rare but several do survive. Due to steeply sloping ground the two-cell church at Dutisbourne Rous, Gloucestershire, has a crypt under the chancel that is entered from the churchyard. The most impressive church crypt, however, is the three-aisled example at Lastingham, Yorkshire, which was begun in 1078; its windows are small for fear of weakening the wall structure. The chancel at Barfreston has a blind arcade linking its narrow windows.

Often the most decorative part of a church is the doorway, which may be deeply recessed and flanked by jamb shafts and surmounted by a carved tympanum. At Barfreston, amid the other strange carvings, we find Samson opening a lion's jaw, a bear playing a harp and a monkey with a rabbit. On the centre of the tympanum sits Christ with his hand raised in blessing, as in contemporary

Kilpeck, Herefordshire: church with typical Norman apsidal termination to the chancel.

Romanesque churches in France. The south door at Kilpeck is surrounded by reddish sandstone carvings of animals, birds and monsters, perhaps suggesting the theme of creation. The door jambs depict Eden, with man being tempted by the fruit from the Tree of Life. Both churches also have strange heads carved on to the corbel blocks beneath the eaves of the roof.

Some Norman churches had a small bellcot rising from the west gable or a square western tower. In Norfolk and Suffolk, where the ground was soft or waterlogged, builders resorted to constructing circular towers of flint bonded in mortar and pierced with narrow openings. St Margaret, Hales, Norfolk, is a fine example. By the mid-12th century churches had become more grand, with an increasing number of cruciform plans incorporating a squat tower above the crossing, sometimes allowing a choir area between the nave and chancel. Occasionally the tower was inserted, but without transepts, as at Iffley, Oxford, and Studland, Dorset. While at Iffley the tower is richly embellished with bands of semi-circular headed arcading, at Studland it hardly rises above the level of the nave roof, and possibly was never completed due to insubstantial foundations.

Where side aisles or clerestory are in evidence it is likely that the church once formed part of a monastic complex that may even have been dissolved long before the Reformation.

The finest example of this is Melbourne, Derbyshire, for a time the seat of the Norman bishops of Carlisle. Here the plan is cruciform with flanking aisles, a central crossing supporting a tower and two western towers against the nave. The interior is like a miniature cathedral with the massive drum pillars supporting scalloped capitals and chevron decorated semi-circular arches. At the east end there were originally three apses, the arches of which now remain blocked in the walls. An unusual feature is the three-stage elevation with triforium and clerestory.

While in many churches the finest carving was reserved for the door jambs and tympanum, sometimes the chancel arch was highly embellished, as at Tickencote, Rutland, with its impressive six bands of concentric semicircles displaying hundreds of beak-head motifs.

Tewkesbury, Gloucestershire: the west front of the former Abbey church c.1100.

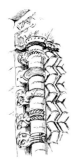

Norman ornament: Chevron and dog-tooth (Romsey Abbey, Hampshire); cable (Ely, Cambridgeshire); beak head (Lincoln); billet (Canterbury).

Each band is supported by a jamb-shaft, or pier, and is a magnificent illustration of the thickness of some Norman walls. The west front of Tickencote is dressed with bands of blind arches and intersecting blind arcading, possibly as the result of some rather inaccurate restoration in the 1790s.

During the 12th century the circular church plan was introduced in England for the churches of the Knights Templars or, to give the Christian military order its full name, the 'Poor Fellow-Soldiers of Christ and the Temple of Solomon'. This plan replicated that of the Church of the Holy Sepulchre, in Jerusalem. Three such churches survive in Britain, although they have all been subject to later extensions and heavy restoration: they are St Sepulchre, Cambridge, Holy Sepulchre, Northampton, and the Temple Church, London. St Sepulchre was built c. 1130, with a central cell supported on massive drum pillars surrounded by a low ambulatory, and a small chancel built on to the north end. Holy Sepulchre has been virtually rebuilt above arcade level, with pointed arches. The Temple Church in London is the most famous example as it also serves as the chapel for the members of the Middle and Inner Temple Inns of Court. It was consecrated in 1185 by Heraclius, Patriarch of Jerusalem, and demonstrates the architectural advances since the building of the Cambridge church: the piers are slender and of polished marble with rings of annulets dividing the shafts; the Arcade is pointed and above, forming a narrow triforium, is a band of intersecting arches; finally, light is admitted through round-headed windows that form a clerestory in the upper shell. But for the richly carved west door entered beneath a later porch we might think we have arrived at the Gothic. Beyond the Round, housing effigies on the floor of associate knights in full armour, is the triple-aisled vaulted chancel added in about 1240, which displays triple-lancet windows in each bay. Severely damaged by bombing during World War II, the church has been magnificently restored.

Few examples of domestic architecture from this period survive, since most houses must have been of timber infilled with wattle and mud, and straw daub. Stone was expensive and used only by rich merchants, in particular by the Jewish community: there are records of stone houses in London, Winchester, Canterbury, Norwich, Lincoln and Southampton. Two houses from the Jewish community in Lincoln survive on Steep Hill. Their basic construction is similar: the ground floor was used for storage, an arched doorway allowed access to the rear with a staircase to the upper storey, which was a communal hall. One, the so-called Jew's House (c. 1150), is similar to a surviving 12th-century house in Cluny, Burgundy—even down to the positioning of a chimney over the ground-floor entrance. Windows were small, twin-arched openings on the upper floor, with slits for the storage space below. Another stone building in Lincoln is the St Mary's Guild House (c. 1180). This has a moulded semi-circular central entrance, and the facade was strengthened by strip buttresses. The upper hall floor has been largely destroyed, so today we see only about half its original elevation. Southampton has the remains of another stone house, known as King John's House but dating from about 1150, some 16 years before the king was born. Little survives in this case, apart from an outstanding fireplace.

Lincoln: The Jew's House,
c. 1150. Dotted lines represent
later alterations, including the
insertion of shop fronts.

2

The Transition to Gothic

It is hard to pinpoint a precise date for the adoption of the Gothic in Britain. The features that make up the style—pointed arches, ribbed vaults and flying buttressing—were first seen at Durham Cathedral, from 1093, yet this building has the weight and solidity of a Romanesque cathedral. The fully developed style employed these features but reduced them to structure-bearing devices, so that the walls could be pierced by openings of ever-increasing proportion. This process began in France in the quire of the Abbey of St Denis, outside Paris, in the 1140s and reached maturity in the cathedral of Notre Dame, Paris, in about 1200.

In Britain, the transition was more gradual. The most frequently found feature was the pointed lancet arch; however, ribbed vaulting and exposed flying buttressing were first found in the reconstructed quire of Canterbury Cathedral after 1174. The pointed arch has the obvious advantage of directing pressure either side of its centre and towards the point of a wall, where it can be supported by a buttress. Adoption of the pointed arch feature spread across France, Germany, Italy and Britain through the influence of religious orders, in particular the Cistercian order, which oversaw the building of churches influenced by their existing monastic houses in Burgundy. Fountains Abbey, Yorkshire, under construction in stone for the Cistercian order from the 1140s onwards, reveals a two-stage elevation with a pointed arcade that is supported on drum pillars in the nave. However, it differs from Burgundian examples in having a clerestory and, originally, a wooden roof instead of a stone barrel vault. The crossing was also covered by a low tower, common in Benedictine establishments but in contravention of the Cistercian rule governing towers. At Kirkstall Abbey, now in a suburb of Leeds, the

Opposite page: Fountains Abbey, Yorkshire: The West Front c. 1175 with the arch of a later window. The tower to the left is c. 1490.

drum pillar was abandoned in favour of the compound pier with clustered shafts forming an eight-point star. The aisle bays were also covered with ribbed vaults, instead of the lateral barrel vaults characteristic of Burgundian architecture, and also found at Fountains Abbey. Roche Abbey near Sheffield, founded in 1147, shows a striking structural advance in the introduction of a triforium stage of blind arches between the lower arcade and clerestory, and also rib vaulting throughout, supported on shafts rising from the pavement.

Since the second half of the 12th century was a great age of monastic building, especially among the orders seeking solitude (not only the Cistercians, but also the Augustinians and Premonstratensians), it is possible that much important transitional work during this period took place, but was lost as a result of the Reformation and the consequent sacking of monasteries. Indeed, Byland Abbey, another Yorkshire Cistercian house, which at the time of its consecration in 1195 was the longest church in England, has sometimes been called the first truly English Gothic building. Byland remains as an impressive ruin, with its west front incorporating a large wheel-window standing jagged against the skyline. However, it was the French cathedrals of Noyon, Laon, Sens and Chartres that really forced the transition and had an influence on English cathedrals such as Canterbury, Durham, Rochester, Worcester and Hereford (all Benedictine communities) and Chichester, Lincoln and Wells (administered by secular canons).

In September 1174 the quire of Canterbury Cathedral was destroyed by fire. This was interpreted by the monks of Christ Church Priory as a message from God, telling them to build a new church worthy of the shrine of Becket (at that time buried beneath the small Trinity Chapel projecting from the east of the choir). The monks brought over William of Sens, who had supervised the rebuilding of Sens Cathedral in the 1160s. The quire, eastern crypt, Trinity Chapel and Corona were completed by about 1190, and show a lightness of construction which is new. Naturally, the quire is very French in feeling: the paired columns, the double arches in the triforium and the sexpartite rib vaulting are all similar to those in

Opposite (top): Canterbury Cathedral: the east end of Trinity Chapel showing the transition from Romanesque to early Gothic. In the lower right corner is the 15th-century St Edward's Chapel.

Trinity Chapel c. 1185–9, showing apsidal termination. The paired pillars supporting early use of pointed arches The shrine of Becket stood here from 1220–1538.

Above: Byland Abbey, Yorkshire: the original floor tiles in front of the side aisle altar, c. 1200.

Sens. The apsidal east end also has a French feel, with the external
appearance of the windows showing a mixture of pointed and semi-
circular headed arches.

A more definite adoption of the Gothic style can be seen in
Chichester Cathedral, built in the 1190s, with its pointed arches and
deep bands of moulding. Piers and columns are also dressed with
detached marble columns that are anchored by their capitals and
bases to the pier or column. At Rochester Cathedral the quire has a
fine array of lancet arches, although the elevation is of only two stages
with no intermediate triforium. The shafts dividing the bays rise from
the pavement to the springing of the vault, which starts at about the
midpoint of the upper, clerestory stage; as at Canterbury, the vault is
sexpartite. At both Canterbury and Rochester we also see the
introduction of another popular repetitive ornament known as the
dog tooth, which gradually supplanted the chevron of the Norman
style.

The cathedral that best exemplifies the change from Norman to an
English adaptation of Gothic is Lincoln, rebuilt from about 1195
following an earthquake that damaged the Romanesque building, of
which only the west front now remains. Here we find not only lancet
windows but also the evolution of plate and bar tracery, brought over
from France. The vaulting introduces additional ribs, creating the
effect of an avenue of trees with their branches linked across the
centre. Lincoln definitely has that feeling of lightness associated with
Gothic. Advanced as it is, the cathedral also retains a feature from the
French influence on British development: sexpartite vaulting in the
western transepts. Lincoln's development was to take it through the
Early English period to the dawn of the Decorated style in the 14th
century.

In Scotland, the transition from Romanesque to Gothic was helped
by the zeal of King David I (1124–53) who wished to bring Scotland
closer to Latin Christendom and create a sense of national identity.
He also wanted to block any claims made by the archbishops of York
to lands beyond the Tweed. Consequently, vast sums were spent on
church building until prolonged wars with England in the 14th

century diverted money to castle building. David's reign coincided with the dramatic spread of the monastic orders in England, not least the Cistercians. As Prince David he had founded a Benedictine community at Selkirk in 1113, which was later moved to Kelso, and as king he founded at least nine more monasteries. The first Benedictine priory was Dunfermline, founded by Queen Margaret in 1070 with monks from Canterbury. She was buried there in 1123 and a few years later, in 1128, King David re-founded the community as an abbey and royal palace, using masons from Durham to rebuild it. The first Cistercian house was Melrose, founded in 1136 as a daughter-house of Rievaulx, in Yorkshire. The Augustinian canons built a number of major houses including Holyrood, in 1128, which is now incorporated into the royal palace at Edinburgh, and Jedburgh, in 1138. Although these communities adopted the layout of conventional buildings, common across Europe and first set out in a surviving parchment plan from St Gall, Switzerland, that dates from c. 800, the Scottish monastic churches were generally smaller than their English counterparts and rarely received a large income from pilgrimages to a saint's shrine, as was common in England. (The two exceptions were Dunfermline and St Andrews, the latter refounded in about 1145 by King David I of Scotland to serve as a cathedral and priory of Augustinian canons.) Even though the quality of craftsmanship was extremely fine these churches were on a simple cruciform plan with a square eastern choir or chancel, and the crossing crowned by a squat tower. At the Augustinian Abbey of Jedburgh, founded by King David in 1138 and built on a grand scale to match the English, the nave is nine bays in length and has three clearly defined stages with no intermediate vertical bay-division shaft. The lower arcade has piers with clustered shafts supporting water-leaf capitals. Above this, the triforium has paired openings beneath a moulded arch, the plate of which is pierced by a small circular opening. The clerestory, originally supporting a wooden roof, is pierced by a row of lancets. The choir to the east of the crossing has a somewhat different bay elevation in that the triforium is set within a two-storey arcade with chevron moulding, supported on massive drum pillars. This is unusual outside southern England but is found at Oxford Cathedral and Romsey Abbey, from where masons were possibly 'exported' to work at Jedburgh and elsewhere.

The Tironsian, or reformed Benedictine abbey at Kelso was the most impressive and richest of the Scottish monastic houses founded by King David in 1128. The abbey was also unique in having a double-cross plan: that is, the choir and nave both had a set of north and south transepts, each set with a tower at its crossing, and with projected westwork. The building therefore had two towers surmounted by low pyramids. The nave elevation was of three stages with the lower arcade supported by massive drum pillars and scalloped capitals. The division between arcade and triforium is marked by a cornice of chevron moulding. The triforium and clerestory are of equal height.

In parish church architecture the transition to Gothic was slower, and many Romanesque features were retained into the 13th century. For instance, at Barton-on-Humber, Lincolnshire, the Saxon tower adjoins a nave with an arcade of pointed arches on drum piers decorated with chevron patterned carving. At the Temple Church in London there is a fine Romanesque arched doorway leading into the Round, dedicated in 1185, with an arcade of pointed arches rising from Purbeck marble piers of clover-leaf pattern. Thin marble wall shafts rise through the bays at triforium and clerestory level to support a wooden ribbed vault. The Quire at Canterbury, then under construction, may have been an influence here.

3

The Gothic Cathedral

Just as thousands of parish churches survive in the Gothic style, so there are numerous cathedrals that remain as witnesses to the highest standards of medieval craftsmanship. Fortunately, most cathedrals were preserved at the Reformation to become seats of the dioceses of the Anglican Church; they were not subject to the destruction inflicted on the monastic churches, such as Fountains in Yorkshire and Tynemouth in Northumberland, both examples of the early adoption of the Gothic style. The only major medieval cathedral to be destroyed was St Paul's in London, and this was by fire in 1666.

The earliest pure Gothic cathedrals were Wells and Salisbury; the latter is an excellent example of a cathedral built wholly in one style. As the mother church of New Sarum, the town that had recently moved from its windswept and cramped site on the edge of Salisbury Plain, construction of Salisbury Cathedral was started in 1220, on a new site. This meant that there was no need (as for example at Canterbury and Lincoln) to build over, or on to, existing remains. The building's plan is cruciform, with double transepts and a square eastern termination in a low Lady Chapel rather than an apse with radiating chapels as in its contemporary, Rheims. Most of the stone is local from quarries at Chilmark in south Wiltshire.

As one enters through the north porch one senses that very English characteristic—length, as opposed to height. One's eyes are drawn down the relatively low nave to the crossing beneath the tower and spire. The proportions of the elevation have changed: the lower

Opposite: Norwich Cathedral from the south east showing the Norman crossing tower with spire added 1464–72, and late 15th-century clerestory above the 12th-century quire. The flying buttresses were introduced to support the wall against the pressure of the vault.

Below: Salisbury Cathedral cloister c.1263–84: upper stage of tower and spire c.1330–70.

arcade is almost half the height and the triforium has been reduced as the clerestory grows in height to be pierced by triple lancet windows. The horizontality is more than usually emphasized by the lack of shafts between each bay (also the case in the nave of Wells Cathedral). Both Salisbury and Wells have simple quadripartite rib vaulting in nave and transepts, but the quire of Wells was rebuilt in the 14th century with the most advanced lierne pattern. Dramatic scissor arches were inserted to take the weight of the projected crossing tower.

Salisbury provides an excellent example of the use of clustered shafts of Purbeck marble against the piers, divided by annulets and surmounted by roll-moulded capitals. In the Lady Chapel the marble shafts are actually detached from the pier or central column. Externally, the bays are clearly marked by boldly projected buttressing, taking the pressure of the vaulting over the side aisles through a system of flyers. Internally, the weight of the tower is taken by strainer-arches, dating from c. 1460, that link the crossing piers against the transepts.

The interior of Salisbury was drastically restored by both James Wyatt (1746–1813) in c. 1790, and Gilbert Scott (1811–1878) in c. 1860, resulting in the destruction of chantry chapels, medieval glass, pavements, and the stone pulpitum at the entrance to the quire. This gives the cathedral today a rather severe and perhaps overly 'tidy' aspect. But while Salisbury was under its original construction, to be served by a bishop and chapter of secular canons, Westminster Abbey was under reconstruction, from 1245, in the more advanced Early English style, known as Geometrical but heavily indebted to Rheims and Amiens. It was Henry III's intention that Westminster should serve as the English coronation church and royal mausoleum.

One supposes that the master mason for the building, Henry of

Rheims, was a Frenchman, since Westminster's reconstruction resulted in a short quire with the French chevet ending, consisting of a number of polygonal chapels radiating beyond the ambulatory. The height is emphasized by the unbroken rise of the Purbeck marble shafts from pavement to vault spring at the base of the clerestory. The elevation is of three stages; lower arcade, narrow triforium and a clerestory of geometrical traceried windows, similar to those at Rheims. The richness of the work can be observed in the treatment of the spandrels of the arches of the pre-1270 work, which is decorated with a diaper pattern. By 1270 the transepts and four bays of the nave had been reconstructed before work was brought to a halt due to lack of funds. Work recommenced in about 1380, with the remaining bays of the nave being completed in a simplified form but close to the earlier work. Externally, the south wall of the nave is supported by a system of double flying buttresses which cover the south aisle and north cloister walk. It is only with the west window that we see the by then contemporary Gothic Perpendicular. (The west towers were only completed in the eighteenth century.) The chapter house at Westminster, rebuilt for the community of Benedictine monks in about 1253, beautifully exemplifies this development, with large windows filled with pointed arches of bar tracery supporting foiled circles or occuli, after the development at Rheims and Paris. The chapter house at Salisbury is close in detail to that at Westminster: both are octagonal, with a central column of clustered shafts supporting the ribbed vault.

The west front at Salisbury appears rather like a large screen placed across the nave and side aisles. It is without flanking towers, as in many other English examples, but is terminated by low spiralets.

Wells Cathedral: crossing strainer-arches to withstand the weight of the new tower, c. 1338.

The nave bay is filled with triple lancets, rather than a circular oculus as in French cathedral fronts. Also, little is made of the portals, which lack the magnificent carved gables, jambs and tympana of the French cathedrals. The Early English style can also be seen in many other cathedrals and monastic churches, among them York, Ripon and Beverley, Worcester, Peterborough, Southwark, Hexham, Tynemouth and Whitby.

In South Wales the original Norman construction of Llandaff Cathedral, Cardiff, was rebuilt in the early thirteenth century, with a long nave and short choir but no transeptal crossing. At the west front were two flanking towers. Internally the building had no triforium and was covered by a wooden roof. Unfortunately it partially collapsed in the fifteenth century and was severely damaged during the Civil War. Much restored in the 18th and 19th centuries, it was

Chapter houses.
Left: Westminster Abbey,
c.1253.

Right: Salisbury Cathedral,
c. 1263.

again severely damaged during World War II.

In Scotland, the Cathedral of Glasgow, dedicated to Saint Kentigern (Mungo), was rebuilt from 1136; nothing remains of this building because from about 1200 a further rebuilding was underway, with a new nave exhibiting the current state of Gothic development. The plan of the cathedral is rectangular and incorporates a crossing with short transepts within the perimeter of the aisle walls. The aisles continue round the east end of the choir as an ambulatory. With the ground dropping away steeply to the east, a vast undercroft or crypt was built beneath the choir, dating from about 1240. Here Bishop Bondington built a shrine over the presumed burial place of Kentigern, which became a major place of pilgrimage. The crypt has a magnificent array of piers with clustered shafts and stiff-leaf capitals from which spring ribs intersecting at large richly carved bosses, to form quadripartite patterned bays. Light is admitted through single and paired lancets in each bay. Also at ground or undercroft level is the Blackadder Aisle, built by Bishop Blackadder in the late 15th century, and displaying the flamboyant tracery of the period and richly carved pier capitals— this is the first and only part of the intended extension of the south transept, which was to have supported a large chapel above.

The nave, with its imposing lines of clustered shafts supporting the arcade, is basically of two stages with the clerestory of lancets combined with the panelling below. The west window has a geometrical tracery pattern, similar to tracery development at Lincoln Cathedral. The roof remains as a wooden open-timbered version, so there is little pressure on the outside walls. Beyond the 15th-century stone screen or pulpitum (the only one to survive in a major Scottish church), the choir has a triforium, similar to that at Lincoln, and a clerestory of lancets behind a gallery passage. As in the nave, it appears there was never any intention to introduce a stone vault; instead, the covering is a wooden barrel ceiling, again reducing the pressure on the walls. The disposition of the choir with ambulatory beyond the high altar recalls the similar termination at Wells, though in that case there is an extension into a retrochoir. The squat tower and spire over the crossing is 15th century, and the West Front was flanked by two

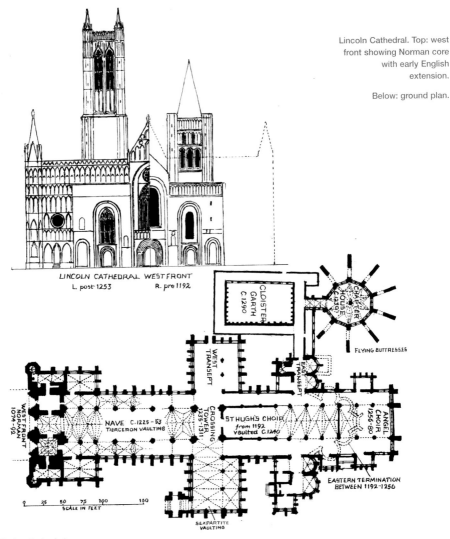

Lincoln Cathedral. Top: west front showing Norman core with early English extension.

Below: ground plan.

LINCOLN CATHEDRAL WEST FRONT
L. post-1253   R. pre 1192

CLOISTER GARTH C.1290

CHAPTER HOUSE C.1240

FLYING BUTTRESSES

WEST TRANSEPT

EAST TRANSEPT

WEST FRONT NORMAN 1074-92

NAVE C.1225-53
TIERCERON VAULTING

CROSSING TOWER 1235-1311

ST HUGH'S CHOIR from 1192 vaulted C.1240

ANGEL CHOIR 1256-80

EASTERN TERMINATION BETWEEN 1192-1256

SEXPARTITE VAULTING

0 25 50 75 100   150
SCALE IN FEET

towers (one of which remained incomplete) until their demolition in 1846. A late 15th-century square-planned chapter house survives at the north-east corner and is entered from the choir ambulatory.

About 130 miles north-west of Glasgow lies the island of Iona, the birthplace of Christianity on the British mainland with the coming of Columba and his monks in 563. Here the abbey, the burial place of early Scottish kings, was sacked by Viking raids and may have been abandoned for several centuries. In about 1200 it was rebuilt to a simple cruciform plan with low crossing tower but, unlike English monasteries, it remained quite small. The abbey survived until the Scottish Reformation in 1560. Extensively restored between 1902–10, the building we see today faithfully reproduces the church as it appeared in the 15th century. Externally it is without buttressing, as there is no internal vaulting. A further sense of austerity is added by the small dimension of the windows, which were perhaps influenced by Irish models; even the traceried windows of the south transept and the 15th-century choir are small. Inside, there are late Romanesque drum pillars against the south quire aisle and a finely embellished semi-circular headed arch on the north, now leading to a vestry. The cloister has been restored on the north side of the nave. As in Glasgow Cathedral there is sloping ground to the east which allowed for a low undercroft in the initial construction. However this undercroft was removed in the 15th century with the reorganization of the short quire, incorporating windows with flamboyant patterned tracery.

The cathedral church of Edinburgh is St Mary's, with all the appearance of a 13th century Gothic building but actually designed by Sir George Gilbert Scott (1874–79), and not St Giles, as many visitors assume. However, the church of St Giles did have cathedral status in 1634–39 and 1662–68. Although the earliest church on the site of St Giles was founded by monks of Lindisfarne in 854, it was subsequently rebuilt at least twice, in about 1120 and, after burning by the English army, in 1385. The plan is cruciform with a relatively low nave and chancel divided across the middle by transepts. There is no triforium and the clerestory is low. The ceiling is vaulted with a tierceron rib pattern, and in the nave this springs from corbels in the wall rather than shafts rising from the arcade pillars, which are polygonal and stout. The chancel vault, however, is supported on slender wall-shafts rising from just above the pier capitals and so giving more of a feeling of Gothic thrust. The square crossing tower, built in about 1480, is crowned by the crown-steeple formed by the flying buttresses springing from each corner that converge in the middle to support a slender spire. Heavily restored in the nineteenth century, the windows display fine examples of Flamboyant, or curvilinear, tracery.

By about 1300 the Gothic style had been fully assimilated in Britain. Previously lagging behind France in development, Britain now took the lead at a time when the great cathedral building campaign of the Ile-de-France area was largely over. The next phase of development is known as 'Decorated' and may be considered to have lasted for much of the 14th century. As the name implies, it was a period of rich ornamentation when much of the carving was highly naturalistic. But it was not a period of complete building so much as one of addition or alteration. Only one cathedral, Exeter, is largely in this style. Just as Lincoln's nave, choir and transepts herald the early Gothic, so in the same building's eastern extension—the so-called Angel Quire, of about 1280—we see the transition to the Decorated. The windows have geometrical tracery but the sides exhibit ball-flower ornament. The vault also seems more complex, with the introduction of tierceron and ridge ribs; this creates the sense of a stone forest of branches—an effect seen at its best in Exeter, which has the longest unbroken area of vaulting in Europe, running the length of both nave and quire. At Bristol Cathedral the introduction of lierne ribs to create a star-like pattern adds even more complexity. At York,

Iona Abbey, Argyle & Bute: the 13th-century Abbey reconstructed between 1902–10. On the right is St Oran's Chapel from about 1160.

INTERNAL VAULT LINE
CLERESTORY
TRIFORIUM
NAVE ARCADE
N. AISLE
NAVE
S. AISLE

Exeter Cathedral: west front, 1346–75. As at Salisbury, the buttressing against the nave is hidden by a screen of masonry. The western portal is relatively insignificant and is overwhelmed by tiers of figure sculpture.

the nave was rebuilt between 1291 and 1324, a wooden vault was constructed in the 1350s.

Window design of the period seems to know no bounds as the tracery twists and curves to form leaf and flame patterns, hence two other terms for the style: 'Flamboyant' and 'curvilinear'. Again this is seen at Exeter, in the large west front window, although the most impressive west front encasing a huge Flamboyant traceried window of the period belongs to York Minster. At Dorchester Abbey, Oxfordshire, the tracery curves into branches, to delineate the Tree of Jesse in coloured glass, while in the example at Canterbury Cathedral the window is cut out of the Norman wall of the St Andrew Chapel. Another form of window tracery of this period was 'reticulated', in

York Minster: west front, c. 1291–1345, a fine example of a Decorated style cathedral West Front.

York Minster. Top: ball-flower ornament. Below: pier with clustered shafts and roll-moulded capitals.

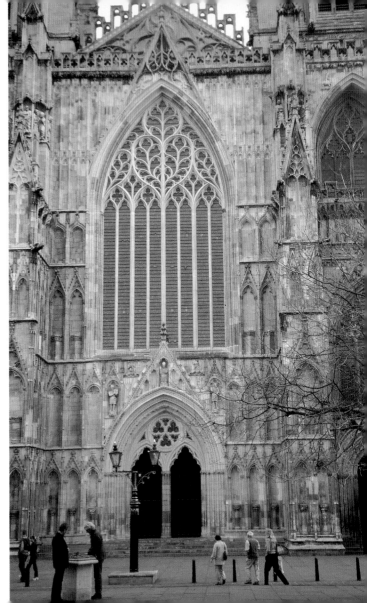

which the pattern resembles a spreading net, as in the Lady Chapel at Wells Cathedral.

Carved decoration moved forward from the stiffness of Early Gothic to a highly naturalistic and delicate phase. In Southwell Minster Chapter House the leaves seem to all but grow away from the capitals; a similar high standard of naturalistic carving occurs in York Minster Chapter House and its ambulatory, possibly hailing from the same workshop. This delicacy of carving can also be found on wall arcading, for example at Ely Cathedral Lady Chapel, and grand tomb canopies such as that of Lady Eleanor Percy in Beverley Minster. At Ely the all but detached Lady Chapel still exhibits a wonderful range of decoration in the wall arcading. Each bay is capped by an ogee arch, from the edge of which curving leaves seem to sprout. Unfortunately the figures, which include the Holy Family, angels and saints, were mutilated by the Puritans; what remains nevertheless bears adequate testimony to the virtuosity of the craftsmen, and traces of paint that survive on the decorations give an idea of this once colourful interior.

Externally, buttresses were often more than mere wall supports, displaying life-size figures set into canopied niches, and frequently

Southwell Minster, Nottinghamshire:
Top: four-leaf flower ornament.
Bottom: foliated capitals on chapter house entrance.

Left: Beverley Minster, Yorkshire: vault bosses from the mid-14th century.

Exeter Cathedral: decorated style nave, 14th century. The north and south Norman towers were retained and incorporated into the transeptal division between the nave and quire.

terminating in pinnacles sprouting foliated crockets. Parapets on walls were also filled with curving tracery, which when viewed from the ground gave them an added degree of delicacy. Sculpture rarely played a major part in the external treatment of English medieval cathedrals, although the west front of Wells had several hundred figures set into canopied niches, a number of which have been restored. At Exeter the west front has a band of figures representing ancient kings; these look rather awkward and certainly do not compare with those adorning the great west fronts of French cathedrals. Lichfield Cathedral is a splendid example of Decorated Gothic in its red sandstone but sadly it was severely damaged in the Civil War siege of the City, enduring three sieges between 1643 and 1646. Consequently most of the external sculpture at Lichfield is largely 19th-century restoration. The West Front, dating from about

Norwich Cathedral:
15th-century clerestory and
lierne vault built above the
12th-century Norman apsidal
east end.

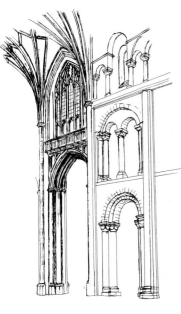

Winchester Cathedral: the nave Gothic bay construction c.1394–1450 (left) encasing the partially demolished Norman bay, c. 1100 (right).

1280, is impressive for its geometrical blind arcading, but its flatness without buttressing divisions reveals the smallness of the portals, in contrast to those of the classic French cathedrals. The late 13th-century nave is covered by a tierceron vault, but the extraordinary feature is the clerestory, with its series of triangular-shaped windows. At the east end of the cathedral, beyond the Quire, the Lady Chapel projects as a smaller version of Ste Chapelle, Paris, or the contemporary choir at Aachen, in Germany. The tall windows of the Lady Chapel enclose trefoil roundels that create a feeling of movement. Lichfield is unique among British medieval cathedrals in retaining three slender spires, punctuated by bands of gabled lucarne openings.

The last phase of Gothic, the Perpendicular, also lasted the longest, and includes the Tudor phase, which overlaps with the dawn of the Renaissance. When the Perpendicular style began is open to scholarly debate, although in general terms it is regarded as the prevalent style of the 15th century. For a long time the end of the Decorated style was attributed to the Black Death of 1349–50, although this is not actually so: the earliest surviving examples of buildings with Perpendicular Gothic characteristics are the gateway of St Augustine's Abbey, Canterbury, dating from around 1306, and Gloucester Cathedral quire, rebuilt from about 1337. St Stephen's Chapel, in the Palace of Westminster, constructed from about 1306 and destroyed by fire in 1834, and the chapter house of Old St Paul's Cathedral, c. 1332, were both built under the direction of the master mason William de Ramsay, and were virtually the first complete buildings in the style. At its simplest this phase may be seen as consisting of walls and windows divided by vertical mullions and horizontal transoms, hence its secondary title, 'rectilinear'. And if it was not quite as inventive as the Decorated, it was certainly more prolific.

As in the Decorated period there was little complete rebuilding of greater churches during this phase, with the exception of Sherborne and Bath Abbeys. It was more a period for rebuilding of major areas of cathedrals (such as naves), as happened at Canterbury and Winchester—for the latter, this involved encasing the Norman piers in a Perpendicular outer skin. At Norwich Cathedral the Norman

Above: Oxford Cathedral Quire, Norman, c. 1150–80, with fan and pendant vaulting added c. 1480–1500.

Right: Cambridge King's College Chapel, interior from ante-chapel showing the fan vaulting constructed c. 1500–1515.

Cambridge: King's College. The chapel was constructed of stone brought by sea and river from Yorkshire and Northamptonshire to adjacent quays on the River Cam. On the left is the Fellows' Building c. 1724–31 by James Gibbs, constructed of stone from Portland, Dorset.

clerestory was replaced; at Oxford Cathedral, then St Frideswide's Priory, a fan and pendant vault was built over the Norman quire, while Peterborough received a fan-vaulted Lady Chapel. Numerous crossing towers were built, including those at Canterbury, Gloucester, York and Durham (that at York was rebuilt as a result of an earlier tower's collapse in 1407). Near York, the master mason William Colchester also completed the western towers of Beverley Minster. At Lincoln the Norman western towers, partially hidden by the addition of a Gothic screen to the Norman Front, were increased in height with the addition of two stages enclosed by tall pinnacled buttressing; this was then given spires, which survived until 1807. At Malvern Priory a delicate central tower was built, perhaps by the same masons as at Gloucester, while at Fountains Abbey, in defiance of the

Cistercian rule, Abbot Huby ordered the construction of a tall north transeptal tower in about 1500, which survives almost complete.

As well as St Stephen's, Westminster, several other royal foundations were to have magnificent chapels in the Perpendicular style: examples include St George, Windsor; the twin foundations of Eton and King's College, Cambridge, and that built for Henry VII at the east end of Westminster Abbey. The building that perhaps most typifies the style is King's College Chapel, Cambridge (1446–1515). This was a royal foundation made by Henry VI in 1441, in which no expense was to be spared. However, due to Henry's deposition in 1461 and subsequent vicissitudes, progress was slow and work halted for some years. Even the original quarry that provided materials was worked out. The chapel somewhat resembles a huge glass cage or stone-framed greenhouse, with each of its bays divided by huge buttressing that in turn flanks windows rising above low side chapels to below the battlemented parapet. The building's sense of verticality is further enhanced by the numerous mullions. Inside, the ante chapel is divided from the quire by a wooden screen. Each bay in the ante chapel has a division of clustered shafts, rising to the transverse division of the fan vaulting of the ceiling, while in the quire the vaulting shafts spring from corbel stops on a level with the window transoms. The fan vaulting, which is used here to such superb effect, was mostly likely developed from that in Gloucester Cathedral cloister, of about 1360; but it has also been suggested that a lierne vault was originally intended, and that John Wastell, master mason at King's College (1508–15), was in fact influenced by the fan-vaulted quire of Sherborne Abbey, dating from about 1460.

Eton College, the sister royal foundation from 1440, is dominated by a large stone-built chapel on the north side of Lupto's Quadrangle —had it been completed according to the original intentions it would have rivalled that of King's College Chapel in length. What stands is the quire of eight bays. Had it been built, the ante chapel would have extended out across what is now Eton High Street, making a total length of 17 bays. But after the King's deposition, in 1461, the endowments were curtailed, including the provision of chantry priests

and sequestration of land, and the chapel treasures were transferred to St George's Chapel, Windsor. In 1480, the Provost of the time, William Wayneflete (also founder of Magdalen College, Oxford), finished the quire with a low, single bay ante-chapel. The intention was to provide a stone fan vault to cover the interior, but the ceiling we see today is stone-faced concrete, and was only completed in 1959.

Behind the ramparts of neighbouring Windsor Castle is St George's Chapel, started by Edward IV in 1478 and completed during the reign of Henry VIII, in 1525. It was largely paid for out of the royal exchequer, although Sir Reginald Bray, a Knight of the Garter, gave additional funds so that work did not stop in time of economic difficulty. Occupying the site of an earlier chapel it is cruciform in plan with a short transept at midpoint dividing the nave or ante chapel from the quire. Both sections are flanked by side aisles, which appear as screens of glass, divided by thin flying buttresses from the clerestory wall above. Here, beneath a forest of fan and pendant vaulted bays are the stalls of the Knights of the Garter, from the 1480s: a cluster of pinnacles and canopies, they provide some of the most intricate examples of late medieval carving. In its carefully measured spacing of bays the nave seems light and uncluttered: the character of the Perpendicular style is enhanced by shafts on the piers, rising unbroken from pavement to vault-spring, by the division of wall space in aisles, triforium and beneath the west window and by the continuation of the line of window mullions as blind panelling. Beyond the Quire, and linked by a low passage through the doorway surviving from the previous chapel by Henry III, is the Chapel of Henry VI, perhaps inspired by the construction of the Lady Chapel

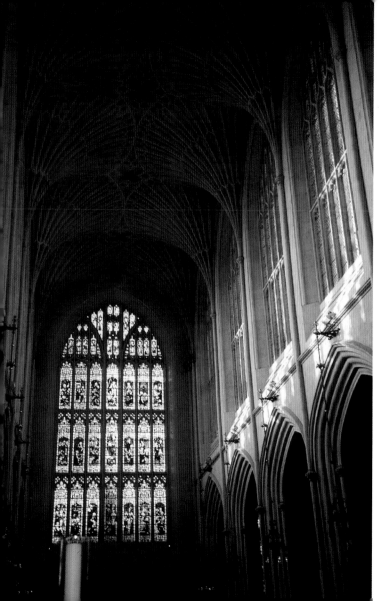

Bath Abbey: interior of abbey church reconstructed between 1501—39, the last major reconstruction of any English church before the Reformation. The elevation is of two stages, the intermediate triforium having been eliminated.

Opposite: Canterbury Cathedral Nave, c. 1380–1405, and crossing tower, c. 1480–1506. Originally intended as a single stage lantern tower like York, it was raised by another stage necessitating the insertion of strainer-arches between the crossing piers. To reduce weight, it was constructed of 480,000 bricks faced in Caen limestone. The master mason was John Wastell who designed the fan vaulted ceiling and supervised the completion of King's College Chapel, Cambridge.

beyond the Quire of Gloucester Cathedral. This chapel was intended to be the final resting place of Henry VI, but he remained undisturbed in Westminster Abbey. In the nineteenth century it was converted by Queen Victoria to become the Albert Memorial Chapel.

Just as few people can fail to be moved by these magnificent royal chapels, it is difficult to remain unmoved by the clean and simple lines of the naves of Canterbury and Winchester Cathedrals. By now much of the light comes in through tall side aisle windows, and the triforium is reduced to little more than an intermediate gallery. In both Canterbury and Winchester, however, the clerestory windows are relatively small, but at Sherborne and Bath Abbeys they comprise almost half the total elevation; at Gloucester and York Cathedrals about three-quarters of the east end of the quires is filled by enormous traceried windows in rectilinear style.

On the exteriors, parapets and towers in Perpendicular style invited a further display of rectilinear panelling: at Canterbury Cathedral, Bell Harry Tower, built to replace an earlier crossing tower known as the Angel Steeple, has decorative motifs of Tudor roses as well as a cardinal's hat set into the surface between vertical mullions and ogee hoods, as a punning reference to both the royal house and the patron of the tower-building campaign, Cardinal Henry Moreton. Originally intended to be a single stage lantern-tower, Bell Harry Tower was increased in height by another stage in the 1490s, and masked at the corners by clustered buttressing that enhanced the vertical thrust to culminate in four highly decorated corner pinnacles, rising some 8 metres (25 feet) above the open parapet. When seen from a distance the creation of this tower shows remarkable visual judgement in relation to the length of the cathedral.

In general, decoration and moulding of the Perpendicular is shallower than in earlier periods, and tends to be rather repetitive. Yet the style could sometimes rise above this to a highly complex and delicate form, as in the fan and pendant vault of Oxford Cathedral, and in Henry VII's Chapel, at Westminster. But by the time Henry's royal chapel was nearing completion, in 1520, the first Italian Renaissance ornament was appearing in England—on the tomb of Henry VII, beneath that very same chapel's remarkable vault.

4

The Medieval Parish Church

Thousands of churches survive with a substantial structure dating back to before the Reformation. While no two are the same, there are regional similarities in planning and ornament: the flint and stone churches in the Perpendicular style of Norfolk differ from the small moorland churches of north Yorkshire; in Cambridgeshire, church builders sometimes mixed flints with the soft local stone known as clunch; spires abound in Northamptonshire and Lincolnshire but are rare in Somerset and Devon—indeed, Somerset is renowned for its elegant towers in golden Ham Hill limestone; in Cornwall, churches are of local granite that, unlike limestone, does not yield easily to the chisel and is too hard for intricate external decoration; in Cheshire there are complete timber- framed churches, with that at Marton making claims to be the oldest wood and plaster structure in Europe. Churches also reflect the wealth of a region, as well as local patronage: it is no coincidence that the largest parish churches are in Hull, Great Yarmouth and Boston, once flourishing ports trading with the Hanseatic ports of Flanders and the Baltic. On the other hand, some churches survive in splendid isolation to bear witness to one local wealthy sheep trader, such as the numerous churches on Romney Marsh. Local patronage, whether it came from a nobleman, merchant or trade guild, often led to the rebuilding of a chancel or nave, or the construction of a chantry or burial chapels that, in some cases, as for example at Cirencester, Gloucestershire, almost doubled the area of the church.

As we have seen, Norman churches were usually relatively simple in plan with a rectangular nave and chancel terminating in an apse. If the church was cruciform, a tower would mark the crossing. With the coming of the 13th-century, churches were enlarged but rarely

Opposite: Chipping Camden, Gloucestershire: interior of this famous Cotswold church looking from the nave, rebuilt from 1488. The window above the chancel arch is typical of the region.

Below: Stamford, Lincolnshire: St Mary's church, early English tower and broach-spire. The only external change is the insertion of a window in the Decorated style in the 14th century.

entirely rebuilt. Perhaps the first expansion would be the addition of a south aisle, or perhaps one on both sides of the nave. Clerestories were still rare but they do occur, for example at West Walton, Norfolk, where there is a band of alternating open and blind lancets.

With the coming of the Early English period chancels were often rebuilt to provide more space and light. Windows were at first lancets, but by the mid-13th century increasingly displayed plate and then geometrical bar tracery, under the influence of contemporary cathedral architecture. At Uffington, Oxfordshire, the splendid cruciform church is pierced by a set of lancets that identify its period from a considerable distance. The transepts have small, rudimentary eastern chapels, and the crossing is unusual in that it supports an

Uffington, Oxfordshire: early English church with lancet windows and octagonal crossing tower. The entrance is through the south porch (left). The now familiar rectangular chancel end is seen to the right.

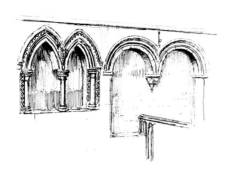

octagonal tower, the lower stage of which originally supported a stone spire. The spire was destroyed by a storm in the 18th century, after which an upper octagonal stage was then added to the tower. At West Walton the tall west tower of about 1240 is detached, and clasped by polygonal corner buttressing. Its faces are dressed on the first stage by a band of lancets and on the upper or belfry stage by plate-tracery openings.

By the 13th century aisles were increasingly added to naves, which sometimes necessitated either the destruction of earlier walls or cutting through and underpinning them with pointed arches set on piers. If Salisbury Cathedral and the quire of Westminster Abbey stand as the finest examples of greater church architecture of this period, the church of St Mary at Stone, near the southern approach to the Dartford Bridge, in Kent, must rank on the same level for the parish church. It was perhaps built in the 1250s, possibly under the patronage of Bishop Robert of Wendene, later buried in Westminster Abbey. Constructed in Caen and Reigate stone and Purbeck marble (as well as flint for much of the exterior), the nave of St Mary is large and of three bays, flanked by side aisles beneath a single sloping roof. The piers are slender and dressed with detached Purbeck marble shafts, divided by annulets or rings and rising to stiff-leaf foliated capitals. The nave is covered by a plain open-timbered roof that

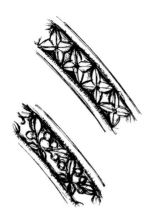

directs the gaze to the chief glory of the church, the chancel. Here, the interior rises above the height of the nave and is crowned by a quadripartite ribbed vault, and lit by large geometrical traceried windows that are similar to those in Westminster Abbey. Another connection with Westminster is the trefoiled arcading along the chancel walls, that on the south incorporating the sedilia and piscina. The foliated carving in the spandrels is most elaborate and on the north wall incorporates dragons entwined in branches and leaves— possibly the carving came from the abbey's workshops at Westminster. The west tower of the church is incorporated into the west bay of the nave and appears somewhat squat; it has a massive buttress at the south-west corner that was perhaps intended to support a spire that was never built.

At Hythe, also in Kent, the chancel was reconstructed in about 1210 with side aisles over a large crypt and is therefore one of the earliest examples of parish church Gothic, perhaps influenced by the nearby and newly completed Canterbury Cathedral quire. The interior of Hythe is unusual in that it is of three stages including a triforium and clerestory. Short shafts of local Bethesden marble support the triforium arcade and a vault that, although intended from the start (as evidenced by the massive exterior buttressing) was only constructed during J L Pearson's restoration in the 19th century. Dog-tooth moulding was increasingly prevalent at this time, as seen here at Hythe, but exists on a more spectacular scale at West Walton, where bands rise between the jamb-shafts of the porch.

Where towers were erected at the west end they might now support an octagonal spire, splayed on four sides with broaches or half pyramids to link with the corners of the tower. The Midland counties have numerous examples of this, as at Raunds, in Northamptonshire, Ketton, in Rutland, and Kirby Bellars, in Leicestershire, while at Barnack, the octagonal spire is added to a Saxon tower. All these churches are built of the famous Clipsham and Ketton limestone.

As with cathedrals, the 14th-century Decorated period was not one of significant new building, but rather of embellishment. Perhaps the two most notable, almost wholly Decorated churches are those at

Heckington, Lincolnshire and at Patrington, Yorkshire. Both have tall towers with spires that rise from behind a parapet and are flanked at each corner by tall pinnacles. The corners of the spire display sprouting crockets, such as leaves, and the surfaces are pierced at intervals by lucarnes, a kind of gabled opening that allows air to circulate inside the spire. At Oxford, the beautiful tower and spire of St Mary the Virgin soar above the curve of the High Street with a most complex display of buttress pinnacles sprouting crockets and delicate finials.

The style is characterized by large geometrical and flamboyant windows that pierce the walls, and fill the complete wall space

Left: Ketton, Rutland. St Mary's church, a fine example of the early English style showing lancet windows and broach spire pierced by lucarnes.

Right: St Patrick, Patrington, East Yorkshire, c. 1320–1410. The chancel is lit by a large rectilinear window of the later Perpendicular period.

The Medieval Parish Church 67

between buttresses. Grantham, Lincolnshire, is an excellent example of this, while Higham Ferrers, Northants, has two reticulated traceried windows at the east end, resembling those in the Wells Cathedral Lady Chapel. Another characteristic feature of this period, especially in adorning window tracery, is ball-flower ornament, as seen at Badgeworth, Gloucestershire and Ledbury, Herefordshire. Indeed, interior ornament sometimes compared to that of cathedrals in the quality of its naturalistic carving. Appropriately for Nottinghamshire, with the nearby work at Southwell Minster Chapter House and perhaps York Minster Chapter House, is the sanctuary at Hawton, where the decoration may be from the same workshop. Hawton has an elaborately canopied sedilia and piscina beneath ogee hoods on the south wall, and the Easter Sepulchre opposite this, on the north. The donor for this work was Sir Robert de Compton, whose effigy lies,

Cirencester, Gloucestershire: St John the Baptist. Although the original church dates from c. 1180, it was largely rebuilt in the 15th century. The triple-storey porch dates from c. 1500.

appropriately, in the tomb recess between the Priest's Door on the left and the Sepulchre on the right. At the base of the Sepulchre are panels enclosing four recumbant knights beneath ogee hoods. Above is a wide and deeply recessed opening with the relief figure of Christ rising from the dead. On the left is a narrow bay for the reservation of the sacrament, and on the right there is a recess depicting the three Maries coming to the tomb. The hood with its ogee is lavishly embellished with oak leaves and scrolls, above which there is a row of apostles looking upwards toward heaven.

The Perpendicular Gothic phase is more than adequately

represented in parish churches, all the more so since the second half of the 15th century was a period of great rebuilding and enlargement. Some of the so-called 'wool churches' of the Cotswolds, such as those at Cirencester, Burford, Fairford and Northleach, attain considerable size and lightness, with large aisle windows and the introduction of a clerestory, sometimes carried across the chancel arch (as at Cirencester and Northleach). In eastern England, in particular in Norfolk and Suffolk, churches were built in a combination of stone and flint; the lines of window tracery sometimes continued across walls with stone strips inserted into a flint ground, a treatment known as flushwork. There are no better examples than the Suffolk churches of Lavenham, Long Melford and Blythburgh, the latter built as one unit that combined nave and chancel, divided internally by means of a delicate wooden screen.

Burford, Oxfordshire: St Mary's is a fine example of a parish church with a Norman core visible in the crossing tower. During the 13–15th centuries the body of the church was largely rebuilt on an expansive scale with a triple-storey porch (just visible) and a number of chantry chapels.

Lavenham, Suffolk: detail of Spring Chantry chapel on the south side of church showing late 15th-century use of flush-work. The lattice balustrade should also be noticed.

Opposite: Lavenham, Suffolk. The parish church from the south. The church was rebuilt from 1486 with lavish financial support from the de Vere and Spring families. The huge tower, typical of East Anglia, is of flint with dressings of stone on buttresses and openings. Pinnacles were originally intended to surmont the tower.

In rare instances brick might at this period be used for additions: Holy Trinity, Hull is unique in having been rebuilt largely in brick. In the county of Essex a number of small two-cell churches in brick survive, adorned with a wooden bell turret over the western gable: Woodham Walter is a good example. Also in Essex, at Greensted the chancel was rebuilt in brick against the surviving Saxon nave in wood, with a wooden weather-boarded tower supporting a small spire at the west end. Another wooden tower is at Margaretting, which has a simple covered belfry supported on oak beams. Across the border in Cambridgeshire, Diddington church has a west tower built in Tudor brick in the early 16th century.

Windows of this period have increasingly slight curves towards a central point and are sometimes rectangular, with a rectilinear tracery pattern within. Roof pitch is radically reduced, sometimes to less than ten degrees, thus allowing the tracery of an open parapet to be silhouetted against the sky: battlementing was a favourite form. Whilst it was often the fashion to leave the tall side aisle windows clear-glazed during the fifteenth century, there were exceptions. At Fairford, in Gloucestershire, the church was entirely glazed with coloured glass, which has fortunately survived in its entirety.

Churches were now often entered through majestic south or north porches. These would be flanked by buttresses and, if part of a major town church, might have an upper storey for use as a grammar school room or place for guild meetings, as in the three-storied porch at Cirencester. The provision of an upper storey also allowed for the embellishment of the walls with canopied niches filled with statuary. Much of this was destroyed during the Reformation, but at Northleach, also in Gloucestershire, the south porch still retains its statue of the Virgin above the ogee-hooded entrance. The money given for the provision of a school might be part of the endowment for a guild or chantry chapel, in which masses would be celebrated for the repose of the souls of the benefactors. One of the finest examples, certainly in terms of external decoration, is at Tiverton, Devon. It was built for the London merchant and draper John Greenaway who built the south aisle and porch of the church and his chapel of two bays.

Tiverton, Devon: Greenaway chantry chapel.

Above the windows is an appropriately decorated carved frieze depicting ships on waves, woolpacks and horses, while the parapet is in the form of battlementing pierced with quatrefoils. There are other excellent examples of such chapels, which are almost like stone cages in their lightness, at Burford and North Leigh in Oxfordshire, Cirencester and Lavenham.

Most parish churches were covered by a timbered roof, and stone vaulting was used sparingly, if at all, for memorial chapels or side aisles. Only one English medieval church, St Mary Redcliffe, is vaulted throughout, paid for by William Canynge, a wealthy Bristol merchant who owned a large fleet of ships. Similarly, at Cullompton, Devon, the clothier John Lane paid for fan vaulting of the south aisle in 1529. Roof types ranged from the simple tie beam to the complex hammer beam, with the richest examples culminating in the magnificent double hammer beam roof, adorned with over one

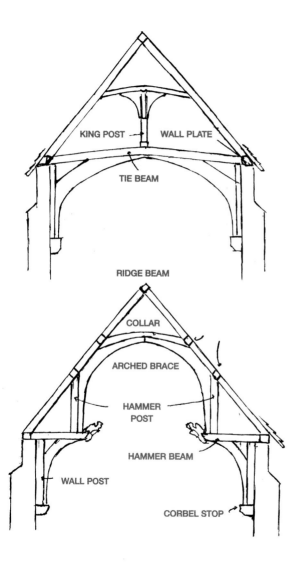

KING POST → WALL PLATE

TIE BEAM

RIDGE BEAM

COLLAR

ARCHED BRACE

HAMMER
POST

HAMMER BEAM

WALL POST

CORBEL STOP

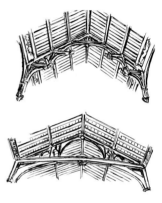

Below: Roof types.
Upper: Woolpit, Suffolk,
hammer beam
Lower: Addlethorpe,
Lincolnshire, tie beam.

The Medieval Parish Church 75

hundred angels with outstretched wings, at March in Cambridgeshire.

Seen from afar across open country some churches of this period take on the appearance of cathedrals in miniature as they dwarf the surrounding cottages of a village, or the roofscape of a small town. As with cathedrals, towers became objects of pride, and even of rivalry. Those towers in the Cotswolds and Somerset are in particular outstanding for their height and delicacy: some are crowned with open-battlemented parapets and corner pinnacles of tracery similar to that of the crossing tower of Gloucester Cathedral. Notable examples are St Stephen's, Bristol, St Mary's, Taunton, and Malvern Priory. The tallest tower in England is that of St Botolph, in Boston, Lincolnshire: it is surmounted by an octagonal lantern stage, also seen on a smaller scale at St Mary's, and All Saints, Fotheringay, in Northamptonshire,

and All Saints Pavement, in York. Boston's huge tower, with its tiers of windows and soaring lines of blind tracery and panelling, must have been inspired by those in Flanders, such as that of the Cloth Hall in Bruges and the church towers at Malines or Utrecht, or in the Baltic ports such as Danzig.

Today it is hard to envisage the original colour and atmosphere of a pre-Reformation church, and only glimpses remain. Originally the walls would have been painted with biblical themes and the chancel arch adorned with a large Judgement painting. The earliest surviving example of the latter is at Clayton, Sussex (c. 1100), where a painting of 'Christ in Glory' is set directly above the crown of the chancel arch, but the best and most dramatic example is in the church of St Thomas of Canterbury, Salisbury (c. 1470), in which Christ sits on a

Opposite left: St Botoph, Boston, Lincolnshire: dominating this once-flourishing port, the tower was constructed over a peiod of two hundred years from 1309. The third stage, with its single opening, is perhaps a little heavy, but the design is redeemed by the octagonal lantern stage at the summit. Opposite right: York, All Saints Pavement.

Far left: Nantwich, Cheshire,15th-century octagonal crossing tower. Left: Taunton, Somerset, St Mary, a wonderful example of a tower adorned with open-battlemented parapet and corner pinnnacles of open-tracery, typical of Somerset and south Gloucestershire.

Salisbury, St Thomas of Canterbury: this magnificent interior displays to the full the power of a Doom painting above the chancel arch.

rainbow throne above his twelve apostles. He is flanked by angels holding symbols of his Passion, against an architectural backdrop of the heavenly Jerusalem. The dead rise up on Christ's right and those condemned, on his left, are drawn down by devils to the jaws of death. On either side, at the foot of the painting are St James, patron of pilgrims, and St Osmund, bishop of Salisbury from 1078 to 1099.

Elsewhere in a pre-Reformation church the walls above the nave arcades might be adorned with representations of local saints or miracles. A most popular figure until the 15th century was St Christopher, who was not only the protector of travellers but the sight of whom would protect the viewer from sudden or evil death. Splendid examples of his image adorn the south wall of Haddon Hall, Derbyshire (c. 1427), and the north wall of the nave at Breage, Cornwall. He was, however, superseded by St George, who had been elevated to patron saint of England as early as 1350 and whose feast day was by now a major festival. The depiction of the legend of St George fighting the dragon was a favourite motif for church wall painting, one of the finest examples being in St Gregory's church, Norwich (c. 1500). At Pickering, Yorkshire, we find St George, along with St Christopher, on the north nave wall. Other popular saints included St Michael, St Nicholas, St Catherine, St Margaret (popular as patroness of the family), and depictions of the martyrdom of Thomas Becket were also relatively common. Beneath the chancel arch there would have been a rood screen displaying exquisite carving and painted panels. A few of these screens survive, for example in Dunster, Somerset, and Plymtree, Devon. The top of the screen would have had an overhanging platform or loft, beneath which would have been carved vaulting. Access to the loft was often by a newel stair within the side piers of the chancel arch; sometimes a door or arch with steps beyond is the only remaining evidence of a rood. Above the loft there would have been a large crucifix and statues of the Blessed Virgin and St

Plymtree, Devon: surviving rood screen, one of a number of impressive examples of medieval craftsmanship in the county.

Right: Hastingleigh, Kent, 12th-century font.
Far right: East Dereham, Norfolk, 15th-century font depicting the Seven Sacraments.
Below: Nantwich, Cheshire: Ambo or stone pulpit, 15th century.

John, which would have been covered by a purple cloth during Lent. The walls of a chancel or that of the arch might be pierced by an oblique passage called a squint, so that worshippers could see the High Altar, and occasionally see the side altars and the priest elevating the host during Mass.

Some chancels in large churches have stalls with tip-up seats, called misericords, bearing grotesque carvings of humans, animals and monsters. Above them are highly decorated hoods sprouting pinnacles almost up to the height of the clerestory and comparable in craftsmanship to those in any cathedral—as at the churches at Ludlow, Shropshire, and Nantwich, Cheshire. Beyond the chancel, on the right or south side of the sanctuary, there are usually three arcaded recesses, or sedilia, in which a priest, deacon or sub-deacon could sit during Mass. Further beyond these is another smaller recess, the piscina, with a basin for washing and draining the sacred vessels.

Wooden features encompassed rood or parclose screens (enclosing a small chapel), choir stalls and nave benches with ends overlaid with traceried panels, topped with poppy heads. But the most outstanding feature in wood was often the ornate and heavy font cover, designed to protect the holy water in the basin from theft, sometimes placed over an existing older font situated near the west end of the nave. Some of these font covers resemble church spires supported on miniature octagonal open-work screens like Perpendicular windows, and with flying buttresses clasping each angle, while others rise in diminishing tiers of traceried arches beneath ogee hoods. The finial at the summit is linked to a pulley and counterweight by a chain, enabling the cover to be raised at the appropriate occasion—although the hood at Ufford, Suffolk is so high that the lower stage has to retract into the upper when the font is needed. The finest font covers are in East Anglia: at St Gregory, Sudbury, St Edmund, Southwold and St Mary, Ufford, although the cover at St John, Halifax, in Yorkshire is also outstanding.

Much medieval glass was destroyed by the Puritans, and where it does survive it is often not in its original position, or is simply a jumble of coloured fragments. Very little survives in parish churches before the 13th century, other than fragments. Decorative roundels of St Catherine and St Mary Magdalen in the east window of West Horsley church, Surrey, date from between 1210 and 1225, while the glass in the east window at Westwell, Kent, also dating from the early 13th century, is among the oldest surviving in an English parish church. At Westwell, figures in deep red and blue toned medallions are surrounded by branching scrollwork of the Tree of Jesse, not unlike the glass at nearby Canterbury Cathedral. In the 13th century there was much use of so-called 'grisaille': windows made up of fragments of white and grey glass interspersed with panels of deep colour, but without any specific pictorial theme. Gradually the properties of sulphide of silver were more fully explored, to enable the use of a wider range of colours, such as orange and yellow. The introduction of new colours was particularly useful since more naturalistic settings appeared in glass at this time, involving foliage and architectural detail.

In the glass of the 14th century figures appear set beneath canopies and pinnacles, appearing somewhat like brass effigies. The colours also become lighter around this time, along with the wider range of colour. By the 15th century not only are there straightforward representations of popular saints such as St Christopher, St Margaret or St Mary Magdalene, but there are also representations of groups engaged in action: the depiction St Helena presenting the nails and part of the True Cross to the Emperor Constantine Heraldic, from Holy Trinity, Tattershall, Lincolnshire (1482), serves as a fine example. Heraldic devices also begin to appear in panes or lozenge-shaped quarries of glass. It is rare for a complete cycle of church glass to have survived the subsequent iconoclasm of the Reformation intact; perhaps one of the finest examples of a complete series of early sixteenth-century windows is that of Fairford, Gloucestershire, which was probably made by Anglo-Netherlandish glaziers in London. The windows at Fairford depict scenes from the life of Christ and the Virgin Mary. Sometimes church windows are filled with panes of medieval glass brought from elsewhere, either from cathedrals and dissolved religious houses or saved from the Puritans by local families in the 17th century.

Although generally not as large or as lavish as those in cathedrals, tombs in parish churches reflect local patronage and wealth and are often masterpieces of figurative sculpture and decoration, sometimes as recumbent effigies of the deceased raised up on a table or chest-tomb. Some tombs retain traces of their medieval painted decoration, while the earliest tombs were simple 12th-century tomb slabs incised with foliated crosses. But starting from the 13th century we have recumbent knights in Purbeck marble, dressed in crusaders armour that acts as a faithful record of the military costume of the period, as seen in the tombs of Knight Templars in the Temple Church, London, or at Croft, Herefordshire, and Winchelsea, Sussex. There are also effigies of ecclesiastics in their priestly vestments and, dating from the 14th century, double tombs in Nottinghamshire alabaster, the most lavish bearing vaulted canopies in which husband and wife lie beside each other in prayer, sometimes with lap-dogs at their feet. Some church tombs from the 15th century are as grand as those in any cathedral and were set within a chantry chapel where 'masses would be said in perpetuity for the repose of their soul'. The finest example of these is that of Richard Beauchamp, Earl of Warwick, Henry VI's 'Governer of the Roialme of Fraunce and of the Duchie of Normandie', which is cast in gilded bronze in the Beauchamp Chapel at St Mary, Warwick (c. 1440). Richard rests on a Purbeck marble tomb-chest with fourteen niches for bronze weepers. At his feet is his emblem of a muzzled bear, and also his second wife's emblem, a griffin.

Another outstanding tomb is that of Lady Alice de la Pole at Ewelme, in Oxfordshire, who, with her husband William, rebuilt the church in the 1430s and founded the neighbouring almshouse and school in 1437. Set within an arch between the chancel and chapel of St John, her tomb lies beneath an ornate canopy adorned with angels and bands of foiled and leaf decoration. With the Order of the Garter adorning her left arm and wearing a coronet, her alabaster robed figure lies on an elaborate tomb-chest with weepers in niches. The lower stage is open to reveal a cadaver figure, as a remembrance of mortality—perhaps it was executed by the same workshop as the similar figure on Archbishop Chicheley's tomb at Canterbury Cathedral, and also the one on the tomb of Sir John Golofre in Fyfield Church, in Berkshire. For the nobility, coats of arms might also be displayed in a richly decorated canopy or on the tomb chest itself, supported by spiral-columns, as on the Fitzalan tombs at Arundel, Sussex. Increasingly, personality was introduced into effigies of noblewomen, carved wearing the latest female fashion of the period. At Lowick, Northamptonshire, there are charming alabaster effigies of Ralph and Katherine Green (c. 1420), he in armour with feet resting on a dog, she in current fashion, including an elaborate embroidered headdress and cloak tied across the shoulders by a cord, and resting on a cushion. Unlike on many effigies, where hands are joined in prayer, he rests his left hand in gauntlet on his sword whilst his right unclothed hand holds his wife's hand. In the 15th century, merchants and civil leaders such as mayors were increasingly represented dressed in fur-edged gowns with their feet resting on a lamb. The tomb of William Canynges and wife in St Mary Redcliffe, Bristol (c. 1470), donors of money for the building of the clerestory and the church's beautiful vaulting, is a good example of a tomb that has been restored to its original painted colour scheme.

With the close of the Middle Ages and the coming of the Renaissance tombs became increasingly grand, and were sometimes quite out of scale with their setting—as if status could only be confirmed by size of monument. Among the finest early Renaissance tombs must be that of the 9th Lord Cobham and his wife, at Cobham, Kent (1561). The tomb-chest supporting the couple's effigy is adorned with scallop-shell headed niches flanked by Ionic pillars, containing effigies of their ten sons and four daughters. The tomb of the Fettiplace family at Swinbrook, Oxfordshire (c. 1613), occupies the south wall of the chancel and has six effigies in two stacks, lying on their sides in recesses beneath a pediment. As the century progressed the most lavish tombs might be adorned with miniature obelisks and flanked by standing figures in Classical robes—although perhaps suitable for a Hawksmoor or Gibbs interior this appears somewhat out of place in the average medieval church.

As in cathedrals, tombs are also marked by monumental brasses set into a stone matrix that is either set into the pavement or raised on a tomb-chest. Many of these, sadly, only survive in part. The earliest examples, from the 14th century, are deeply-engraved brasses representing life-size effigies of knights lying crossed-legged, such as Sir Robert de Bures (c. 1302) at Acton, Suffolk, and Sir Robert de Septvans (c. 1306), at Chartham, in Kent. Other early examples represent ecclesiastics. The earliest extant brass of a lady is at Trotton, Sussex, and dates from around 1310. Over the next two centuries merchants and their wives were increasingly represented, as well as knights and ecclesiastics, but the effigy becomes smaller at the expense of a pinnacled canopy. From about 1400 children are sometimes represented, with boys and girls on separate panels below their parents. The sides of slabs were inset with strips or fillets of brass incorporating an inscription in Latin or Norman-French. From the late 14th century a separate inscription might be placed immediately below the figure, and crests might be set above the hood (but within the outer border-strip). Sometimes effigies were produced abroad, for example in the German states; the craftsmanship reached a very high degree of sophistication, with borders incorporating an architectural framework of pinnacled niches enclosing miniature figures. By the 16th century engraving is shallow, and cross-hatching was introduced to increase the suggestion of depth. The brass survived as a memorial throughout the 17th century and in the 19th century underwent a revival.

Fortunately, churches did not suffer the destructive fate of monasteries although an Act of 1549 that allowed the destruction of chantries and rood screens was a grievous blow to the skills of the medieval sculptor, wood carver and painter. The Puritan destruction in the 17th century was spasmodic rather than total, due in some cases to the intervention of local families who hid removable objects and furnishings, but nevertheless left tombs desecrated and windows smashed. There was, however, to be an additional period of neglect, particularly in the 18th century, when some buildings partially collapsed. In Kent, the west towers of Goudhurst and Wye collapsed and were rebuilt in what may be described as a charming Gothic pastiche, with the tower at Goudhurst entered through a Classically framed west door. The 19th century was the greatest age of restoration and rebuilding, sometimes to the extent of destroying original furnishings and ornament in favour of what were presumed to be more faithful replicas of the original.

Leaving aside King's College Chapel, which has been discussed in the previous chapter, a number of other Oxford and Cambridge colleges retain the original chapels that formed a major feature of their layout: that of Merton College, Oxford may be taken as typical. Founded in 1274, the original Mob Quadrangle at Merton was completed by about 1300. Work on the chapel in the Perpendicular style continued throughout the 14th century until work stopped, with only the quire and transepts completed and crowned with a large

Oxford: Merton College Chapel.

crossing tower. The resulting T-shaped plan was adopted at nearby New College and Magdalen, and allowed for a large ante-chapel. A number of chapels remain as simple rectangular boxes, and several absorbed buildings from an earlier foundation, as at St John's, Oxford, where the chapel of the Cistercian St Bernard's College was absorbed into the new foundation of the 1550s. Similarly, the chapel of Jesus College, Cambridge, was originally the church of the former Benedictine priory on the same site. The Gothic continued in academic architecture well into the 17th century, and the external

appearance of the college chapels at Jesus (c. 1617) and Lincoln, Oxford (1629–31), may be described as Perpendicular, although the interiors introduced Classically ornamented panelling. At Brasenose, Oxford, the exterior of the new chapel, begun on a T plan in 1656, looks superficially Gothic, but on closer examination reveals Corinthian ordered pilasters, cornices and pediments. Inside, the quire is divided from the ante chapel by a Classical screen. It is at Cambridge that the first pure Classical chapels are seen, at Clare and Pembroke colleges.

Oxford: New College quadrangle c. 1380–1400 with the chapel on the immediate left, and the hall beyond. The only addition since is an upper storey to the range to the right of the tower in about 1684.

5

The Castle and Medieval Manor House

The Normans laid the firm foundation of national defence with their early fortifications—a castle keep set on a mound or motte. At first these keeps were surrounded by wooden walls, but eventually stone came to replace what must have been regarded as a weak point of defence. Stone curtain walls enclosing a rectangular bailey were interrupted at intervals by projecting mural towers. These were square in plan at first but subsequently became polygonal or semi-circular, to reduce the risk of collapse due to attempts at tunnelling underneath them. The castle at Dover remains an excellent example of a well-developed system of stone curtain walls, flanked at intervals by mural towers. One of the corner towers of Rochester Castle's keep collapsed as a result of mining during the siege of 1215 and was rebuilt in semi-circular form. Another excellent example of an early flint and stone outer wall defended at frequent intervals by rectangular mural towers is at Framlingham, residence of the Bigods, earls of Suffolk.

The ultimate protection against mining was a broad moat, which needed to be fed by neighbouring rivers or streams. One of the finest examples of this must be Leeds Castle, Kent, begun in 1119 with a main bailey, or inner compound, protected by high walls and set within a moat. The inner bailey, or 'Gloriette', is separated from the outer bailey by a narrow channel, traversed by a stone causeway.

By the late 13th century the castle complex of inner and outer bailey courtyards, and especially the main building, the keep, often proved cramped. A general desire for more room led to the building of a detached hall and chapel within the bailey. The windows in these were now much larger than those built by the Normans and would follow the geometrically patterned bar tracery fashion of churches since, after all, the outer walls would act as first defence. Some halls,

Opposite: Bodiam Castle, Sussex. The wide moat provides perfect defence.

Dover Castle, Kent: its system of double curtain walls made it virtually impregnable.

such as those at Oakham and Winchester castles, were aisled, and were large enough to accommodate many guests at high table and in the body of the hall. By parish church standards, castle chapels were small; they were usually rectangular in plan, although the chapel at Ludlow Castle, Shropshire, is circular. In some instances, for example at Durham, the castle chapel had a high degree of carved ornament, especially on the entrance portal; however, the buildings were more usually small and austere.

Entry to a castle was through a gatehouse; as an obvious area of weakness in the curtain walls, it had to be very strong. Gatehouses were often flanked by tall drum towers, which were splayed at the base and crenellated at the top. These towers contained spiral staircases that provided access to each floor, their treads supported in the thickness of the wall. Above the entrance the parapet might have been machicolated or projected so the platform could be pierced with 'murder holes', from which stones or boiling fat could be dropped on assailants. The entrance itself could be barred by a portcullis of wood studded with iron. It is romantic to think of all castles as having been surrounded by a wet moat; in reality, conditions might not have allowed this, and a ditch would have sufficed to stop an assailant placing a ladder or belfry near the walls.

If the castle was the residence of a powerful lord who may have had to entertain the king, more room than the keep could provide would have been needed. For this reason, and as already mentioned, by the end of the 13th century the inner bailey might have contained a hall and chapel, and other ancillary buildings specifically intended for the lord's use. In the outer bailey there might have been a certain duplication of these buildings with, for example, an additional hall, and a chapel for the garrison; by then the defence of the bailey had improved, with thick curtain walls rising well above these buildings.

All of these developments may be perfectly observed at Windsor Castle, where the Norman motte and bailey structure, including the circular shell keep, had been converted from wood to stone under Henry I, who also built the first stone chapel dedicated to St George. In about 1175 Henry II built a second bailey or upper ward to accommodate a new royal lodging protected by not only a high stone wall but also a steep cliff. Henry II also built a hall and chamber within the keep. By the beginning of the 14th century there was a need for greater comfort in these lordly residences: Edward III was responsible for massive building works at Windsor when 'masons and carpenters throughout the whole of England were brought to that building'. The first building campaign, between 1350 and 1356, involved both the remodelling of Henry III's chapel in the Lower Ward and the provision of chambers for canons who served the chapel and lodgings for the Knights of the Garter, the order of chivalry founded by King Edward in 1348. During the second building campaign, between 1357 and 1377, the Upper Ward or bailey received further alteration; this included the building of a new hall and the conversion of the old hall into a great chamber, kitchen and chapel. It was Edward IV who started the third rebuilding of St George's Chapel in 1475—by the time of its completion in about 1525 it had become one of finest examples of late Gothic ecclesiastical architecture in Europe.

The greatest castle-building campaign in Britain was that of Edward I between about 1280 and 1300, in order to guard the

Caernarvon Castle: it is said to have been inspired by the walls of Constantinople.

coastline of Wales and the Welsh marches, or English border counties. These castles introduced a new form of plan in which the keep was dispensed with (except at Flint) in place of enlarged domestic apartments within very high curtain walls: for example, as at Caernarvon, Beaumaris and Conway. The walled enclosure was further divided by a list (a space between inner and outer walls), into an upper and lower ward. At Caernarvon, said to have been modelled on the walls of Constantinople, the mural towers are polygonal and some are surmounted by turrets for increased observation, while those at Conway are circular drums.

At Harlech and Beaumaris (c. 1280–90) we see examples of the concentric plan, perhaps first used at Caerphilly, with a double rim of walls and the defensive stronghold in the gatehouse, with its residential apartments. The outer gate was not aligned with the inner gatehouse, lessening the chance of an assailant mounting a charge. At

Beaumaris Castle the southern gatehouse was approached at an angle, to avoid both a concentrated attack and the risk of being fully exposed to fire from above; to get to the outer gate necessitated crossing a drawbridge. Caerphilly, held for the King by the Clare earls of Hertford and Gloucester, and built just before Edward I's castle-building campaign, is, even in its ruined state, a most impressive sight. It was originally set within a large moat and protected from approach by land on its narrow flank by a wide walled platform.

The concentric plan at Caerphilly consisted of an outer wall enclosing an outer ward, and a narrow passage between the enciente (precinct) and inner wall, and an entrance through the great gatehouse to the inner ward. In the inner ward, as at Harlech Castle, the great hall and domestic apartments were protected by a high wall. On the opposite side of the inner ward another gatehouse led across the narrow outer ward to the outer wall, from where a bridge led to an enclosed semi-triangular shaped island. Sadly the so-called south lake has been drained, so the castle now seems marooned on land.

With the increase in wall height, castles became virtually impervious to assault by trebuchet, catapult or battering ram. The only way to reduce a castle to submission seemed to be by starving the garrison by means of a lengthy siege. To allow more concentrated fire power, embrasures or arrow loops were increased in number, from single openings through the merlons of the battlements to lines of openings for firing galleries behind the walls. These openings were splayed on the inside to allow for the angling of the crossbow. Such was the confidence in castle defence that a second lesser entrance or postern gate was now cut through the curtain wall. This might allow a garrison the opportunity to launch a counter-attack against the assailant, who was prevented from concentrating an attack at any one point due to the need to surround the whole perimeter closely.

Although the great age of castle building could be said to have ended with the death of Edward I, in 1307, many castles still underwent extensive rebuilding or addition. An excellent example is the Tower of London, where the seemingly massive Norman White Tower became immersed within a complex series of concentric walls

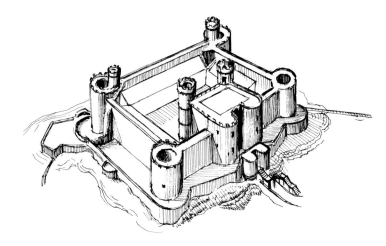

guarded every few yards by cylindrical or polygonal mural towers. Surrounded by a broad moat, the Tower was reached through an outer barbican and then across the moat by a stone causeway and drawbridge. At Warwick, the castle founded in 1068 and fully reconstructed in stone by Henry II, underwent extensive reconstruction under the Beauchamp Earls of Warwick between 1356 and 1401. Work included strengthening the curtain wall against the approach from the town and flanking at either end by two prominent towers, one, Guy's, is multi-angular and the other, Caesar's, has a clover-leaf plan and is splayed at its base. In the middle of the curtain wall there is a huge gatehouse of three storeys, positioned over the entrance arch, which is approached from the town through an outer barbican gate and between flanking walls. Two drawbridges provide a further defence, the outer one over a wide ditch. Along the south side, overlooking the Avon, there is an enormous series of apartments with their foundations buttressed into the hillside. These include a great hall lit by large windows, well above the walls and out of reach of danger. The castle at Lancaster has an almost equally impressive gatehouse, built in 1405 and again entered from the town, where any would-be assailant had to run the gauntlet of oil or projectiles dropped through the machicolations. At Warkworth, Northumberland, the castle built in the early 12th century, and for a time captured by the Scots, was given increasing strength in about 1390 when Henry Percy, Earl of Northumberland was granted permission to raise an enormous Greek-cross planned keep, which was not only to provide a vantage point for defence but also an ingenious array of domestic apartments pierced by large windows. The centre of this unusual plan is dominated by a tall turret, intended both for observation and the collection of rainwater for the private apartments and garderobes. For all the expenditure on the keep, the building proved uncomfortable and a spacious mansion was constructed in the bailey in 1461.

Although the major danger of a serious revolt against English rule had been suppressed by Edward I's castle-building campaign, Welsh castles continued to receive modifications or extensions. At Raglan, Monmouthshire, however, a new castle was built on the site of a Norman motte and bailey between 1435 and 1460 for Sir William ap Thomas, the 'Blue Knight of Gwent'. Its massive irregular enclosure of high walls, divided at frequent intervals by polygonal mural towers, was divided across the middle by a hall and chapel; the two enclosures that resulted, the Fountain Court and Pitched Stone Court, each had their own gatehouse. The Pitched Stone Court was entered through a truly monumental gatehouse with flanking towers, heavily machicolated and built by Thomas's son, William Herbert (later, Earl of Pembroke). Both the hall and chapel were linked to the domestic buildings ranged within the perimeter of the walls. This plan allowed space for a more comfortable and imposing domestic layout, with both the hall and chapel being well lit from the two courts. The final stronghold is the hexagonal donjon known as the Yellow Tower of Gwent, surrounded by a wide moat and linked by a stone causeway.

The medieval castle had become so impregnable that it had largely outlived its purpose. In any case the nature of warfare had changed, and was increasingly waged by open battle in the field, or even across the Channel in France. There were still a few new castles built in the 14th century, especially in the Scottish border country, such as Etal (c. 1340), a keep and bailey type. Nearby, the castle at Edlington (c. 1350) also has an outdated keep. Another familiar defensive feature of this region is the so-called stone Pele Tower, which was little more than a rectangular tower of perhaps three or more storeys that provided room for both storage and a residence. Although for the most part built to guard against cattle and crop thieves, the most impressive of these towers, such as that at Belsay, have corner turrets, machicolation and crenellation.

In Scotland there had been the need for defence against the English as well as protection against tribal warfare between clans. At first, as elsewhere in Britain, castles were in the form of a motte supporting a timber structure and bailey enclosed by timber palisading. However, as elsewhere by the 13th century, stone had come to replace wood as a secure form of protection, as well as providing a display of status and wealth by local magnates. Sometimes, as at Bothwell, Lanarkshire (c. 1290), a circular 'donjon' on a mound guarding a river bend was linked to a system of high curtain walls, enclosing a courtyard. During the course of the 14th century Bothwell suffered repeated sieges and occupation by the English. After 1400, no doubt under the influence of Welsh castle development, the walls were strengthened to incorporate a new hall, lodgings and a chapel with appropriately larger windows cut through the wall overlooking the river. A huge circular tower with a machicolated parapet guards one corner. Another impressive early stone castle is Caerlaverock, Dumfriesshire (c. 1260–70), which is a triangular enclosure within a wide triangular moat. Its gatehouse has massive twin drum-towers guarding the entrance across a bridge, and the two other corners are protected with circular towers. The courtyard was actually rather cramped, with lodgings in the gatehouse, and a hall and chambers against each wall. For all its strength it was actually captured in less than two days by Edward I, leading the English army, in 1300. However, many castles were small in area and depended on a compact tower house with adjacent range for a hall and ancillary apartments. One such example is Brodick Castle, Arran (c. 1500), which has the corner turrets, or bartizans, that would be a characteristic of Scottish defensive architecture for several centuries to come.

As in England, Scottish castles in the 15th and 16th centuries became more palatial, in an attempt to emulate the luxury of the royal manors of England and France. The first building to emulate this luxury was Linlithgow palace (c. 1425), built for James I, in the form of a tall rectangular mass with sheer walls and no mural towers. James IV was a great palace builder and also added lodgings to existing buildings. At Stirling Castle he built a great hall (1503) with decorative machicolation and stepped gables; the bay window incorporates mullions that curve at their midpoint to form a U-shaped intersection. When his successor, James V, married Madeleine de Valois, the eldest daughter of Francis I, a Renaissance influence was brought to Scotland with the importing of French masons and pattern books. As in England, Classical form was not to be correctly understood or applied for many years but the resulting mannerism did bring a certain exoticism and a release from the bleakness of stone walls: an admirable example is seen at Falkland Palace, Fife, where the chapel (c. 1538) is divided into bays by Corinthian ordered pillars mounted on tall pilaster bases. Here, roundels containing Classical portrait busts are also inserted between the pillars and windows, a feature also being added at the same time to the walls of Hampton Court. The new palace block at Stirling (c. 1540) shows a further development of the cult of decoration, with panels set between the windows. These panels are inset with spiral-fluted shafts that are mounted on wall-brackets supporting statues and capped by cusped arches. But defence was not entirely forgotten: in 1530 at Kirkwall, Orkney, Bishop Reid added a tall round tower to his palace, complete with gun loops.

At the other end of the country, in Sussex, far from the threat of the Scots but somewhat nearer the threat of French nuisance raids during the Hundred Years War, Bodiam Castle was built between about 1385 and 1400. One of the most picturesque (and

Above: Penshurst Place, Kent. Great Hall with its fireplace.
Below: Stokesay Castle, Shropshire. Medieval window retaining wooden slats and shutters.

photographed) castles, it is set in a broad lake fed by the River Rother and reached by means of a right-angled causeway, through a barbican, and across a double drawbridge. Its plan is quadrangular, with each corner marked by a huge drum tower and a gatehouse flanked by machicolated towers. From outside it appears to be impregnable, with the chapel window providing the only visible hint of the domesticity within. Most of the area inside is now in ruin but it once contained a continuous range of apartments around the four walls that included a great hall, kitchen, buttery and chapel, built so as to provide an inner rectangular space. Chambers survive over the gatehouse, giving some indication of the size and structure of the apartments, which would have been lit by narrow windows and heated from a simple fireplace. Garderobes that discharged directly into the moat also survive.

By the time Bodiam was finished, in about 1400, the fortified manor house (from the French 'manoir' meaning 'a dwelling') had been introduced. The manor allowed for a far greater degree of comfort while at the same time providing limited protection from unrest. But, most importantly, a grant by the king of a 'licence to crenellate'—giving permission to build and live in a fortified house—gave the owner immense political and social status. Sir John Poultney provides an excellent example: a merchant from London who contributed financially to the wars of Edward III, he was granted the manor of Penshurst in Kent, and a licence, in 1341. The dominant surviving feature at Penshurst is the Great Hall, entered through a porch. The floor is of hard brick but the central hearth is of stone to allow a fire, the smoke of which rose to a louvred exit in the ridge of the roof. At the entrance or lower end of the hall was a vestibule divided by a screen from the body of the hall. Beyond the screen, which in effect provided a barrier against the smell, the outer wall was pierced by doors to the now-destroyed kitchen. Behind the upper end of the hall, where a high table raised on steps was placed, was a parlour, with a solar and other domestic apartments

Penshurst Place, Kent.

above it. In some cases, as at Penshurst, there may also have been a cellar beneath.

The solar, from the old French 'solier', an upstairs room lit by the sun, was the private living and sleeping chamber of the household. By the end of the Middle Ages the solar may have been just one of a number of domestic chambers that would also have included a chapel and chamber for the chaplain. As at Penshurst, the solar would usually have a spy-hole to allow the family to watch the hall below.

Glass was rare as a permanent filling to windows, even in royal residences. Royal accounts record frequent payment for the insertion and removal of glass panels as the kings moved from one palace or manor to another, taking the expensive panels to their new abode. Lacking glass, windows were either closed by shutters, as can still be seen in Hemingford Manor, Cambridge, or by lattice panels composed

Opposite: (top) Oxburgh Hall, Norfolk; (left) Little Wenham Hall, Suffolk c. 1250, one of the first medieval manor houses to be built substantially of brick; (right) Tattershall Castle, Lincolnshire, c. 1440. Tall and narrow, it looks more like a toy fort than a building for serious defence.

Below: Ightham Mote, Kent.

of diagonal strips of wood, as at Stokesay Castle, Shropshire. In order to combat the fierce winter cold, an additional fireplace might be built into the side wall.

Most manors would be entered across a ditch, or broad moat as at Ightham, Kent, and through a gatehouse as at Stokesay (later rebuilt). Gatehouses were sometimes of considerable grandeur, such as those in brick at Oxburgh Hall, Norfolk (1482), Lullingstone, Kent (1497), and Layer Marney, Essex (1525). The courtyard beyond would have contained stables and a well. The hall may have been in a tall L-shaped tower block, as in Little Wenham, Suffolk, which is one of the

earliest buildings in brick. In this case the chapel with solar above is at right angles to the hall. Some families instead used the nearby parish church as their chapel or built a substantial addition to the church for their own use, as at Kedleston, Derbyshire, where the church has a chapel dedicated to the de Curzons. Adjacent to Great Chalfield Manor in Wiltshire, the church of All Saints was refashioned in the fifteenth century by Thomas Tropenell, a successful politician and landowner who added a family chapel, as well as a spire and bellcote over the west front.

Two other impressive brick-built manors are Tattershall Castle, Lincolnshire (c. 1440), built for Ralph Cromwell, Treasurer to Henry VI, and Kirby Muxloe Castle, near Leicester, built for William, Lord Hastings (c. 1480). Tattershall is very tall and narrow and is rectangular in plan, with polygonal corner turrets, and what can only be described as exaggerated machicolations beneath the parapet. Inside the building there are four chambers with enormous brick fireplaces. The castle was originally part of a large complex that included a grammar school, a chantry chapel (served by choristers educated in the school) and almshouses for poor men. Kirby Muxloe shares Bodiam's picturesque qualities, with its surviving brickwork shimmering in the

broad moat. Commissioned by William, Lord Hastings, the moated rectangle was to have been enclosed with high walls; they were never completed after Hastings was executed by Richard III. The gatehouse is impressive with the entrance flanked by broad bastions. It was to have been machicolated like Tattershall, no doubt for show, as is the fine black-brick diaper-work inserted into the gatehouse and surviving red brick corner tower.

By the close of the period some manor-castles, for instance Haddon Hall in Derbyshire, had a hall dividing the enclosure into an upper and lower court, with ranges of chambers on all sides. The arrangement was similar at Eltham Palace, in what is now south-east London, where the royal manor had a Great Hall (c. 1480) with a splendid hammer beam roof, dividing courts, and also a substantial chapel (c. 1500) built out into the Great Court. Perhaps the ultimate proof that the castle was now largely regarded as a backdrop to courtly grace and leisure was the building of the Great Chapel of St George, in the lower ward of Windsor Castle.

Like parish churches, manor houses exhibit fine craftsmanship in the variety of timber roofs spanning halls and the carving of screens and panelling, the so-called linen-fold pattern being particularly prevalent at the close of the fifteenth century. But, like churches, they have been subject to change and alteration as the demand for comfort, and the display of wealth, increased at the expense of protection. In some cases the changes were drastic, with the insertion of floors, particularly in halls to make more room, or the concealing of an elaborate timber framed roof by a decorated ceiling. Even more dramatic might be the demolition of the medieval hall to make way for a Georgian dining room and private suite.

But it was not only courtiers and rich merchants who were granted the right to live behind crenellated walls: senior churchmen, and especially archbishops—who wielded immense power and wealth— were allowed to build palaces that rivalled royal residences in size and splendour. At Canterbury, the palace built by Lanfranc in about 1080 was rebuilt between 1193 and 1228 with an aisled banqueting hall, second only in size to that of Westminster Palace. The palace, including

Opposite top: Great Chalfield Manor, Wiltshire, c. 1470. To the right of the manor house is the small parish church which also acted as the chapel for the Tropenell family.

Opposite (bottom): Eltham Palace, south London. Originally built in 1305 by Anthony Bec, Bishop of Durham, it ceded on his death to the Crown and became a favourite royal residence near London until the 16th century. The surviving Great Hall was built by Edward IV in about 1480.

hall, was demolished in the 1650s but several arches of the southern aisle were incorporated into the rebuilt palace, and the north entrance porch and two adjoining bays containing blocked-up geometrical windows were incorporated into an eighteenth century building, now part of the King's School. At Lambeth, the great brick gatehouse dates from about 1495, but the buildings beyond, including the Great Hall, have been rebuilt. Significant remains of other palaces of the archbishops of Canterbury survive at Lambeth, Maidstone, Charing and Croydon; Archbishop Bouchier's manor at Knole near Sevenoaks, from the 1450s, was given to Thomas Sackville Earl of Dorset in 1586.

Apart from Lambeth, the most substantial medieval bishop's palace still surviving is that at St David's, in Pembrokeshire. Here the palace occupying the site of earlier buildings was perhaps rebuilt as a result of encouragement from Edward I, on his visit to Bishop Thomas Beck in 1284. No expense was to be spared, and work continued under Beck's successor, Bishop Henry de Gower, until about 1350. Set within a large courtyard and entered through a gatehouse, the range on the left or south side of the courtyard was built first under Bishop Beck and incorporated a hall, kitchen, solar and chapel, immediately inside the gatehouse. Perhaps this was not grand enough for Gower who set about building a Great Hall and chapel in 1328, situated opposite the entrance gate on the west side of the courtyard. Set over a barrel-vaulted undercroft, it was entered through a highly decorated porch. The stone walls, originally plastered and painted white, are topped with multi-arched crenellated parapets incorporating chequered stonework of white, purple and green blocks. Within the gable of the south wall is a perfectly preserved circular wheel-tracery window.

Many bishops had London palaces, but all have been destroyed except for the chapel of Ely Palace, from about 1290, which survived to become St Ethelreda's Roman Catholic church in Ely Place. In Southwark a small section of the hall of the Bishop of Winchester's palace survives and incorporates a Flamboyant traceried circular gable window. The bishops of London had a palace at Fulham from 691 but the oldest surviving building, still in a quaint quadrangle, is the Tudor brick Great Hall that dates from about 1510, and is not unlike a contemporary Cambridge example. At Eltham, the medieval royal palace started life as the moated manor of Bishop Anthony Bek of Durham, in 1305. It was handed to the crown on his death in 1311. Much of Bek's stone retaining wall survives, overlaid with fourteenth and fifteenth century brickwork.

Just at the point when courtiers and merchants were seeking an increasing show of status and wealth in ever larger stone or brick houses, England witnessed the last campaign of castle building. In the 1530s, as a result of Henry VIII's break with Rome and split with Catholic Europe, there was a new threat of invasion from the continent. For this reason, as John Lambarde, historian of Kent wrote, Henry 'builded Castles, platfourmes and blockhouses, in all the most needfull places of the Realme', which meant along the south coast from Sandown near Deal, to Pendennis and St Mawes, in Cornwall. These castles were built between 1540 and 1542. They were unlike previous castles in that the plan, devised by Stefan von Haschenperg, an Austrian, formed a concentric clover-leaf of low stone bastions set behind the shore line and protected by a moat (a plan copied on a smaller scale in the brick martello towers built during the Napoleonic wars). These bastions were pierced by embrasures for cannon, set within chambers with air vents for smoke and shelves for ammunition. Above, the ramparts were platforms for further cannon, providing a wide angle of fire. The garrison had primitive living quarters in the central block, but these were not intended for permanent residence. If danger arose it would be easier for the garrison to hit an enemy ship than for the ship's crew to score direct hits on the castle, due to the latter's low-lying position. The finest preserved examples of such castles are those at Deal and at Walmer, both in Kent, but other fine examples survive at Southsea and Calshot, in Hampshire, and St Mawes, in Cornwall.

When the enemy did finally appear, from Spain in 1588, defence relied on a fleet instead, but a number of the castles were seized later by the Parliamentarians during the Civil War, and, much later still some were even garrisoned in the two World Wars.

6

The Medieval House

For obvious reasons a house in continuous use is likely to be subject to frequent alteration. If situated in a town its existence might be threatened by pressure to maximize the use of the site, leading to rebuilding perhaps several times in a century. In medieval times, additional threats of destruction came from fire, siege or flooding. Before the 15th century few houses were constructed in stone, apart from those originally built by the Jewish community or for rich merchants in the port towns. Of houses built by the Jewish community, the most celebrated is in The Strait, Lincoln, dating from about 1150. Moyses Hall, Bury St Edmunds, built over a vaulted undercroft is another, but is heavily restored: two gabled flint-built wings front the market, and a pair of two light windows beneath semicircular arches remains in one wing. Remains of a 12th-century stone house survive in a yard behind 48–50 Stonegate, York, and there are remains of the ground floor of a stone house from the early 14th century at King's Yard, Sandwich, and also at Hythe, where they are incorporated into a later building. After a fire in 1189 Richard I issued building regulations to the citizens of London, requiring the building of stone party walls of at least three feet in thickness. However, it was not until the Great Fire of 1666 that rules against building in wood were fully enforced.

Where medieval timber town houses survive unaltered in any number, as in Canterbury, Shrewsbury, and York, they were built no earlier than the 15th century, and are on deep rectangular plots with a narrow frontage to the street. They were constructed as two or more storeys, which were jettied or projected at each stage, with the top storey being within the gable of the roof. At the corner of the jetty a bracket might be carved into a grotesque figure with its head acting as

Opposite: The Shambles, York, 15th century and later.

a support for the over-hanging stage above. Where possible, a foundation of stone or brick was used to avoid damp causing sill beams to warp prematurely. The ground floor of a town house might serve as a shop with a timber panel opening out to the street to display wares for sale. A fine example of a row of houses with shops is in Church Street, Tewkesbury; one of the houses has been restored to give an idea of the cramped conditions for medieval commercial life. Generally, a door led directly into the front chamber, or alternatively to a passage through to a yard behind, which might have been used to keep animals or fowl. In another surviving three-storey house in Church Street the second storey retains evidence of wooden 15th-century tracery forming a continuous window, which was subsequently blocked in.

At Chester the famous Rows remain, although heavily restored, to give us a unique idea of a medieval shopping mall. The shops, or rows,

Chamber
Open hall
to roof
Parlour

Wealden Hall House, Kent /Sussex: numerous examples of this type of late-Medieval house survive in the wooded regions of the Weald.

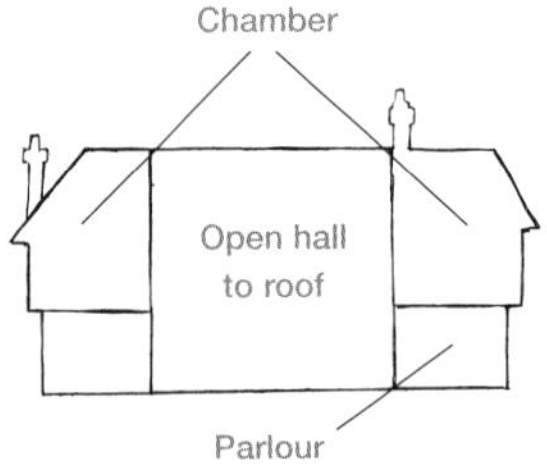

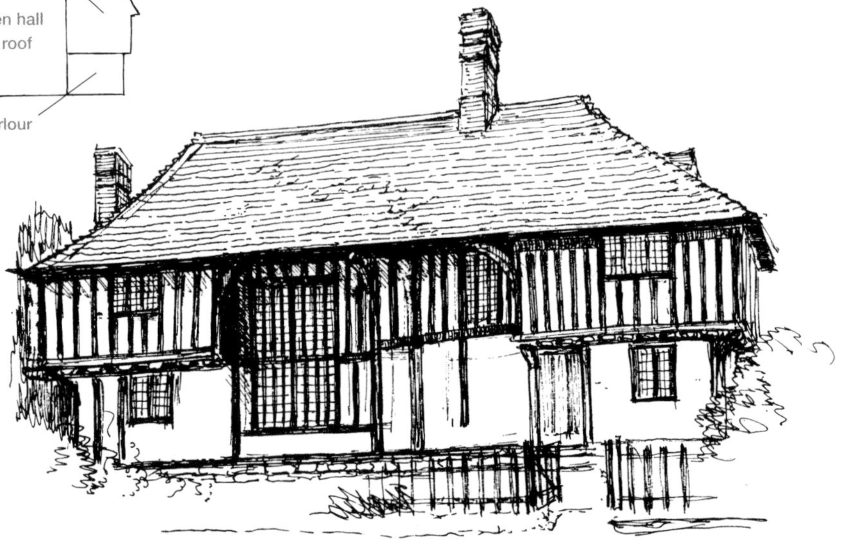

are set back beneath a solar or living chamber, built gable-on to the street, and behind a walkway raised above street level on an undercroft. The ground floor was covered with stone flags supported by wooden joists over the undercroft, which was used for storage. Access was by steps from the street, built between the stout wooden piers supporting the structure above. There were variations in planning and, where a town or village was not confined by walls or a ditch, houses were sometimes oriented lenghways to the street, as for example in Lavenham, Suffolk, and Coggeshall, Essex.

The upper stages of medieval buildings were jettied on immensely thick joists that ran through the house and acted as a support for the floorboards of each chamber. Heavy furniture was placed against the outer walls or at points where the joists were supported by a wall or frame below. Windows might also project outwards, the sill supported by brackets. The party wall of stone or brick would have a fireplace

Lavenham, Suffolk: Guildhall. A fine example of a late-medieval jettied structure.

on each floor and a flue to the chimney stack above the level of the roof ridge. Thatch was widespread as a roof covering until at least the 13th century, when the use of tile became more widespread, especially in towns where there was a more obvious risk of fire spreading.

The term 'half-timbered' is very apt for these buildings, as there were numerous vertical studs, horizontal transoms or curved and diagonal struts placed within the area of the structural timbers. The frame of the roof structure was held rigid by a horizontal wall plate, an intermediate purlin and a ridge rib linking the gable-end frames. Depending on the length of the internal structure, support might be added at intervals by cross-frames in which the main post in the outside wall supports the wall-plate, which itself is linked to that on the opposite wall by a tie beam. At the junction of the tie beam and wall plate is the principal rafter, thicker than the common rafters that support the outer roof timbers. The principal rafter, supporting the purlins running the length of the roof, may be supported or trussed by a horizontal beam known as a collar. A structural variation on this arrangement was the cruck support in which two huge beams, slightly curved towards their base, supported the weight of the roof with a horizontal collar beam acting as a lateral support; this was particularly favoured in barns. The timbers were held together by wooden nails or pegs, or by mortise and tenon joints. There are many regional variations, in some of which the timbers were filled with rectangular panels intersected by a diagonal strut, or vertical studs placed a few inches apart: hence the term close studding, quite common in East Anglia.

The most common form of infilling was wattle and daub in which vertical oak staves were woven horizontally by hazel wattles. This frame was daubed with a mixture of clay, dung and chopped straw, and the panel was then limewashed or painted. Regional variations included a filling of stone chippings plastered over, or, increasingly from the later Middle Ages, brick laid in horizontal courses, as in the Midland counties, or, in East Anglia, the herring-bone pattern found at Paycocke's, Coggeshall, and elsewhere in the South East. The pattern of exposed timbers could be simple, such as walls of close-studded

Above: Canterbury, Kent. Herringbone brick in-filling to jettied stage of half-timbered house.

Opposite: Coggeshall, Essex, Paycocke's House, c. 1450.

Below: Lower Brockhampton Manor, Herefordshire, 15th century.

Above: Chipping Campden, Gloucestershire. Grevil's House c. 1450, a fine example of a stone house of a wealthy Cotswold wool merchant. It has a bay window.

Above right: Didbrook, Gloucestershire. Cruck cottage, c. 1500. The dormer window is a later insertion.

vertical posts without any diagonal struts for additional strength that were especially favoured in East Anglia and Warwickshire. Or, as often found in counties such as Berkshire, Surrey, and Sussex, the panels might be square and large, with curved struts for additional rigidity. In the wooded areas of Kent, Cheshire, south Lancashire and Shropshire the timber patterns could be extremely complex, with quatrefoil patterns set off against white-painted plaster.

In the country, houses ranged from the simplest timber-framed cruck cottage as seen at Didbrook, Gloucestershire (c. 1500) to the yeomans 'hall house' of the Kent and Sussex Weald. The hall house was originally open in the middle from the ground floor to the roof. At the upper end was a parlour with a jettied chamber above and, at the opposite end, kitchen, pantry and larder with a chamber above. As this type of house was refined, so a stone or brick chimney might be introduced through the end walls or at the side. Solid brick was increasingly used for the lower stages of the side chambers towards the end of the period. Sometimes, and especially in eastern England, the upper floor might be covered in plaster over the frame of studs and infilling (such as thin lathes). The wet plaster would then be sculpted into relief decorations known as pargetting, seen at its finest in Suffolk and Essex.

In the wool areas of the Cotswolds and south-west of England merchant houses were built of stone. At Chipping Camden, Gloucestershire, Grevil's House of about 1490 had an open hall with a tall bay window filled with Perpendicular mullions. As the period closed so brick was increasingly widespread, and windows filled with glass increased in size. At Ockwells Manor, Berkshire, the hall is filled on both sides with an almost continuous row of windows, like a gallery, as also suggested at Tewkesbury, but here much larger. Unlike the majority of citizens whose houses, whether in town or country, would have had earthen floors at ground level, the houses of wealthy merchants had floors made of coloured tiles forming geometrical patterns, such as those at Canynges House, Bristol, and Clifton House, Kings Lynn, supported on a brick lined undercroft. Their houses

Speke Hall, Liverpool, c. 1530. Although technically speaking not medieval, it is a wonderful tribute to the art of timber-framed houses and typical of the style of late medieval house building in south Lancashire, and Cheshire. The characteristics of the region include diamond patterned panels created by repetitive diagonal struts.

might also have had a certain degree of sanitation, or at least a primitive privy in a small room off a stair well, in which the waste emptied by way of a chute to a pit or drain. For the majority of the population, however, waste emptied into the streets or back alleys.

Uniformity is not a quality generally associated with a medieval town, indeed planning as such was rare before the 17th century. However, at Wells a complete street of medieval stone houses survives, built to a scheme of Bishop Ralph Beckington between around 1445 and 1465, and intended to accommodate 42 vicars, facing each other in 22 two-storey houses across a narrow street. Each house had a ground floor room and an upper room for sleeping, and the cold Somerset winters were taken care of by fireplaces whose position is today indicated by the line of tall chimney stacks. It was a self-contained community with hall and kitchen at the lower end adjacent to a bridge that provided direct access from the cathedral and chapter house. At the upper end is a small chapel and library. As inhabited residences today, concession has been made to light with the replacement of the original medieval windows by quite acceptable sash windows, except for one house which has been restored to its original appearance. An examination of Mob Quad, Merton College, Oxford, also provides a good idea of the original treatment of wall openings. Perhaps this idea of community living, not unlike that of an Oxbridge college, was behind later schemes at Hereford, and also at Windsor Castle where, in about 1480, 21 timber framed houses were built round Horseshoe Cloister for the song-priests of St George's Chapel.

When seeking examples of medieval architecture it must be remembered that what would have been a substantial building at the time might well now be buried behind a brick or even a stone frontage dating from the last hundred years or so. As the years went on, towns tried to create a degree of smartness with uniform facades and buildings that occupied the floor space originally in front of the medieval shop or ground floor chamber. Conversely, what may look convincing as a late medieval half timbered facade may well be a largely 19th-century restoration, as is the case in some of the buildings in Chester.

Opposite: Wells, Somerset, Vicars Close, c. 1445–65.

Below: Ludlow, Shropshire, The Feathers Inn.

7

Tudor Architecture

While the period 1485–1603 was one of dramatic religious and political change, in architecture the transition from the Gothic to the Classical was much slower, and the appearance of most towns outside London would have shown little evidence of the Renaissance. Because of its geographical isolation, Britain followed Western Europe in its absorption and true understanding of the principles of Classical ornament and proportion. The religious troubles of the Reformation and subsequent suspicion about the Roman Catholic continent discouraged much contact with the Classical south. It was in the fields of literature and the theatre that the Classical world had the greatest impact on the general public. Both Marlowe and Shakespeare wrote plays based on Classical history and mythology. There was no national school of painting and most artists at this time were Flemish or German by birth, and their subject matter largely confined to portraiture.

Renaissance architectural form was developed in Florence from the 1420s by Brunelleschi and was the subject of a number of learned treatises, from Alberti in the 1450s to Serlio and Palladio over a hundred years later. As in France, it was the court which was responsible for the early use of Classical form in Britain: Henry VIII imported craftsmen from Italy and France to work on his numerous hunting palaces and manors, including Nonsuch, in Surrey (demolished c. 1685). The earliest surviving actual use of Classical ornament in Britain is on the tomb of Henry VII, in Westminster Abbey, which was designed by the Florentine sculptor Pietro Torrigiano (1472–1522) in c. 1512. Torrigiano had actually been a fellow student of Michelangelo in the school run by the Medicis.

It was more as ornamentation that the Classical style began to appear, as for example in a Classical capital in Chelsea Church,

Opposite: Montacute House, Somerset, c. 1595: an H plan house erected for Sir Edward Phelips, a West Country lawyer. The porch, however, is from the earlier Clifton Maybank, c. 1546, inserted into the west front in 1786.

London or the wooden pulpitum screen in King's College Chapel, Cambridge (c. 1535). The latter, made by Italian craftsmen, has a strong flavour of the Lombardic Renaissance. The Loire chateaux building programme of François I contributed a number of craftsmen, who worked at Hampton Court, St James's Palace and Nonsuch. St James's Palace, now much altered, was created out of a former leper hospital. Its frontage is dominated by a tall brick turreted central gatehouse topped by a belfry.

The 16th century was no exception in showing royal favour to those who had supported the monarch in times of difficulty, particularly during the struggle with the Church. Size emphasized status rather than convenience and encouraged the possibility of a visit by the monarch, which might bestow extra favour. Due to the Dissolution of the Monasteries, building material was quite plentiful, especially stone, which was pillaged for re-use for stately homes such as Fountains Hall, Yorkshire, Longleat, Wiltshire, and Burghley, Lincolnshire.

As the century progressed, the traditional quadrangular plan, as seen at Ightham and Haddon, was gradually superseded by the open E plan. Perhaps one of the last great houses on a quadrangular plan was Cowdray House, in Sussex, which was rebuilt between c. 1530 and 1540 for Sir William Fitzwilliam, later Earl of Southampton. Entered through an imposing gatehouse, it was one of the most impressive houses of Henry VII's reign, with a great hall almost as big as those of Hampton Court and Christ Church, Oxford; unfortunately it was burnt down in 1793 and survives only as a gaunt ruin. The change to the open E plan created the need for an imposing front, with the entrance set into a central projected bay against which the Classical orders were displayed in ascending stages, with the Doric on the lowest. However, not all E planned houses exploited Classical grandeur on such a scale: at Loseley Park, Guildford (c. 1560), built of ragstone from the former Waverley Abbey, the entrance is in a flanking wing so that the central projected bay can incorporate a bay window to light the high-table end of the hall within. At Parham, in Sussex, built in lovely warm brick in the 1570s, there is a similar

Hampton Court, Greater London: brick chimneys.

elevation, but here the entrance is through the central bay, with the high hall to the left, lit by enormous mullioned windows and with a projected high table bay at the opposite end. The beautiful plaster ceiling retains an intricate interlaced pattern with dropped pendants.

The proportion and accuracy of architectural detail and ornament varied according to the source, which was usually a pattern book published in France or Flanders. The first book in English on architectural practice was the *First and Chief Groundes of Architecture* by John Shute, published in 1563 as a result of a visit to Italy. Other books were not published until later, such as Sebastiano Serlio's scholarly treatise on architecture, translated in 1610, and Andrea Palladio's *Quattro Libri dell' Architettura*, not available in English until 1715. Although there were increasing numbers of published engravings of ornament (some copying another source, leading to inaccuracy of detail), those books with a substantial text were in a foreign language, and would only have been collected by those with a working knowledge of Italian or French.

Stone was a costly material, unless plundered, so many 16th-century houses used brick extensively, often of a reddish hue and inset with a chequer pattern of black or white bricks. Terracotta was sometimes used instead of stone, as in the centrepiece of Sutton Place, Surrey (c. 1529), which is richly decorated with friezes of diamonds and quatrefoils. Increasingly there was an emphasis on symmetry, with flanking wings at each side. Windows were large and rectangular with lead glazing bars set between mullions and transoms. A horizontal band of brick coursing might be used to define the level of the floors from the exterior. Roofs were still often steeply pitched but were now projected out over eaves instead of falling behind battlemented parapets. As roof spaces were utilized for additional servants' quarters, light was admitted through gables projecting at intervals from the main roof line. Other memorable features of the roof line of Tudor houses are the batteries of tall cylindrical brick

Charlecote Park, Warwickshire: although extensively altered internally in the 19th century, the exterior, with its characteristic Tudor bay windows and stair turrets on the wings, date from Sir Thomas Lucy's rebuilding in 1558.

chimneys exhibiting intricate pattern work. Excellent examples include Hampton Court, Charlecote Park, in Warwickshire, and Sawston Hall, Cambridge.

The reign of Elizabeth I witnessed the building of a number of so-called 'prodigy houses', remarkable for their size as well as a more serious approach to Classical form. Most notable were those attributed to Robert Smythson (1535–1614), who was described on his tombstone as 'Architect and Surveyor unto the most worthy house of Wollaton and diverse others of great account'. In addition to Wollaton, Smythson was responsible for Longleat, Hardwick, Worksop (now demolished), Burton Agnes and possibly Fountains Hall.

Wollaton Hall, Nottingham: a great Tudor house dominated by its hall rising above the surrounding ranges. The tower gables, hiding chimney stacks, are adorned with Flemish strapwork patterns.

Longleat, in Wiltshire, built for the Lord Protector Somerset, was begun in 1541. Although not completed until 1580 it is memorable both for its symmetry and its enormous windows, 'more window than wall', as the saying about Hardwick Hall goes. The building has Classically ordered pilasters applied correctly to the three stages between each window. Each floor is defined by a cornice and the main entrance is defined by means of a Doric pedimented doorcase. The roof is flat and hidden by an open parapet adorned with triumphal arch motifs and lions. The chimneys are in the form of Tuscan columns surmounted by an entablature and cornice. As the roof now served as a promenade for the household and guests, domed pavilions known as banqueting houses were introduced, from which wine and sweetmeats could be served.

Wollaton Hall (1580–88), now in a suburb of Nottingham, was built for Sir Francis Willoughby, Sheriff of Nottinghamshire. At first sight it has a superficial resemblance to Longleat but is only of two stages over a raised basement. However, square towers are introduced at the four corners, which rise to three stages and so incorporate the three orders. Gables adorned with Flemish strapwork top each side and cunningly hide the chimneys behind. Normally a rectangular planned house of this proportion would have an open court within, as

Burghley House, Lincolnshire c. 1564-86: built by William Cecil to impress the Queen when she visited. The court is dominated by the gatehouse displaying the classical orders surmounted by a pyramid. The date of completion is carved above the clock.

Opposite: Hardwick Hall, Derbyshire, 1580–88. A great rectangular pile of stone flanked by towers displaying the cypher, 'ES' for its creator, Elizabeth, Countess of Shrewsbury.

at Longleat, but here the hall is placed in the centre with direct access from buttery, pantry, and kitchen. In order to admit light the walls of the hall are raised above the surrounding roofline to accommodate a clerestory. As if this is not enough, the hall walls are raised by a further stage to incorporate a 'great chamber', and the corners are adorned with domed turrets supported on buttresses. Finally, Smythson makes full use of the flat roofline with the addition of groups of chimneys in the form of Doric columns.

By now the great hall had in many cases become one of many large apartments, or even just an entrance chamber used only on special occasions. As such it cannot always be identified from outside unless it still uses the full height of the house, as at Wollaton and also at Burghley, near Stamford. At Burghley the mansion, which incorporates remains from a former religious house on the site, is attributed to its founder William Cecil, Lord Burghley, who took a keen interest in architectural progress although he had the advice of an Antwerp mason named Henryk. Burghley was begun in 1553, and its great hall retains medieval proportions with a steep pitched roof supported by the now almost outdated hammer beam construction. Like Longleat, the building retains a courtyard plan, with the inner ground stage originally arcaded like an Italian palazzo. Also like Longleat, the roof line is punctuated by columned chimneys, obelisks and turrets. However, the most memorable feature is the tall courtyard entrance to the hall, which rises in ordered stages, perhaps inspired by Philbert Delorme's centrepiece for the chateau of Anet, c. 1550 (this centrepiece is now preserved in the courtyard of the Ecole des Beaux Arts, in Paris). Burghley's entrance is surmounted by a clock with a single hour hand and bears the date of completion, 1587; above this rises an enormous obelisk.

Hardwick Hall, also by Smythson, is rectangular in plan and has a rather insignificant entrance beneath a Doric colonnade that leads into a screen-passage of the hall. The building is notable not only for its enormous windows but also for the earliest use of the long gallery, which took over from the hall as the social centre. Not only could household and guests talk and walk here, but portraits could be

Above: Hardwick Hall,
Long Gallery.

Right: Knole House,
Sevenoaks, Kent, Great Hall.

displayed. Family pedigree was very important to the Elizabethan gentry and not least to the owner, Elizabeth of Hardwick, who even had the parapet of the six towers adorned with her cypher, ES. Like Longleat and Burghley, the roof at Hardwick is flat and hidden by a parapet.

Although the courtyard plan was fading by the third quarter of the 16th century, one example, Kirby Hall, Northamptonshire (1570–75), built for Sir Humphrey Stafford, deserves a mention rather for its ornament. Possibly designed by Thomas Thorpe (c. 1569–1635), who had evidently culled various illustrated books on Classical ornament for ideas, it is the first building in Britain to display the 'giant order', that is pilasters rising through more than one stage—in this case at the north entrance range and the hall and kitchen at the opposite end. We may associate giant orders with Michelangelo, who was of course fully conversant with Classical rules, but here it is Classical form adapted for the enhancement of a building. For instance, the pilasters displaying the Ionic order flanking the centre bay of the entrance to the north range are ornamented with candelabra and floral decoration, which might have come from a drawing by Bramante in his 15th-century Milanese period. Other pilasters are incised with fluting, and the ground stage has an arcade whilst the floor above has windows adorned with alternating triangular and semi-circular pediments. If this is making a dramatic departure with the past, the hall at the opposite end, on the other hand, is lit by mullioned and transomed windows, and crowned by a steep pitched roof. This hall is divided from the kitchen by a passage entered beneath a triple-staged centrepiece, which displays paired Ionic pilasters on the ground stage, raised on ornamental bases. Above these are two stages of Corinthian, the upper incorporating a gable embossed with eight mini pillars in front of a highly decorated stone backdrop set against the steep-pitched roof behind. Sadly, in the early 1800s the house was abandoned and most of the interior has fallen into ruin.

Another great courtyard house was Sissinghurst Castle in Kent, from the 15th century the seat of the Baker family. It was rebuilt in the 1560s by Sir Richard Baker, who entertained Queen Elizabeth

Cambridge, Trinity College:
Great Court Fountain, 1601–2.

Cobham Hall, Kent, c. 1594

Opposite: Oxford, Bodleian
Library c. 1600: Tower of the
Five Orders.

there in 1573. Built of brick with mortar dressings it was demolished in the late 18th century, apart from the entrance range and a tall turreted tower, both of which were incorporated into the home created on the site in the 1930s by Harold Nicolson and Vita Sackville-West.

A fine example of the English adaptation of the triple-staged porch adopted from France is that of Cobham Hall, Kent. Dated 1594, it led into the hall. The third stage lacks an order and paired piers support urns. A final Classical touch is added by the pediment surmounting this stage. Often central portals are only of two stages, incorporating the Doric order on either side of the doorway and the Ionic flanking the window of the stage above, as at Charlcote Park, Warwickshire, built for Sir Thomas Lucy in 1585. In this case there is still a pitched-roof punctuated by batteries of tall chimneys.

Away from the mansion, several academic buildings in Oxford and Cambridge began to show signs of the Classical style towards the close of the 16th century. At Cambridge these include the Gate of Honour at Gonville and Caius College, perhaps by Dr John Caius (1510–1573), physician to Edward VI and Queen Mary: Caius had studied medicine in Padua, and so would have been exposed to the latest Classical developments in northern Italy. In the Great Court of Trinity College there is a fountain beneath a canopied octagonal arcade supported on Ionic columns, dating from about 1601. It also exhibits Flemish strapwork on each side, and the canopy is surmounted by a rampant lion clasping a shield displaying the Tudor arms. Yet the Gatehouse to the court, from a few years earlier, shows no evidence of the Renaissance. The first college in either university that was built wholly in the Classical style was Clare, Cambridge, rebuilt c. 1640–80. At Oxford, the Tower of the Five Orders (c. 1600), which forms the entrance to the Bodleian quadrangle, was the first example in Britain to exhibit the Composite and Roman Doric orders, inspired by the Italian architect Sebastiano Serlio (1475–c. 1554) who authoritatively described the Classical orders in the early 1500s.

8

The Jacobean House

To a certain extent the period between 1603 and 1620 was a continuation of the Tudor age, at least architecturally, and witnessed the building of another batch of prodigy houses. These include Hatfield, Audley End, Charlton, Bramshill and Holland House. These buildings suggest a more settled period of design, with a greater sense of mass and silhouette rather than a show of great windows. As in the later years of Elizabeth's reign, large numbers of continental craftsmen were at work in Britain, including at the Scottish court of James VI. There were of course additional sources of architectural inspiration from pattern books which had detail from the Netherlands, or exotic distortion or reinvention of Classical forms from the Nuremberg craftsman, Wendel Dietterlin. The most widely used ornamentation was strapwork inspired by the architectural paintings of Flemish artist Vredeman de Vries, as seen on the centrepiece of Charlton House, south London.

Opposite: Chastleton House, Oxfordshire, c. 1612, Long Gallery with barrel vaulted ceiling with roses.

Left: Charlton Park, Wiltshire: a fine example of plaster strapwork with pendants, c. 1625.

Charlton House, south London, 1607–12. The lead-capped turrets at each end are typical of Jacobean houses.

The standard plan for the large house was either the so-called H plan or the E plan. The H plan was perhaps first used at Wimbledon House (c. 1588), which had deeply projecting side wings, and again a few years later at Condover Hall (c. 1598), in Shropshire. The square or rectangular plan, as seen at Chastleton, near Oxford, and Bolsover Castle, Derbyshire, was also popular. Blickling Hall in Norfolk also has an unusually elongated rectangular plan with a narrow entrance front.

Although Audley End near Cambridge, built for the Earl of Suffolk, was started a few years earlier in 1603, Hatfield may be taken to exemplify the character of the period. In 1607 work started on a new house to replace the old palace which had for a time been the childhood home of Elizabeth I. Robert Cecil, Earl of Salisbury, had exchanged the manor of Theobalds with James I for the royal manor of Hatfield, and now, like his father (William Cecil, Lord Burghley),

set about building a mansion worthy to entertain the king and queen. Just who created Hatfield House is slightly confusing, as with many great houses of the 16th and 17th centuries. Robert Cecil, like his father, took a keen interest in architecture and might have dreamt up the basic design; after all it was an exercise in image building and status seeking in the game of politics and courtship. Robert Lyminge (c. 1580–1628) is thought to have been the main designer but others, including Simon Basil, who served as Surveyor of the King's works between 1606-15, and Inigo Jones (1573–1652), who succeeded Basil after the latter's death in 1615, may also have advised.

Hatfield is built to an E plan, with separate apartments in each wing for the royal guests—the king in the east wing and the queen in the west. It has a central linking block built of stone, some of which was pillaged from St Augustine's Abbey, Canterbury. The ground floor had an open Italianate loggia (subsequently enclosed) divided by

Chastleton House, Oxfordshire, c. 1612. The most perfectly preserved of early 17th-century manor houses, it was built for Walter Jones, a wealthy Witney clothier, in local honey-coloured limestone. The rectangular body is flanked by battlemented stair towers. The entrance is in the left of the two projections on the front. The Long Gallery runs across the top of the house.

Hatfield House, Hertfordshire:
the grand staircase.

Doric pilasters. On the upper floor the bays are divided by Ionic pilasters. The centrepiece, emblazoned with the completion date of 1611, rises three floors to include paired triple orders after the French manner, seen earlier at Burghley. The roof line behind is broken by Dutch gables, another feature from the Netherlands, and a central clock and belfry tower in receding stages. The projecting wings are of red brick and are three rooms wide on the front between the staircase turrets, which are capped in lead. These turrets are a familiar feature of the Jacobean style and may have originated at Theobalds, built by William Cecil and dating from the 1560s.

Inside, one of the most impressive parts is the Marble Hall. This rises through two floors and is dressed with wooden wall panelling of exquisite craftsmanship. The fireplace is flanked by carved grotesque terms (sculpted posts) supporting an ornamental cornice—the type of feature found in a pattern book. At the upper end of the hall is a gallery, which is a visual riot of carved strapwork panels surmounted by arched openings. Access to the upper floor is by the oak grand staircase—dating from the age when a stair changed from being merely a means of access to a feature designed to create the expectation of splendours to come, through a show of virtuosity from the woodcarver and the hanging of paintings on the walls.

Hardwick Hall is one of the earliest houses to have a grand staircase, but while it is spacious it is relatively austere compared to the elaborate wooden square newel type, examples of which at Knole, Kent, and Stonyhurst, Lancashire, pre-date Hatfield's by perhaps five years. At Hatfield, elaborately patterned newel posts support carvings of putti (winged cherubs) and monsters. A few steps up from the bottom, gates prevent dogs straying to the apartments above. These rather practical additions are divided into panels decorated with carved fleurs-de-lis. No great house of the 17th century was without its long gallery: Hatfield's, directly over the loggia, ranks among the finest and remains unaltered, being panelled throughout and with a plaster ceiling of the most intricate strapwork. The two fireplaces in the gallery are flanked by paired columns of alabaster on two levels, in the manner of a triumphal gateway.

Robert Lyminge, who gave Hatfield its magnificent entrance front, also worked at Blickling Hall, Norfolk, where the local church register of deaths confirms him as 'the architect and builder of Blickling Hall'. Built originally for Sir Henry Hobart, this house is approached between two long wings of outbuildings containing the kitchens and stables. The house, in lovely red Norfolk brick, is then reached via a bridge across a dry moat. Its narrow frontage is defined in the centre by a projected stone-arched porch, flanked by Doric pilasters and crowned by an entablature. The bay window above is flanked by the Ionic order and has the conventional vertical mullions and horizontal transoms, as in the windows at Hatfield. The brick entrance front is crowned by three Dutch gables; lead-capped brick stair turrets flank each corner. The triple-staged clock and belfry is also similar to that at Hatfield. Throughout, there is a magnificent blend of reddish brick and stone dressing for windows, gables and quoining. Beyond the entrance, a small courtyard led to the Great Hall. This was considerably altered in the 18th century to become a hall for the grand staircase, which is similar to that at Hatfield and therefore probably by Lyminge.

The H plan was used at Charlton House, near Greenwich, for Sir Adam Newton, Secretary to Henry, Prince of Wales. Not as large as Hatfield or Blickling, Charlton is also predominantly of red brick with stone reserved for windows, quoining, plat-bands, balustrade and the ornate centrepiece with arched porch. The plan of the house may have been by John Thorpe (1563–1655), clerk of the royal works from 1584 to 1601, to whom other Jacobean houses are attributed, including Audley End. The magnificent stone centrepiece was borrowed from patterns by German, Wendel Dietterlin; such a riot of uninhibited Classical distortion is also seen above the entrances to Bramshill, Hampshire, and Aston Hall, Birmingham. Like the Elizabethan Hardwick Hall, the hall at Charlton House is placed axially, that is across the body of the house, and so entered directly from the porch. As at Blickling, the roof line is broken by tall brick chimneys of elaborate patterning, while its Jacobean identity is firmly secured by the tall, lead-capped turrets placed to each side of the house.

Opposite: Blickling Hall, Norfolk, 1616–25, one of the most charming examples of 17th-century domestic brick architecture in England.

Below: Charlton House, south London, 1607–12. Projected centrepiece with pilaster adorning first storey derived from book of orders by Wendel Dietterlin of Nuremberg.

9

Inigo Jones

As we have seen, Classical detail had been introduced into British architecture from the middle of the 16th century. However, it was Inigo Jones (1573–1652) who first produced a scholarly interpretation of the Classical style through his two visits to Italy and his deep study of the writings of Vitruvius, a Roman architect of the 1st century BC. Unfortunately, many of Jones's plans did not get beyond the drawing-board stage due to either expense or the political upheaval of the Civil War, or possibly they were destroyed. Because of his enormous significance as an architect, the name of Inigo Jones has inevitably been linked with buildings where there is actually no documentary evidence of his involvement.

Inigo Jones was born in Smithfield, London, in 1573 but nothing is known of his education and training before 1603, when he is recorded in the Duke of Rutland's accounts as a 'picture maker'; by then he had already made his first visit to Italy. Jones was employed at the court of James I as a designer of scenery and costumes for masques. Many drawings of these ambitious entertainments survive, showing moveable scenery and the first use of a proscenium arch. His earliest excursion into architecture may have been in 1608 with a design for the New Exchange in the Strand, London (the Royal Exchange, destroyed in the 18th century). In 1611 he was appointed surveyor of works to Henry, Prince of Wales, heir to the throne. This post, involving the maintenance of all buildings and property owned or visited by the prince, was short-lived due to Henry's premature death in 1613.

At this point Jones was invited to go on a second visit to Italy as artistic adviser to Thomas Howard, Earl of Arundel—a trip that was to prove most influential. Jones took with him a copy of Palladio's *I Quattro Libri dell'Architettura*, published in Vicenza in 1570, which

Opposite: Queen's Chapel, St James's Palace, London, c. 1623–27. A double-cube hall covered by a magnificent wooden coffered ceiling is based on Palladio's restoration of that of the Temple of Venus and Rome. The east window is a so-called 'Venetian', rarely seen in Venice but adopted and used by Palladio in the Veneto.

he may have purchased on his first visit to Italy. With Palladio's work in hand, he diligently studied the buildings of Palladio in Vicenza as well as the antique remains of Rome. He was not, however, to become a slavish imitator of Palladio but an interpreter who had due respect for other Italian masters as well.

On his return to England in 1615 Jones was appointed surveyor to King James I; he was also to hold the appointment during the reign of Charles I until the Civil War. His first major work, and one which survives, is the Queen's House, Greenwich. Built originally as two rectangular blocks on either side of the Woolwich Road and connected by a central bridge on the upper floor, it combines features from villas by Palladio and Sangallo, without being a copy of any particular building. The building is constructed of brick, faced in plaster and with the lower stage rusticated. Stone is reserved for the window architraves, cornices and Ionic pilasters of the loggia, and a stone balustrade hides the roof. Started for Anne of Denmark, wife of James, the Queen's House was completed for Charles I's queen, Henrietta Maria, in 1637. However, after the Restoration, in the 1660s, its appearance was radically altered by John Webb (1611–1672), Jones's nephew, at the bidding of Charles II: by adding short connecting galleries on each side he converted the building into a rectangular block. Doric colonnades were added in 1807, when the building became a naval asylum. Today it is part of the National Maritime Museum.

Jones's next work and arguably his most formally Classical one was the Banqueting House, Whitehall (c. 1619–22), built to replace an earlier house in wood at the heart of the palace of Whitehall. This building of double cube proportion is loosely derived from Palladio's Palazzo Barbarano, Vicenza, but Jones was not a copyist. The facade displays the Ionic and Corinthian orders, raised on a rusticated basement and crowned by a balustrade. The windows have the formality of Italian Classicism, with cornices over those on the lower floor and alternating triangular and semi-circular pediments on the upper. The centre of the facade is emphasized by half pillars, and the end of the facade is closed by paired pilasters, as was the manner of 16th-century Italian public buildings. Since the staircase from

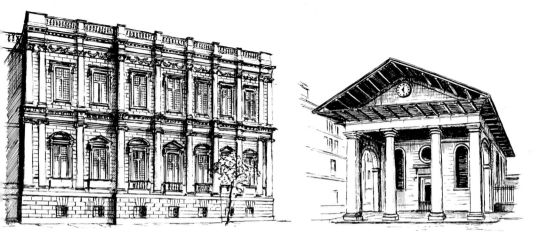

pavement level is set in an annex at the north end, the interior floor space is an unimpeded double cube. Even the balcony running round three sides is cantilevered on brackets so as not to impede the floor space below. The painted ceiling with panels by Rubens, glorifying the reign of James I, was inserted in 1635.

Jones was also responsible for the first example of formal town planning in Britain, that of Covent Garden, dating from the 1630s. Said to have been inspired by the piazza at Livorno, it certainly bore a close resemblance to the Place des Vosges, Paris (c. 1605). On land leased from the Earl of Bedford (and formerly a garden owned by Westminster Abbey, hence the name), the design comprised terraces over ground level arcades on the eastern and northern sides, while the west contained the church of St Paul. An eastern portico was of the Tuscan order, said by Vitruvius to be the most primitive of the Classical orders. The terraces were of brick, with plaster pilasters dividing the windows from each other. The idea of a ground floor arcade was found not only in the Place des Vosges (formally Royale) but also in the Place Dauphin, from c. 1607. Jones's name has also been linked with the layout of the west side of Lincoln's Inn Fields, without documentary evidence, although the builder was probably Nicholas Stone, who worked under Jones at the Banqueting House at

Left: Banqueting House, Whitehall, 1619–22: the only surviving remnant of Whitehall Palace. The drawing shows the original appearance with casement windows.

Right: St Paul's Church, Covent Garden, c. 1631. The east portico overlooking the piazza looks rather top-heavy after the raising of the street level to obliterate the steps shown in 17th-century engravings.

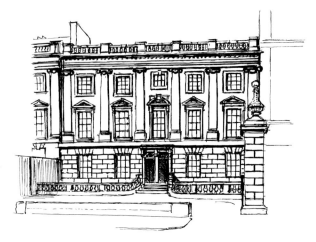

Lindsay House, Lincoln's Inn
Fields, London, c. 1640.
Original brick with stone
pilasters dividing the windows.
Its brick was plastered over in
the 18th century when the
double doorway was
introduced. It was then the
residence of the Marquis of
Lindsay.

Whitehall. Here on Lindsay House, the only surviving building of the
layout, we find the use of giant ordered pilasters and triangular
pediments over the windows of the piano nobile (main floor).

As court architect Jones was responsible for the design of the
Queen's Chapel, built as an adjunct to St James's Palace between 1623
and 1627, for Charles I's French Catholic bride, Henrietta Maria, and
her retinue. The chapel is externally austere, with a Venetian window
at the east end. Inside, a coffered barrel ceiling survives. Another royal
commission that did not go beyond the basic planning stage was the
rebuilding of Whitehall Palace. Drawings survive in the hands of Jones
and John Webb, showing a building that, if built, would have rivalled
the Escorial in Madrid and the Louvre in Paris. The elevation of two
major floors was to be broken at intervals by pavilions displaying the
orders and formal entrances flanked by towers capped by domes.

Jones was also responsible for a major programme of restoration of
St Paul's Cathedral: this included encasing the Gothic walls of the
nave in a Classical style skin, with semi-circular arches replacing the
Gothic windows. At the western end he designed a huge Corinthian-
ordered portico of ten columns based on Palladio's restoration of the
antique Roman Temple of the Sun and Moon. This was flanked by

two low towers, one (on the south side) incorporating the medieval towers of St Gregory the Great. Although the portico survived the Great Fire, it was demolished in 1668 as Wren's new cathedral arose in its place. But we can obtain some idea of its appearance by looking at the west front of St John's church, Northampton (c. 1680), which must have been influenced by St Paul's.

Outside London, Jones has been associated with many country houses, including Castle Ashby and Stoke Bruerne, in Northamptonshire, and Wilton, in Wiltshire. Stoke has the plan of a Palladian villa and was built for Sir Francis Crane, who had established the tapestry factory at Mortlake, near London. A central block was linked to the pavilions by curving colonnades. At Castle Ashby Jones may have advised on the addition of a gallery to link the two Tudor wings, thus enclosing a front court. Here he uses the Doric on the ground level and Ionic on the first stage pilasters and half pillars.

Jones's involvement in Wilton is hard to unravel. The south front was begun in about 1632 and is attributed to Isaac de Caus (1590–1648), possibly with Jones as consultant since it has a similarity to detail in his design for the Prince's Lodging at Newmarket. Wilton was severely damaged by fire in 1647 and restoration was put in the hands of John Webb. The restored interior includes the famous Single Cube and Double Cube rooms, which are decorated in a rich Flemish-French manner, although the doorcases are derived from those at Jones's Banqueting House.

Wilton House, Wiltshire, c. 1630: south front.

10

17th-Century Mannerism

Outside London the impact of the revival of Classicism in architecture was varied. Much that passes within the term 'Classical' was designed by masons and craftsmen, and even by amateur gentlemen who had read foreign texts on architectural proportion and usage. Results varied, from the absorption of the Whitehall court style of Jones and his circle to a mixture of styles from the Netherlands and France. The works of individual masons are not well documented: Nicholas Stone (1586–1647) has been linked with Lindsay House, Lincoln's Inn Fields, and the use of giant ordered pilasters, while in the provinces one of the most notable masons was John Jackson of Oxford, to whom is attributed the Baroque south porch of St Mary the Virgin (1637) and the Canterbury Quadrangle in St John's College (1632–36).

The porch at St Mary is a curious addition to the medieval church and shows the first use of twisted columns supporting the Corinthian order. Although such a feature had been used in around 1625 for the baldacchino (the canopy covering the altar) in St Peter's, Rome, it is likely that Jackson's source was either those depicted in a panel by Rubens, in the Banqueting House ceiling, or the cartoons by Raphael, then recently acquired for the Mortlake tapestry factory.

At St John's, where the college founded in 1555 incorporates buildings from the former St Bernard's College, the 17th century is marked by the building of another quadrangle. Here on the east and west sides of the Canterbury Quadrangle are ranges supported over an arcade of Tuscan Doric pillars. The centrepieces of two stages have paired columns of the Doric and Ionic orders, surmounted by a semi-circular pediment. The east front has a bronze figure of Charles I by Hubert Le Sueur (1580–1658) set into a niche flanked by Corinthian pillars and surmounted by a triangular pediment. The west side is

Opposite: Belton House, Lincolnshire, c. 1684–86, a fine example of classical symmetry in honey-coloured limestone.

identical except that the figure is of Queen Henrietta Maria. The upper stage of the range on either side, with rectangular windows with stone mullions and the battlemented parapet above, might seem to be a continuation of the collegiate style of the previous hundred years.

This reluctance to adopt the Classical style at Oxford can be seen at Brasenose College. Here the chapel and library of about 1656–59 have windows filled with Gothic tracery set within walls divided by Corinthian-ordered pilasters and crowned with pediments. The parapet is partially battlemented and adorned with pinnacles and urns. The inside of the chapel has a 15th-century plaster fan and pendant vaulted ceiling that was brought from the former St Mary's College. At Christ Church the Great Staircase to the dining hall has a remarkable fan vault of about 1640 in which most of the weight is supported on one central pier. At University College the original buildings were replaced by two rectangular blocks in the Gothic style, with building dating from the 1630s but interrupted by the Civil War. Here there were no concessions to the Classical: the gate lodges on the High Street front are battlemented and the roof-line of each range is punctuated with ogee-headed gables with a distinctly Flemish flavour. It was at Clare College, Cambridge, originally founded in 1338, that the first complete college rebuilding was undertaken. This began in

1638 with the east range and entrance to the court, and then the west range facing the Fellows Garden and Backs in 1640. Work was interrupted by the Civil War and not resumed until the 1660s. The entrance includes triple orders, a rusticated arch and an oriel window projecting from the middle stage. The west range introduces giant Ionic-ordered pilasters, dividing the facade into seven bays on either side of the gateway to the court, probably under the influence of the Jones-Webb circle, and contemporary with Lindsay House and Lees Court. The balustrade is open so as to admit light to the roof dormers, which are themselves adorned by alternating triangular and semi-circular pediments. In order to facilitate the movement of building materials to the site a bridge was built across the Cam between 1635 and 1640: designed by Thomas Grumbold, a Northamptonshire mason, it was strongly influenced by a design for a triple-arched bridge by Palladio in his *Quattro Libri*, with the substitution of a balustrade instead of a parapet.

Lees Court, Kent, c .1640: Like Lindsay House, it has been linked to Inigo Jones. Here we have a monumental display of giant Ionic ordered pilasters. The roof may originally have been hidden behind a parapet.

Away from the academic environment of Oxford and Cambridge the reigns of James I and Charles I saw the building of a number of houses in a style that the late Sir John Summerson dubbed 'Artisan Mannerism'. Since this style was largely dependent on the adaptation of pattern-book detail, the result can be seen as quaint or unusual, and certainly more reminiscent of the Low Countries than Italy. In the southern counties brick was used extensively: three outstanding examples are Swakeleys, near Uxbridge, from about 1629; the so-called Dutch House at Kew, from 1631; and Broome Park, near Canterbury, from about 1635.

Swakeleys and Broome are built to a pronounced H plan, while Kew is basically rectangular. The principal distinguishing features of this style are the so-called Dutch gables adorning the roof line. The east and west facades of Broome are dressed with giant ordered brick pilasters, and the casement windows are retained. At Swakeleys, stone

Above: Salisbury, Wiltshire: Mompesson House, 1701.

Below: Kew, London, Dutch House.

is used for window cases, doorways, quoining at the wall angles and the framing of gables. At Kew the work is in brick throughout, although the visual harmony has been somewhat marred by the replacement of mullioned casements with later sash windows. The centre is emphasized by an attempt to create the three orders in brick, even to the carving of Ionic and Corinthian capitals. The roof line of Kew is dominated by a battery of eight brick chimney stacks.

Dutch or Flemish gables were also used extensively in eastern England for farmhouses, barns and sheds, as well as almshouses. In northern England Dutch gables were rare; the traditional diagonal facing was retained, and the only hint of Classicism would have been the doorcase. If stone was not ideal for a highly decorative translation of an engraved pattern book plate to the wall surface, plaster certainly was, and the craft of pargetting (found principally in Suffolk) provides a rich variety of Flemish patterns including strapwork swags, naive figures and coats of arms. An outstanding example is Sparrows House, Ipswich.

The degree of Classical influence in houses of the mid-17th century varies from the heavily Italianate in buildings by or attributed to John Webb and his circle, to a Dutch Palladianism, a result of exile during the Commonwealth of builders in sympathy with the Stuart cause. Lees Court, near Faversham, Kent (c. 1640), is an Italianate, long rectangular building dressed with giant Ionic-ordered pilasters throughout its length. The roof is projected out over an eaves cornice of considerable depth supported by brackets. Perhaps this was influenced by the terraces of houses which had recently been built in London's Lincoln's Inn Fields and Great Queen Street, with giant ordered pilasters running through the piano nobile and upper floor. At The Vyne, Hampshire, a house dating from the Tudor period, John Webb made alterations to the interior as well as adding the first giant ordered portico of any house in England (c. 1660).

The Vyne, Hampshire, c. 1660: the earliest example of a projected portico over the entrance to a house.

The Dutch influence in the second half of the 17th century is more formal to the extent that such buildings as the Dutch House at Kew are made to seem rather quaint. A feature that now appears is the hipped roof, sometimes balustraded and adorned in the centre by an octagonal lantern and cupola: a fine example is Ashdown House, Berkshire (c. 1650). Ashdown has been attributed to the Dutch-born Huguenot, Sir Balthazar Gerbier (1591–1667), since it was built for the Earl of Craven, who had commissioned Gerbier to build nearby Hampstead Marshall. Ashdown is virtually a cube of three floors above a basement, divided by horizontal plat-bands. The hipped roof is boldly projected over the eaves, and the east and west fronts are pierced with triple dormers, while tall chimneys rise from the other two sides. The corners of the walls have quoining. In many respects the building seems almost a full-size prototype of the traditional doll's house.

Sadly one of the most famous houses of the mid-century decade,

Ashdown House, Berkshire, c. 1650: rather Dutch in flavour with its hipped roof, balustrade and central cupola.

Coleshill (1650), not far from Ashdown, was destroyed by fire in 1952. It was designed by the gentleman architect Roger Pratt (1620–84), who had travelled on the continent during the Civil War and had stayed in Rome. It seems to have borne a resemblance to Newington House near Oxford (c. 1630), perhaps one of the earliest examples of a hipped roof and central cupola. Coleshill was a double square in plan with a corridor running across the middle of the house on each floor, and rooms on either side justifying its label as a 'double-pile' house. Its harmony of detail was particularly pleasing. The facades were divided into three stages including basement. Ground and upper floors were divided by a plat-band. The wall surface was of ashlar with corner quoining. The nine windows on each floor were spaced into two narrow and one wide set corresponding with the hipped roof dormers. Pairs of chimneys rose from the slope of the roof: two at each side and two marking the longitudinal walls within and the corresponding broad space between each set of windows. The entrance led directly into the stair hall rising through the ground and upper floors. Directly opposite was the great parlour or salon and on the upper floor, entered from the gallery, was the great dining room. The basement contained the service rooms including a kitchen, pantry, larder, dairy, servants' hall and still room. Back stairs each side of the house linked the basement with the upper floors and the servants' quarters in the roof—thus the servants were able to move about unseen.

Red or pinkish brick is always associated with Dutch architecture—Holland has no natural building stone. In this respect Eltham Lodge, in south London (c. 1665), seems the quintessential Dutch house of the period. Like Coleshill, it is a double-pile, but the grand stair has been moved to the centre of the house, beyond the entrance hall. Coleshill was designed by Hugh May (1621–1684), who became a leading figure at the Court of Charles II and who had been in exile during the Commonwealth, mainly in Holland. The influence of Jacob van Campen's Mauritshuis, at The Hague, is easily apparent, but Eltham Lodge is far from being a mere copy. On the north entrance front it has a giant pilastered centrepiece with a pediment on a level with the slope of the hipped roof. The windows on each floor may be an early example of the sash type that from now on came to replace casements, while the sides of the roof, pierced by dormers, project out over an eaves cornice that is supported by small brackets (modillions). From the flat of the roof rise four pairs of brick chimney stacks with the added elegance of recessed panels on each face.

Another fine example of the Anglo-Dutch style of the Restoration is Ramsbury Manor, Wiltshire, with a similar entrance front elevation to Eltham Lodge. Here, however, the pedimental centrepiece is slightly projecting, with corner quoining. As at Eltham, the main pediment is adorned with a cartouche and swags. Pilasters are not used. The main floors are divided by a plat-band and the entrance

Eltham Lodge, south London, c. 1665: Hugh May based the design on the Mauritshuis at the Hague c.1630.

door is surmounted by a pediment. Squeries Court, Westerham, Kent (c. 1680), built for John Warde, son of a Lord Mayor of London, also has a strong Dutch flavour with its pinkish brick and hipped roof. It is also rectangular like Coleshill, but is one bay shorter on either side. A similar house to Squeries is nearby Tadworth Court, Surrey (c. 1694), with a centrepiece beneath a prominent pediment; it displays brickwork of the highest quality.

In the second half of the century the H plan of the Tudor and Jacobean period was again popular. Thus, the entrance front is flanked by projecting wings, at first minimal, as at Honington Hall, Warwickshire (c. 1671), although Groombridge Place, Kent (c. 1661), is a more definite H. One of the most impressive and influential versions was Clarendon House, Piccadilly (1664), by Roger Pratt (1620–1684), also the architect of Coleshill, with which it had a

Squeries Court, Westerham, Kent, c. 1680: beautifully proportioned, even the recessed panelled brick chimneys add to its charm.

distinct visual link. Built in brick, Clarendon had a slightly projected pedimented centrepiece, and the side wings projected considerably. A balustraded hipped roof extended across the whole house, with a cupola in the centre. Although demolished in 1684, it was closely copied in William Winde's (c. 1645–1722) Belton House, Lincolnshire (1684–86), although on a smaller scale. Belton, perhaps the finest example of a country house of the period, has a simple hall and salon division through the body, with the main stair placed in a hall to one side. The walls of the principal rooms are covered with exquisite panelling in oak and walnut, with highly naturalistic fruit and flower carving by Grinling Gibbons and his school. The high plaster ceilings are divided by deeply moulded rectangular and elliptical panels, decorated with flower mouldings.

The first half of the 17th century was not one for major church building: after all, there were many redundant former religious houses now prey to the needs of those seeking building stone. In many instances it was a question of alteration rather than rebuilding, such as the introduction of a pulpit and family pews or a carved screen, and indeed the re-introduction of so-called 'papist' features such as a the canopied font or pulpit, under the influence of Archbishop William Laud. One such example is Rycote Chapel in Oxfordshire, originally built in 1449 in the grounds of Rycote House, at that time the seat of the Quartermain family. In the early 17th century it was changed internally to reflect the new liturgical requirements and has remained unaltered ever since. Beneath its wooden barrel roof the rood screen has been replaced by a wooden frame to support the royal arms. On either side of the aisle are enclosed pews: one for the Norreys family, then the owners of Rycote House, and the other for Charles I. Beyond the screen is a small tiled area in front of beautifully carved communion rails, beyond which is the altar in the form of a table. Behind this is a pedimented reredos in front of the Perpendicular Gothic east window. Another example of church building is the small red brick Groombridge Chapel, adjacent to Groombridge Place, in Kent. It was built in 1625, in thanksgiving for the failure of Charles I's plan to marry the Spanish Infanta. Here again the style is

Above: Belton House, Lincolnshire, c. 1680: salon with wooden panelling in oak and limewood by Grinlin Gibbons workshop.

Opposite: Staunton Harold, Leicestershire, church with porch c. 1653. A perfect integration of latent Gothic with Mannerist pattern-book classicism.

Perpendicular. This was also the style of the largest church of the period, St John's, Leeds (1632–33). In London, the church of St Katherine Cree (c. 1631) is a mixture of Classical and Gothic. The interior has semi-circular arcading resting on Corinthian-ordered pillars. The clerestory is Perpendicular, the east window of the chancel reminiscent of window tracery in old St Paul's Cathedral. The vault is almost flat, forming a star-patterned decoration incorporating large heraldic bosses.

In 1631 Inigo Jones's St Paul's Covent Garden was begun as part of the development of the Earl of Bedford's land, and here we see a primitive Tuscan Doric for the portico and austere brickwork for the sides. Compared with a century earlier—before the parliamentary Acts that permitted Henry VIII's destruction of relics, chantry chapels, and all idolatrous ornament—interiors seem cold. Wall paintings have been submerged under whitewash and statues pulled from niches, rood screens and painted panels demolished, stained glass windows smashed. For the next century or so it was the craftsmanship of the woodcarver and plasterer that was to give many church and chapel interiors their colour and life. The statue of the Virgin Mary with the Christ child holding a crucifix, inserted into a niche over the porch of St Mary the Virgin, Oxford, contributed to the charge of popery levelled against Archbishop Laud by Parliament in 1644.

Church building virtually ceased during the Commonwealth period, although one rare example was built, in stark defiance of Cromwell. This is the Perpendicular church of Staunton Harold, Leicestershire, begun in 1653. It is only when one comes to the west door beneath the tower that one is confronted by the most amazing mixture of Classical Mannerist and Baroque ornament. The arched door is flanked by tapering paired pilasters linked by swags, Flemish in flavour. Above the entablature, tall statues of angels flank a framed inscription that tells us that the founder, Sir Robert Shirley, did 'ye best things in ye worst times'. For this noble action he went to the Tower of London. Apart from the rebuilding of the City of London churches after the Great Fire, major church building did not start again until the 18th century, by which time Britain had absorbed the Baroque and was on the verge of Palladianism.

11

Sir Christopher Wren

The name Wren is synonymous with the rebuilding of St Paul's Cathedral, a building that elevates his status to that of a major architect, worthy to stand alongside his continental contemporaries. His achievements were for the most part enabled by the Great Fire of London in 1666; without this unfortunate circumstance he would probably have kept his academic position in Astronomy at Oxford, and it is unlikely that he would have become surveyor of the king's works, an appointment he held for over 40 years.

Opposite: St Paul's Cathedral, West Front c. 1700.

Wren (1632–1723) was born the son of the rector of East Knoyle, in Wiltshire. His father was soon elevated to the deanery of Windsor and thus he was brought up in an atmosphere with pronounced royal leanings. He was sent to Westminster School and entered Wadham College, Oxford in 1649. Here he excelled as a natural scientist; John Evelyn the diarist called him that 'miracle of youth'. Upon graduation he remained a lecturer in mathematics until 1657, when he was appointed to the Gresham Professorship in Astronomy in London. In 1661 he was appointed Savilian Professor of Astronomy at Oxford and in the same year was a Foundation Member of the Royal Society.

Wren's turning to architecture was perhaps unusual for someone who had not studied the great masters of the Renaissance at first hand. In 1661 he was brought to the notice of King Charles II as an able draughtsman. Appearing to the king as a man of great practical ability, Wren was invited to take charge of the fortifications of Tangiers (part of the marriage dowry of Charles's wife, Catherine of Braganza). He declined this opportunity, perhaps on the grounds of ill health, and remained in Oxford, where he was soon approached to design a building for university ceremonies: the Sheldonian Theatre (built between 1664 and 1669), named after the then Bishop of London and former Warden of All Souls' College, Gilbert Sheldon.

To fulfil its purpose, the theatre needed as wide a space as possible, unencumbered by piers supporting the roof. The inspiration for the ground plan was the antique Theatre of Marcellus, which Wren knew from engravings in Serlio's treatise on architecture. The Sheldonian's exterior is relatively plain, with a formal entrance between Corinthian half columns on the wide south front. The interior has seats ranked in steps round the central auditorium. Further seating is set in a circular wooden gallery, painted to simulate marble. Light is admitted through segmented windows beneath the gallery and a clerestory above. The most ingenious part of the structure is the timber roof construction with each truss dovetailed together to form both triangular supports for the roof above and flat supports for the painted ceiling panels beneath. These ceiling panels are painted to represent the open sky above a folded velarium, or canvas awning. The joints of the panels are hidden behind wooden beading, moulded and painted to simulate rope.

In 1663 Wren was appointed a member of the Commission for the repair of St Paul's Cathedral, which had not only suffered at the hands of the Parliamentarians but still awaited completion of the restoration started by Inigo Jones. Wren's proposals included the reconstruction of the crossing area with a dome supported on eight piers, replacing the rather squat square tower. His initial inspiration probably came from Bramante's dome for St Peter's, depicted in an engraving in Wren's copy of Serlio's treatise. In 1665, the plague gave Wren the opportunity to visit France (the only time he travelled abroad). Most of his time was spent in Paris, and by chance the greatest master of the Italian Baroque, Gianlorenzo Bernini, was there to design an east front for the Louvre. They actually met but, as Wren wrote in a letter to the Reverend Dr Bateman on his activities in Paris, 'the old reserved Italian gave me but a few Minutes of his time'.

Wren studied the Louvre in detail, saw Versailles (just before its expansion under Levau and J H Mansart) and visited numerous other great houses. St Paul's must have been uppermost in his mind and so he would have paid particular attention to the churches of the Sorbonne, by Jacques Lemercier, and Val-de-Grace, by François Mansart and Lemercier. These buildings in turn were influenced by churches in Rome, such as Il Gesu, and had domes raised on drums over the crossing. The sight of these, as well as an engraving of St Peter's, Rome with the dome completed after a design by Michelangelo, must have reinforced Wren's desire to make a radical break with tradition.

Wren submitted his report on the proposed restoration to the Commission in May 1666 along with detailed elevations in pen and wash in his own hand. The opening out of the crossing space from a square to an octagon may have been suggested by that of Ely Cathedral where his uncle, Matthew, had been bishop. The dome raised upon a tall drum owes much to Michelangelo, although the introduction of an inner dome connected to a lantern rising through the outer dome shell was close to Lemercier's church of the Sorbonne. Finally, the lantern was to be capped by a pineapple-shaped steeple. Wren could hardly have known how fortunate he was going to be when just six days after the approval of his plan the Great Fire swept across the City of London between 2 and 6 September.

St Paul's Cathedral: pre-fire dome design c. 1666.

With three quarters of the City destroyed, a Commission was immediately set up to address the problem of rebuilding. By 11 September Wren had produced a plan introducing broad thoroughfares between a civic centre and St Paul's, intersected by a grid pattern of minor streets. The plan combined something of the grandeur of Sixtus V's Rome and Henri IV's Paris. Unfortunately, the need to get the City functioning as quickly as possible had to come before Wren's proposal of a total rebuilding, which was in any case beyond the financial means of Parliament, City merchants and the Crown. Wren's contribution was to be limited to the rebuilding of 53 parish churches, St Paul's Cathedral and the Customs House. In 1669 he was appointed surveyor of works and he subsequently resigned his academic position as Savilian Professor at Oxford in 1671.

Although Wren had been working on plans for the rebuilding of St Paul's since the fire, work did not actually start until 1675. Work on many of the churches began immediately after the Rebuilding Act of 1670, which also imposed a tax on coal shipped to London in order to help raise a steady income for rebuilding. Although it is popularly assumed that Wren designed all the churches himself, this is not quite true. Wren must have deputed work in much the same way that artists left minor parts of a painting to pupils; increasingly, scholars attribute work to his assistants, Dr Robert Hooke (1635–1703), a fellow Oxford mathematician, and Edward Woodroffe (died in 1675), who had been surveyor to the Dean and Chapter of Westminster. Some have even suggested that Wren designed little more than the towers of the churches in any detail and, since many of these were not built until the end of the century, even these may owe much to the hand of Nicholas Hawksmoor (1661–1736), who had come to London to enter Wren's office as 'scholar and domestic clerk' in 1679.

No two churches are alike and all are masterpieces of original planning on a confined scale. All but three were designed in the Classical style; one that survives in the Gothic, St Mary Aldermary, has been found to incorporate portions of the medieval church, which had only been gutted by the Fire. Some of the churches are of the columned basilican plan, such as St Bride, or are a simple box, as in St Benet, Paul's Wharf. Others incorporated a dome; at the destroyed St Antholin, and at St Benet, Fink, the body of the church was surmounted by an elliptical dome. At St Stephen, Walbrook, the circular dome is supported on eight pillars, a trial run for the construction of St Paul's. The richer parishes rebuilt in Portland stone although many churches had bodies constructed in red brick with stone being reserved for the window surrounds, corner quoining and towers. These towers would incorporate a belfry stage dressed with Classical pilasters and surmounted by steeples, the most famous being those of St Bride and St Mary le Bow.

Compared with the grandeur of the church interiors of Roman Catholic Europe Wren's may seem austere, having plain plastered walls rather than walls of coloured marble, altarpieces incorporating tableaux of the lives of saints, coloured marble floors and painted domes focussing on heavenly light, framed by plaster reliefs incorporating floating angels. But the emphasis in the Anglican service was on the sermon from the pulpit; interiors were to be

St Benet's, Paul's Wharf, 1677–83: a simple brick box with classical decoration restricted to swags or festoons above the windows, and pediment over the doorcase surrounding the entrance. The corners, including those of the tower, are clasped with stone quoins. The tower is surmounted by a lead-covered **cupola and spire.**

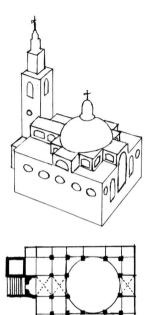

Left: St Stephen Walbrook, 1672–79. Interior showing coffered dome resting on pendentives supported by slender Corinthan pillars.

Above: St Stephen Walbrook, plan.

unencumbered, as far as possible, by piers and columns and to be lit, preferably in Wren's view, by clear glass windows. So, the altar raised on several steps was a simple table set against a carved wooden reredos, perhaps set beneath a carved entablature and pediment. Some altars incorporated an oil painting or were divided into sections by carved and fluted pilasters, and featured the Ten Commandments, Lord's Prayer or Creed. Altar or communion rails might be embellished with spiral bannisters and panels of foliated relief carving by Grinling Gibbon and his assistants. The high quality of woodcarving can be found also on the pulpits, doorways, font covers, and organ cases, sometimes above a galley. Ironwork screens occasionally flanked fonts at the west end of the nave, and certain pews were adorned with elaborate sword rests of iron, dating from the early 18th century. The moulded plasterwork of walls and ceilings were also of exceptionally high quality with perhaps gilding to bring certain areas into higher relief. This plainness came not simply in response to the differing dogmas between Catholicism and Anglicanism but also from the more basic practicalities of money and patronage. There were no Barbarinis, Borghesis or Pamphilis in London and the rebuilt structure, in any case, was restricted to the space occupied by the earlier church and its churchyard. The Coal Tax would only contribute to the basic structure; individual parishes had to raise additional money themselves out of revenue, the sale of building material from the fire-damaged church, subscriptions and by pleading for donations from city companies. Once a parish approached Wren for a design it then had to be approved by the Commissioners for the Act including the Lord Mayor and the Bishop of London.

Design ideas can be traced to various sources. The influence of Italian Baroque is seen in the tower of St Vedast, Forster Lane, and Dutch in the external brick treatment of St Benet and the internal cross-vaulted plans of St Anne and St Agnes and in St Martin, Ludgate—perhaps a result of a strong interest in Dutch architecture from Wren's colleague Hooke. The tower of St Magnus the Martyr bears a strong likeness to that of St Charles Borromeo, in Antwerp, Belgium, while the rusticated and recessed entrance to St Mary le Bow has a striking likeness to François Mansart's design for the entrance to the Hôtel de Conte, Paris. The coffered dome of St Stephen, Walbrook is a simplified version of contemporary Roman examples, but built on a circular rather than an oval plan. A century later, S P Cockerell was to use the idea of a circular dome supported on eight Corinthian columns within a square nave at St Mary, Banbury, Oxfordshire. At St Dunstan-in-the-east, Wren was required to rebuild in the Gothic; the west tower supports a spire raised on four splayed corner buttresses, modelled on the destroyed pre-medieval tower of St Mary le Bow. The church rebuilding campaign

Left: St Magnus the Martyr 1671–76 (steeple 1705).
Right: St Dunstan in the East 1670–71 (steeple c. 1697).

was virtually completed by 1686, although some of the towers and spires were only added in the early 18th century.

The story of the rebuilding of St Paul's is complex, not least because hundreds of drawings from Wren's office survive; some are in his own hand, but many are the work of assistants and are undated. The fact that the completed building differs so much from the Warrant design of 1675 begs the question as to when Wren fixed on the final version: perhaps he redesigned parts and details throughout the 35-year building campaign. One also wonders how much Wren left to his able assistants, Edward Woodroffe, Joshua Marshall and

From left: St Mary le Bow 1670–80; St Vedast 1695–1700; St Bride 1670–84 (steeple 1703)

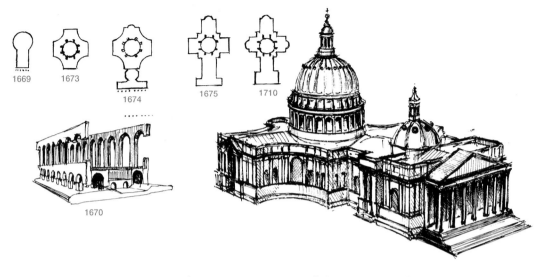

Thomas Strong. However, all this in no way reduces the part Wren played in the project but, rather, emphasizes the support and trust of a close-knit office of work.

Until 1668 the Commission for rebuilding the City believed that old St Paul's could be restored since, although the quire was in ruins, part of the nave encased in Jones refacing had survived, along with his west portico. However, with the collapse of a nave pier Dean Sancroft commissioned Wren, then still in Oxford, to provide designs for a new building, with the cost to be borne by the tax on coal. He was given rooms on the south side of the cathedral in the Old Convocation House, which had escaped the fire, in which to set up an on-site office and workshop. In 1670 Wren produced a wooden model in the form of a rectangular hall with side chambers, or loggias, the latter to provide space for those who previously conducted business in the old nave. A square section surmounted by a dome was to be at the western end of the church.

In 1673 Wren produced the so-called Greek Cross plan, at the

Above left: St Paul's Cathedral,
south west tower c. 1705.
Above: St Paul's Cathedral.

centre of which rose a dome resting on eight piers. He must have
derived this plan from knowing of Michelangelo's ideas for a
centralized St Peter's; François Mansart's design for a Bourbon chapel
of St Denis, near Paris, and a drawing by John Webb for a 'Greek
Cross' church. The following year the Great Model appeared. This
incorporated the Greek Cross design but with a western extension to
include a domed vestibule and giant Corinthian-ordered portico
reminiscent of the Pantheon in Rome. The wooden model survives,
and today can be seen in the crypt of St Paul's, allowing one to
observe the detail that was intended for the interior, with Corinthian
pilasters placed against the eight piers. Light was to be admitted to
the ambulatory circling the dome through large windows in the
concave walls, with additional light coming directly into the central
area from the drum beneath the dome. Some have suggested that had
it been built to this plan, the cathedral would have been rather dark
due to the narrowness of the openings between the piers.
Unfortunately this design, said to be Wren's favourite, was rejected by

Sir Christopher Wren **163**

the Commission on the grounds of cost, practicality and its radical departure from the traditional Latin Cross form.

Some time between its rejection in autumn 1674 and April 1675 Wren produced what is known as the Warrant design, which returned to the traditional plan and included a western portico similar to the one that Inigo Jones had built against the old cathedral in 1635. It is tempting to think of this plan as having been an early 'post fire' idea on Wren's behalf ; hardly a serious intention with its extraordinary saucer supporting a tall Michelangelesque drum and dome, above which is a tall steeple reminiscent of that to be built later at St Bride. In granting the royal warrant for its construction the king was 'pleased to allow Wren the liberty in the prosecution of his work, to make variations, rather ornamental than essential, as from time to time he should see proper' (14 May 1675). In other words, this was an invitation to Wren to build a masterpiece as he saw fit.

The drawings that exist, sometimes referred to as the Penultimate design and perhaps dating from before the end of 1675, bear a striking resemblance at least to the detail of the elevation of the nave as built. So it is likely that Wren finalized much of the design within a few months of the royal warrant. The elevation includes the upper storey screen wall, which hides the buttressing of the clerestory wall behind and adds greater strength to the external appearance. This fundamental alteration to the design could not be carried out before the laying of adequate foundations to absorb the additional load. Indeed, the site was being cleared for the setting out of the foundations in 1673. Strong foundations were also needed for the crossing piers, which were obviously intended to support a heavier structure than that shown in the Warrant drawings and were similar in scale to the dome in the Penultimate design.

The contract for work to commence was signed on 18 June and by 1697 the quire was complete. The nave and west front followed, by 1708, and the dome was built between about 1706 and the completion of the cathedral in 1710. The final result is a triumph of proportion, with the dome and drum rising majestically above. The building's style may be designated as English High Renaissance or muted Baroque: it has articulation derived from Jones's Banqueting House, transeptal porticoes inspired by Cortona in Rome, a west front with a gallery of paired Corinthian columns from Perrault and Levau at the Louvre, and west towers that have a Borromini flavour. The dome itself owes a debt to both Michelangelo and Bramante.

Only by exploring the cathedral can we fully understand and admire Wren's inventiveness which combined his skill as an architectural designer with engineering. The dome we see from outside is no more than a lead shell. The lantern is supported on a brick and stone cone that merges with an inner dome, the combined load then transmitted through pendentives to eight piers. This arrangement allowed for an inner dome that did not create the effect of a funnel due to its height above the floor while the exterior dome was still high enough to act as a focus and landmark from a distance. Wren had perhaps followed J H Mansart's dome construction on the chapel of Les Invalides, in Paris. In order to increase the visual bulk of the nave and quire, as well as to hide flying buttresses (considered unseemly for a Classical building), Wren introduced false walls to the upper stage, dressing them with paired pilasters and niches crowned with pediments.

Despite Wren's work on the City churches and St Paul's, he was also involved in the design of many other buildings in the later 17th century. At the two universities these include Pembroke College Chapel, Emmanuel College Chapel and Trinity College Library, all at Cambridge, and Tom Tower, Christ Church, Oxford. He also collaborated with Henry Aldrich over the design of Trinity College Chapel. The chapel at Emmanuel cleverly forms the centrepiece of the east range of the Front Court and was linked to the earlier north and south blocks by a colonnade supporting a galleried combination room. Indeed the pillared frontage of the chapel hides the continuation of the gallery, from which a door allows access to a balcony over the west end of the chapel proper. At Trinity College Wren had to enclose the west side of Neville's Court with a library, on ground that was only a few feet above water level. His first design was for an isolated square block with a pedimented entrance centrepiece, surmounted by a dome; this was obviously inspired by Palladio's Villa

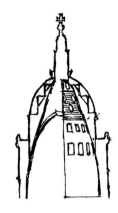

St Paul's Cathedral: dome section.

Rotonda at Vicenza. His next design was for a block linking both wings and raised over a colonnade, probably inspired by the Library of St Mark, Venice, with which he was familiar from engravings. Again there is great originality in the way Wren set the level of the floor below the arches of the colonnade in order to provide enough wall space for the book cases beneath large windows. The facade overlooking Neville's Court is dressed in Doric half-pillars on the ground stage, and Ionic half-pillars between the windows on the upper stage. At Oxford his bell tower above the main entrance to Christ Church is a clever addition, or completion, of the grand entrance from St Aldate's Street. As Wren wrote, 'I resolved it ought to be Gothick to agree with the Founder's Work'. The addition is in two stages between giant flanking turrets covered with Perpendicular blind panelling. The lower stage incorporates a large ogee-hooded arch admitting light to a ringing chamber, while the upper incorporates a clock and, above this, an octagonal belfry stage with eight louvred openings.

Wren's royal contracts included a Palace of Winchester (only partially finished and turned into a barracks in the 19th century); the conversion of Nottingham House, Kensington, for King William III and Queen Mary; apartments for Queen Mary at Whitehall Palace (burnt down in 1698), and apartments for the king and queen, at Hampton Court—where we see the domestic, human scale of English royal building in comparison to the overwhelming grandeur of contemporary Versailles.

Fortunately, royal funds did not run to reconstructing the whole Tudor palace, so Wren was confined to the south-east corner. Here the apartments are built round the Fountain Court in pinkish-red brick above a stone arcade in the manner of an Italian Renaissance palace. The East front, facing a formal drive through the park, has a wide stone centrepiece incorporating Corinthian pilasters and engaged-columns beneath a pediment set against the attic level. The tall windows of the state apartments on the East and South fronts are enclosed within Portland stone window-cases.

Wren was also responsible for a number of small projects, and probably advised on many for which no documentary evidence

survives. One project that was very close to his heart, as an astronomer and mathematician by academic training, was the Royal Observatory. It was built on a hill in Greenwich Park for Sir John Flamstead, who was created first Astronomer Royal by Charles II in 1675. Constructed of red brick and dressed with stone dressings that exhude a Dutch flavour, it consists of a tall block containing living accommodation for Flamstead on the ground floor and an octagonal observational chamber known as the Camera Stellata above, today restored as far as possible to its original appearance. On the corners of the facade overlooking the park are turrets topped with lead-covered cupolas linked by a balustrade. A hint of the baroque is added by the scroll-volutes linking the wall of the observation chamber to the floor below. A walled terrace overlooking the park links two small pavilions such as one might have found in a contemporary garden.

Another Wren project that is now thought to have had an astronomical purpose, though outwardly it was a commemorative monument, is the giant Doric column in Lower Thames Street. Erected in 1676 to commemorate the Great Fire of London, it has also been attributed to fellow Oxford scientist, Dr Robert Hooke. It is surmounted by a great copper ball, supposed to look like flames when caught by the sun, and it is now thought that the basement was to be used as an observation chamber beneath a huge telescope that pointed up to a lense hidden in the summit of the copper ball. Among other buildings attributed to Wren are Morden College in Blackheath, less than one mile from Greenwich Observatory and founded in 1696 for 'decayed merchants in trade with Turkey, Groombridge Place, in Kent, and Winslow Hall, in Buckinghamshire. This wide range of projects might be expected from an architect with many pupils and assistants.

Wren's grandest domestic works were the Royal Hospital, Chelsea, for army pensioners, and the Royal Hospital Greenwich, for naval pensioners. Chelsea Hospital was founded by Charles II in 1682, although it was the inspiration of Sir Stephen Fox who had been Paymaster-General to the Forces and a generous benefactor to the Hospital. The initial inspiration must however have been Louis XIV's foundation of Les Invalides, Paris, in 1670, which was on a far grander

Opposite: Hampton Court. Fountain Court at the heart of the state apartments built for William III and Mary from 1689.

scale and dominated by its domed chapel by J H. Mansart. The Chelsea site was facing the Thames and occupying an unfinished theological college founded by James I. The building plan was essentially in H form but with extended arms on the south to flank the open court facing the river. All range is of the same height and covered by a tiled roof. Construction is largely of two tones of brick: a mauve hue for the walls and a lighter pinkish surround for the windows, the choice of brick being due to the limited funds available. Portland stone is used for the pedimented centrepieces of each block and, in particular, for that of the central block where a Tuscan Doric portico divides the dining hall on the left (west) from the chapel on the right (east). Perhaps out of concern for the health and well-being of the pensioners, who live in cubicles along corridors in each wing, the hall and chapel can be reached from staircases at either the inner end or beneath a loggia to the portico, where the door enters a dividing vestibule. The horizontality of the three blocks is broken by the ranges of brick chimneys and a lantern tower and cupola rising behind the portico.

Greenwich Hospital was founded in 1694 by Queen Mary in thanksgiving for the naval victory of La Hogue, and is positioned at the centre of the dramatic bend of the Thames round Greenwich peninsula. There can be no more splendid set of riverside buildings, which are best viewed from the deck of a pleasure boat, coming into sight with their white stone bathed in sunlight. Wren had to overcome the problem of relating the buildings to both the earlier palace block by John Webb, abandoned in 1669, and to Inigo Jones's Queen's House, some 244 metres (800 feet) to the south. He originally intended to link the two riverside blocks by means of a tall central porticoed block, to house a hall and chapel surmounted by a dome and linked by curving colonnades to an inner set of east and west ranges. Beyond that, the Webb block was to be faced by an identical block across a slightly wider lower or outer court. No doubt Wren had the grandeur of the palace of Versailles in mind. But when this plan was presented in 1694, shortly before her death, the queen objected because it would have obscured the view from the north terrace of the Queen's House. The plan was revised so the Chapel (or

Queen Mary block) and Hall (or King William Block) are built round a quadrangle, enclosed on the east and west side by long Doric colonnades, and face each other across the upper court. The long ranges containing the Hall and Chapel are dominated by domes set on high drums dressed with Corinthian pillars. Queen Mary died before she could see and approve the plan that was eventually built. Indeed a project of this size was likely to go on for many years, and Wren himself did not live to see it fully completed, in the 1730s. The stages of building would have been closely supervised by others, such as Sir John Vanbrugh, who was Comptroller of Works from 1702, and Nicholas Hawksmoor, who became Assistant Surveyor for Greenwich and whose 'architectural hour' was yet to come. Hawksmoor probably supervised the construction of the King William block, which contains the hall with its Baroque interior and a painted ceiling by Sir James Thornhill that commemorates the foundation of the Hospital. The Queen Mary block opposite, containing the chapel, was not begun until 1729 under Thomas Ripley. Sadly the original decoration of the chapel interior was destroyed in a fire in 1779. Even if Wren did not live to see the final result it was his conception and has been depicted by numerous artists, from Canaletto onwards. Ideally the buildings should be admired from the Isle of Dogs, with the blocks and colonnades receding so as to draw the eye back to the Queen's House, from behind which Wren's Flamstead House rises on its green hill.

By the second decade of the 18th century Wren's architectural ideas were going out of fashion. In any case a new generation of architects had been born and were servants of new patrons, not least the Whig landowners who were finally in power by 1715. Distinguished as he was, Wren was none the less forced to resign the office of Surveyor of Work in 1718 as opportunities were given to younger men. His City was rebuilt and his cathedral complete, but the Baroque style was now being superseded by the austere Palladian movement. Wren died at the age of 91, in 1723, and was buried in the crypt of St Paul's Cathedral, where the simple inscription on the wall above his tomb provides the famous, and most appropriate, epitaph: 'Lector, si monumentum requiris circumspice' (Reader, if you seek a monument, look around you).

12

The Baroque Style

In an architectural context Baroque is associated with the Roman Catholic Counter-Reformation and the spiritual zeal of the Church in Italy and central Europe in the 17th century. The term invokes visions of highly ornamented facades and a sense of movement created by a flow of concave and convex surfaces, of interiors in which illusions of heavenly or courtly grandeur are created by the merging of architectural forms into indefinite space. Gianlorenzo Bernini and Francesco Borromini are the supreme architects, and Giovanni Battista Gaulli and Andrea Pozzo the masters of painterly illusion.

Nowhere in Protestant Britain do we approach the architectural complexities of, for instance, Borromini's St Ivo or Bernini's St Andrea al Quirinale, although in Baroque painted interiors there is more feeling of being part of the continental movement: after all, the Italian master Antonio Verrio (1639–1707) decorated apartments at Chatsworth and Burghley, and James Thornhill (c. 1675–1734) painted the apotheosis of William and Mary on the ceiling of the Great Hall of Greenwich Hospital, and on a grander scale than anything Charles Lebrun did for Louis XIV at Versailles. Certainly Andrea Pozzo, the creator of the architectural *trompe l'oeil* ceiling of St Ignazio, Rome, would have approved of Thornhill's ceiling at Moor Park, Hertfordshire, or the surprisingly little-known interior of St Lawrence, Little Stanmore, in Middlesex, built for the Duke of Chandos to serve as a family mausoleum adjacent to his long-since destroyed seat of Canons. The most sumptuous Baroque church interior is that of Great Witley, Worcestershire, built in the 1730s for Thomas Foley, a wealthy ironmaster, and attributed to James Gibbs (1682–1754). Some of the fittings, including the windows, were purchased at the sale of Canons estate in 1747. The ceiling in the

Opposite: Sudbury Hall, Derbyshire. Rebuilt from the 1660s, Sudbury retains some of the most splendid unaltered Baroque interiors in Britain including a grand staircase and long gallery.

form of a shallow barrel is adorned with plaster and papier-mâché moulding and oil on canvas panels by Antonio Bellucci. It is, perhaps, the ultimate in the architectural sublime, and perhaps all the more welcome after a visit to the derelict remains of nearby Witley Court, burnt in 1937. In Britain it was often the private patron, or the aristocrat (such as the Duke of Devonshire at Chatsworth), who was the instigator of Baroque grandeur rather than, with several exceptions, the Anglican Church.

In architecture there are certainly continental Baroque influences, such as Wren's borrowing of windows from Bernini's Palazzo Barberini for the west front of St Paul's, or Thomas Archer's towers at St John, Smith Square, Westminster that are borrowed from Borromini's St Agnese in Agone, in the Piazza Navona. While concave and convex surfaces or the interplay of staggered columns or pilasters on a church frontage proclaim the style in Italy from the early 17th century, it was really only during a brief space of about 20 years at the beginning of the 18th century that Britain witnessed something of a Baroque movement; unlike continental interpretations, here the emphasis was heavy and austere, with a vigorous modelling of contrasting parts or masses into blocks.

While Wren is often regarded as the epitome of the Baroque, he is actually more an architect of the period rather than the style: William Talman (1650–1719), Hawksmoor, Gibbs, Vanbrugh (1664–1726) and Thomas Archer (1668–1743) are considered more 'complete masters' of the latter—in particular Archer and Gibbs, who had the benefit of a Late Baroque architectural education in Rome. William Talman may be considered as the first Baroque architect of the country house and his south and east fronts of Chatsworth House introduced a Classical grandeur that was new to domestic architecture. Inspired by one of Bernini's designs for the east front of the Louvre, the facades are raised on a rusticated basement. The west front, perhaps by Thomas Archer, is dressed with giant Corinthian pilasters and a projected pedimented centrepiece of giant half columns. The south front is dressed at both sides by giant pilasters, and formality is further emphasized by the entablature and balustrade.

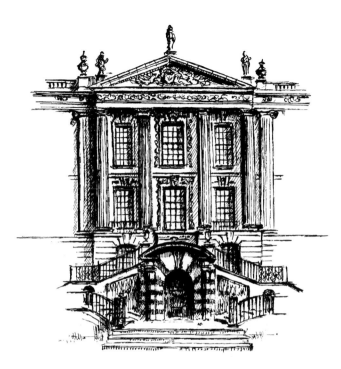

Talman's name has also been mentioned in connection with the much smaller Uppark, built high on the Sussex downs near Chichester for the 1st Earl of Tankerville, in about 1695. Constructed to a rectangular plan of red brick and rising to two floors above a basement it is crowned by a hipped roof that is pierced by elegant chimney stacks. With white stone quoining at the corners and a projected pedimented centrepiece on the south, or garden, front that encloses a pedimented doorcase, the building seems like the perfect model for a doll's house, or the colonial architecture of Williamsburg. The Baroque feeling is muted, with decoration limited to the curved pediment of the doorcase, the frieze above the door and the scroll-

work flanking the central window above. The alignment of the sash windows is continued with the dormers projecting through the roof. Inside, the rooms are restrained—perhaps due to substantial later redecoration by the Fetherstonhaugh family in the 1770s, undertaken in the prevalent Rococo style. Subsequently the interior was beautifully restored after a serious fire in 1989.

Hawksmoor's early years as an architect are rather overshadowed by the presence of Wren, under whom he started his career in 1681. In this capacity he worked at St Paul's Cathedral, Chelsea Hospital, Kensington Palace and Greenwich Hospital. His first independent commission was probably that of Easton Neston, Northamptonshire

Opposite: Uppark, West Sussex, c. 1695. One of the most perfect exteriors of the period and perhaps by William Talman, who was working at Chatsworth at the same time.

Left: Easton Neston, Northamptonshire c. 1699–1702, south or entrance front.

HORA E SEMPRE

Castle Howard, Yorkshire: the garden front by Vanbrugh and Hawksmoor, c. 1720. The centrepiece is dressed with giant Corinthian-ordered pilasters.

(c. 1699–1702), a house that seems to be strongly reminiscent of Talman's work at Chatsworth in its use of giant orders, although here they are of ashlar and not fluted. Easton Neston also has a similarity to the King William block of Greenwich Hospital, which was possibly designed by Hawksmoor as well. The grand entrance front projects out in stages to an entrance that at first may seem almost visually crushed by the giant Corinthian half pillars; above the projected entablature is a carved coat of arms of the patron, Sir William Fermor, set against a semicircular headpiece.

Although Hawksmoor designed much of the detail at Castle Howard and Blenheim, the commissions were given to John

Castle Howard, Yorkshire: the garden front by Vanbrugh and Hawksmoor, c. 1720. The centrepiece is dressed with giant Corinthian-ordered pilasters.

Castle Howard: The giant Mausoleum by Hawksmoor inspired by the tomb of Caecilia Metella on the Appian Way, Rome.

Vanbrugh, to whom the basic designs are also attributed. Both Castle Howard and Blenheim were built more for effect than convenience, and Vanbrugh, being of a romantic disposition and without too great a concern for cost, was the ideal person to create these expressions of power and grandeur. His background, on the other hand, seemed unlikely for such a successful architect. First a soldier, even arrested in France on a charge of spying, he had the pleasure of a short stay in the Bastille. On his return to England he left the army for the stage and wrote ten very successful plays including *The Relapse* and *The Provok'd Wife*. He was a Whig by inclination and a member of the Kit Kat Club, and it was there in 1699 that he probably met Charles Howard, 3rd Earl of Carlisle, who gave him the commission—originally offered to William Talman—to design a new home to replace the Howard family seat of Henderskelfe Castle (destroyed by fire in 1697), sited slightly to the south of the present house. Talman's charges had been too high and his personality unpleasant and pretentious. Vanbrugh had the sense to seek the assistance of Hawksmoor, who may have been recommended to him by Wren.

Castle Howard was planned as a domed central block with

flanking side wings forming a wide garden front on the south. The north or entrance front was to be flanked by projecting wings at right angles for the kitchens and stables. The result was to have been totally symmetrical, and with the dominating central domed block linked by quadrants to the side wings may have been inspired by one of Wren's rejected plans for Greenwich Hospital. The entrance front looks heavy and austere, with rusticated courses and giant Doric ordered pilasters. The south or garden front is raised up on a rusticated basement throughout its length. While the central block is emphasized by height, the salon is marked by a projected pedimented centrepiece. The stonework is ashlar but each window is flanked by fluted Corinthian pilasters running the entire length of the front.

The entrance from the north leads directly into the hall which rises through the house to the drum and dome, supported on four huge piers. The drama is reinforced by shafts of light from the drum as well as through the arches between the piers, truly a hint of the theatrical. It is only after some moments that the true scale registers on the mind as we notice the fireplaces on either side of the hall. Beyond the hall is the salon facing out over the terrace and formal garden. On either side of the salon is an enfilade, or line of rooms, with a sequence of doors in alignment, which in effect creates a corridor through the apartments, as at Chatsworth, and is derived from the French layouts of Vaux le Vicomte and Versailles. The central block with flanking lower wings and the kitchen block were finished according to the original plan; however, the stable block was moved away from the house and its intended position occupied by the library wing, built in the 1750s by William Robinson (1645–1712).

At Blenheim, commissioned in 1705 by John Churchill, 1st Duke of Marlborough, Vanbrugh and Hawksmoor created a mansion covering about three hectares (seven acres). It is a mighty assertion of power and the gift of a grateful nation to one who had reined in the power of Louis XIV, a bust of whom is set above the portico of the garden front. One enters via a huge court, flanked by the kitchen and stable blocks, the majesty of which is intensified by the gradual closing together of the projecting blocks and colonnades. Entrance is made up

two flights of steps and beneath a huge Corinthian portico of truly Roman grandeur. Inside the hall one can see how the admission of light is heavily dependent on the introduction of an attic stage, instead of a drum and dome as at Castle Howard. The ceiling at Bleinhem was painted by Thornhill and depicts the Glorification of the Duke of Marlborough. Beyond, in the salon, a remarkable illusion of space is created by the *trompe l'oeil* paintings of the peoples of the four continents, appearing to look into the room from between a row of columns. Executed by the French artist Louis Laguerre (who charged less than Thornhill), the painted marble of the columns and balustrade merges with that of the doorcases and rusticated marble dado: the painting was quite deliberately based on the wall decoration of the now-destroyed Ambassador's Staircase at Versailles.. Laguerre was also

Blenheim Palace, Oxfordshire, c. 1705 –30: the monumentality and grandeur of Versailles, but on a slightly smaller scale. The curving colonnades draw the eye into the magnificent portico fit for the military hero of the new Augustan age.

Seaton Delaval, Northumberland, 1722–28: John Vanbrugh's masterpiece is made all the more impressive and austere by the enormous rusticated columns flanking the entrance. The interior gutted, by fire in 1822, and with damaged statues still looking down from their pedestals, is the perfect backdrop for a film set in a haunted house.

responsible for an impressive set of wall paintings at Marlborough House that depict the various battles in which the Duke had fought.

From the gardens the facades provide a balance between warm areas of Oxfordshire ashlar and the striking rusticated blocks of the corner towers attributed to Hawksmoor, and surmounted by a heavy cornice and attic stage or what he called 'Emmencys'. The kitchen and stable blocks on either side of the entrance court by themselves occupy an area greater than that of many mansions. On a bleak day they look like prison blocks but on close analysis they are full of Vanbrugh whimsy: for instance, the entrance to the stable block is flanked by heavy paired Tuscan columns and entablature supporting nothing less than British lions crushing French cockerels, while the towers are imaginative creations of two stages, pierced by Vanbrugh-ian arches.

Vanbrugh alone was responsible for Seaton Delaval, Northumberland (1721–28), and Grimsthorpe Castle, Lincolnshire. Although much smaller than Blenheim, Seaton has a similar basic layout. The entrance court is flanked by stable and kitchen blocks, but the central block seems almost oppressive in its weight. The order is Doric, and the paired columns on either side of the door are supported by a bevelled rusticated basement. The interior of the entrance hall has arcades of blind arches set into the walls. Grimsthorpe, also from the 1720s, is the transformation of a 16th-century quadrangular house, and exhibits elements from Blenheim and Seaton that include paired rusticated Doric columns, arcading and block corner towers.

Hawksmoor's most original contributions are the six London churches constructed as a result of the 1711 Act for Fifty New Churches, passed to address the spiritual needs of the newly expanding suburbs of London. Built in Portland stone and rectangular in plan, they all have an austere simplicity that is far removed from the interior of Great Witley: heavy keystones over windows, thick doorcases and a variety of tower designs that rival those of Wren.

Above: Hawksmoor churches, from left: St Mary Woolnoth, 1716–25; St George in the East 1714–27; St George, Bloomsbury 1716–30; St Anne, Limehouse, 1714–30; St Alfege, Greenwich 1712–15.

Left and below: large drawing and plan: Christ Church, Spitalfields, 1714–28.

Wrest Park, Bedfordshire: the banqueting house, 1709.

St Martin-in-the-Fields: west portico.

Thomas Archer was the most Baroque of British architects, having spent some years in Rome. His first commission, the church of St Philip, Birmingham (1709–15), invokes Borromini in the concave surfaces of its tower. St Paul, Deptford, south London (1712–30), offers one of Britain's greatest architectural surprises. Set in a beautiful green oasis of a churchyard with its elegant steeple rising above the trees, it is square in plan with an apse projecting on the east, and raised on a stone podium behind a balustrade creating additional room for a large crypt beneath. Grand staircases give access to doors on the north and south, whilst the main entry at the west is through the door beneath a semicircular portico, reminiscent of Pietro da Cortona's Santa Maria della Pace, Rome. The interior is reminiscent of a great ballroom to a large mansion. Galleries on the north and south sides lead the eye to focus on the altar, which is lit by the clear-glass Venetian Window in the eastern apse. The walls are dressed with giant ordered pillars supporting a bold entablature and cornice. On either side of the altar are beautifully carved wooden vestries. The ceiling is divided into beautiful plastered divisions but without the painted panels of continental examples. The steeple is very cleverly set over a western apse beneath the portico, and rises in receding stages above a circular Doric belfry stage to a slender spire. Pevsner claimed that this church, with its now magnificently restored interior, comes closer to Borromini and the Roman Baroque than any other church of the period.

Archer was at his most original at St John, Smith Square, Westminster (1714). Here, two gigantic porticoes in antis surmounted by broken roof pediments are set in to the north and south facades whilst the four corners are emphasized with towers, derived from Borromini's St Agnese, in the Piazza Navona. Archer's mansion for the Duke of Shrewsbury, Heythrop, Oxfordshire, has the powerful character of Bernini's design for the Louvre front but detail such as broken pediments reversed over pilasters may be traced back to his knowledge of Buontalenti's Porta delle Supplice at the Uffizi, Florence, which dates from 1574. At Wrest Park, Bedfordshire, Archer designed a remarkable domed banqueting house, built largely in brick to a hexagonal plan, with round and square projections on alternate sides.

It is hard to label James Gibbs (1682–1754) as a true Baroque architect: his work varies from the spirit of Roman Baroque to the austerity of the Palladian movement. In his church of St Mary le Strand, London (1714–17), he consciously invokes detail from his master, Carlo Fontana. Rectangular in plan and of two stages raised over a crypt, the sides are divided into bays by pilasters: Ionic (lower) and Corinthian (upper). On the upper stage each alternate bay is crowned by a triangular or semi-circular pediment, so creating an effect of movement. The tower in receding stages is set over a Wren-like belfry stage. Nearby, his St Martin-in-the-Fields (1721–26) resembles an antique temple from the front, with its hexastyle Corinthian portico virtually masking the church behind. The sides are adorned with giant ordered Corinthian pilasters and windows surrounded by alternate courses of projected blocks, the so-called 'Gibbs surround'. The east facade is adorned with a Venetian window, a major Palladian feature.

Above left: St Martin-in-the-Fields, London, 1721–26, East Front.

Above right: Interior with side galleries and magnificent plaster decoration by Italian stuccoists.

Radcliffe Camera, Oxford, 1739–49, lies at the heart of the university and is surrounded on all sides by grand architecture. It is a visual masterpiece almost without equal in Britain.

The interior of St Martin-in-the-Fields retains the side galleries raised half the height of the nave pillars in order to allow light from side aisle windows. The sanctuary is flanked by side vestries and lit by a Venetian arch. The nave has a barrel-vaulted ceiling with delicate imported plaster decoration by the Italian stuccoists Artari and Bagutti.

At All Saints, Derby (now Derby Cathedral, built 1723–25), Gibbs modelled the interior closely on that of St Martin-in-the-Fields. The steeple of St Martin-in-the-Fields is the most Baroque feature of all and was clearly reproduced a few years later by Henry Flitcroft at nearby St Giles-in-the-Fields, and also by an architect whose identity remains unknown, at Mereworth, Kent (1744–46). In Glasgow in the 1740s Allan Dreghorn produced a passable if somewhat heavy likeness of St Martin's in his St Andrew's church; at Edinburgh in St Andrew's, George Street (the first church to be built in the New Town) St Martin's is parodied by a steeple rising behind a portico, designed by William Sibbald. Gibbs's ideas for church design were also quickly transported across the Atlantic to the eastern states of America.

Gibbs's most dramatic building is the Radcliffe Camera, Oxford (1739–49), a development of a plan by Hawksmoor. Raised on a sixteen-sided rusticated base, which formed an open arcade until about 1860, a circular drum wall adorned with paired Corinthian pilasters supports an inner drum that encloses a reading room. This inner drum hides buttress-piers that support a lead-covered dome and lantern. Powerful in its bulk, the building commands attention, as does the domical bulk of Santa Maria della Salute, its Venetian counterpart. However, with the current of restraint running through the English Baroque movement, the Radcliffe Camera stops short of the highly ornate volutes and obelisks of Santa Maria.

A short walk away from the Radcliffe Camera is the imposing church of All Saints', at the corner of High Street and Turl Street, which was built to replace a medieval church between 1701 and 1710. At first it looks like a misplaced Wren City Church but, with its prominent position, it was intended to be seen from several sides— including the churchyard on the north. The building was designed by Henry Aldrich (1647–1710) who was Dean of Christ Church, an amateur architect, and a member of the Wren circle. It has a rectangular body and is dressed with paired Corinthian pilasters supporting a bold entablature and cornice, above which is an attic storey crowned with a continuous balustrade. The main windows are arched without any division, which might indicate the intention to provide an internal gallery. There are two pedimented porticoes, one on the north-west from the churchyard, and the other south-west from the High Street up a flight of steps between tall bases supporting Corinthian pillars. The Tower, built between 1718 and 1720 against the Turl Street front, rises well clear of the roof line with a belfry stage that is reminiscent of Wren's City churches, and is clasped at each corner by rusticated Doric pilasters. Above this is a peristyled temple stage, found for example at Wren's St Mary-le-Bow, and surmounted by an octagonal stone spire.

The interior of the church is light and high, helped by the attic stage beneath a beautifully plastered ceiling. The line of the superimposed pilasters dividing each wall bay is carried across the ceiling in bands of relief plaster, to create squares filled with rosette and floral decorations. Perhaps, as at Deptford, we can almost imagine entering a large ballroom, except that All Saints' is now no longer a church, but a very skilfully converted library for neighbouring Lincoln College; the large crypt that lifts the church so beautifully clear of pavement level has been newly created as a basement reading room, while the floor level above has also been raised to accommodate book-stacks.

13

The Palladian Movement

The full impact and scale of the Baroque could never be imposed on a northern European Protestant nation that, in any case, lacked the patronage of a pope, doge or emperor. By the early 18th century, crown patronage and expenditure were limited by Parliament, so a royal building campaign similar to, for example, that of Louis XIV of France was out of the question. With the completion of the state apartments at Hampton Court, in about 1705, large-scale royal building was over until the Prince Regent (later George IV) commissioned John Nash (1752–1835) to undertake both the Brighton Pavilion, in the oriental style, and the conversion of Buckingham House into a royal palace.

The revolt against the so-called Baroque started in about 1715 and was almost as much about politics as taste. The Baroque was associated with the High Church, the Tories and the House of Stuart. The revolt was essentially a Whig artistic movement although it also had a strong literary foundation. The Baroque had been described by the Whig politician Lord Shaftesbury in his 'Letter concerning the Art, or Science of Design' (1712) as 'frivolous and false style'. In a veiled attack on Wren he wrote, 'Thro several reigns we have patiently seen the noblest publick Buildings perish . . . under the Hand of one single Court Architect'. Wren was now 70 and, although he remained surveyor of works until 1718, had been pushed into the background on the completion of St Paul's.

In their search for a pure architectural style, the Whigs were helped by the publication of two books in 1715 that extolled the virtues of Palladio's style as the architectural 'truth' and Inigo Jones as his disciple. The first of these books, *Vitruvius Britannicus* by the Scottish architect Colen Campbell (1676–1729), was a survey of

Opposite: Stourhead, Wiltshire. The Pantheon by Henry Flitcroft, c. 1740, one of a number of architectural novelties in the classical and Gothic styles, which were to act as visual surprises for the visitor to the garden inspired by the paintings of Claude.

Classical architecture in England from Jones to the present, interspersed with a few of Campbell's own proposals—including his design for a great new London church to rival Wren's St Paul's. The book was published in three volumes that, while clearly preaching a visual message of Classical purity, nonetheless included engravings of the principal works of Baroque masters such as Wren, Vanbrugh, Hawksmoor and Archer. Their names were also included in the list of subscribers, along with a dedication to George I. That Jones was Campbell's hero is made explicit in this statement: 'When those designs he gave Whitehall are published . . . I believe all Mankind will agree with me, that there is no palace in the world to rival it'.

The second publication to give direction to the movement was Palladio's *I Quattro Libri dell' Architettura*, translated fully into English for the first time by Giacomo Leoni, a Venetian, and Nicholas Dubois, an Englishman of French extraction. Hitherto, English architects had consulted editions in French or the original Italian. The Leoni and Dubois translation went through several revisions, culminating in an edition by Isaac Ware in 1738 in which the copper engravings were accurate copies of the original woodcuts in Palladio's work. In 1743 an English translation of Palladio's *L'Antichità di Roma* appeared.

With Campbell praising Jones's faithfulness to Palladio's architectural principles, it was not long before Jones's drawings were published in folios by William Kent (1727), Isaac Ware (1735) and John Vardy (1744). In 1728 Robert Castell published *Villas of the Ancients*, a series of reconstructions of Roman houses based on Classical literature. Lord Burlington, who along with Campbell was to be the leading disciple of the movement, published *Fabbriche Antiche* in 1730, a series of Palladio's drawings specially engraved from the originals in his possession.

While the movement rejected Baroque extravagance and over-ornamentation, this does not mean that Palladian buildings were necessarily austere. Some were extremely grand: the entrance hall at Holkham can hardly be described as anything less than magnificent. Although the first building in this neo-classical Palladian style was Wilbury House, Wiltshire (1710), designed by William Benson, one of

Campbell's circle, as his own house (and modelled on nearby Amesbury by Inigo Jones's nephew, John Webb), it was Colen Campbell (1676–1729) who was the leading architect of the movement.

Campbell was a lawyer by training but had turned his mind to architecture, designing a house for one of his clan in Glasgow, in 1712. With the union with England in 1707 he, like many fellow Scots, saw London as the cultural and social centre of Britain and moved to the capital in search of commissions. Wisely committing himself to the Whig Party and the Hanovarian succession, he launched his *Vitruvius Britanmcus* in the hope of establishment and success. By the time of the publication of the first volume in 1715 he had already been commissioned by Sir Richard Child, heir to an East India Company fortune, to design Wanstead House, Essex. The first version, subsequently rejected by Child, was published in Volume One. As finally built, Wanstead consisted of a large rectangular block flanked by lower wings, some 90 metres (260 feet) long. Originally intended to have a cupola over the centre, it bore a slight likeness to Castle Howard, but without the pilaster divisions throughout its length. Unfortunately it was demolished in 1822.

Lyme Park, Cheshire, c. 1730, transformed from an Elizabethan house by the Venetian architect and translater of Palladio into English, Giacomo Leoni. The south front is severe, and dominated by the Ionic ordered centrepiece and Ionic pilasters dividing each bay.

Wanstead became the prototype for a number of Palladian mansions, including Prior Park near Bath and Wentworth Woodhouse in Yorkshire. A feature of each is the huge hexastyle (six-columned) portico raised above a rusticated basement. This was also a feature of a number of Palladio's villas. The windows of the main floor were capped by triangular and semicircular pediments and the roof was contained behind a balustraded parapet.

One must question how Campbell had absorbed Palladio's vocabulary and detail. He must have been acquainted with an Italian or French edition of Palladio's *Quattro Libri*, and he had visited Italy some time prior to 1715. This is evident from an unexecuted design for a villa rotonda, perhaps for Chiswick Park, the estate of Lord Burlington for whom Campbell worked after publication of *Vitruvius Britannicus*. The famous Villa Rotonda outside Vicenza also inspired James Smith, then Scotland's leading architect, to produce a design based on it.

It was not however in Scotland or at Chiswick that the closest interpretation of the Villa Rotonda is to be found, but at Mereworth, Kent, where Campbell built a villa for John Fane, later 7th Earl of Westmoreland, in 1722–23. It is square in plan with a hexastyle Ionic-ordered portico on each front, raised over a basement. On two opposite fronts there are two flights of steps, unlike the Rotonda, which has steps on each side. The sequence of rooms, like those in its prototype, are arranged round a central circular hall that is surmounted by a coffered inner dome rising just above the level of the roof. Light is admitted through circular windows that are set at the base of the outer dome. Built of lead, the outer dome is constructed to a similar height as that intended by Palladio for the Rotonda (in fact, never built). Smoke from the fireplaces was carried up the dome casing in flues and discharged beneath the cowl of the lantern. Unlike the Rotonda, the windows at Mereworth are of the sash type, without shutters. Also, the sides of Campbell's porticoes are supported by columns, not arches (as in the prototype).

If Mereworth Castle is hidden from the general public by hedges, trees, and a long drive, the more accessible parish church makes up for this, for it too is evolutionary. Commissioned between 1740–46 by Fane, the architect remains unknown. The eye catching steeple has the flavour of St Martin-in-the-Fields, designed by Gibbs, but this rises from a rectangular body with boldly projecting eaves that are similar to those of the church of St Paul, Covent Garden, by Jones; yet the semicircular Doric portico is reminiscent of Archer's St Paul's, in Deptford. The interior is severely neo-classical with a barrel vaulted ceiling supported by eight Roman Doric columns that divide the nave from the side aisles. The sanctuary is simply divided from the nave by communion rails. The columns are painted to resemble marble and are supported by a painted Doric entablature that also runs across the east end, above the altar and beneath a Roman thermal window. The barrel ceiling itself is painted in grisaille *trompe l'oeil* to suggest recessed coffered panels with rosettes. Some have remarked that the overall effect has a Classical severity that is way ahead of its time.

Colen Campbell's other works include Stourhead, Wiltshire (1715), built for the London banker Henry Hoare, which in plan and elevation derives from Palladio's Villa Emo, at Fanzolo. Here Campbell introduces a four-columned portico raised over a rusticated base and

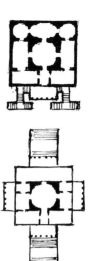

Top: Plan of Chiswick Villa (see next page).

Above: Plan of Mereworth Castle.

Left: Mereworth Castle, Kent, 1723. Colen Campbell's close copy of Palladio's Villa Capra (inset).

rising to roof level. The portico led through an arched entrance to the entrance hall, stair, hall and chapel, with smaller rooms on either side.

In Norfolk, Campbell managed to secure the patronage of Sir Robert Walpole for Houghton Hall (1722–29) which echoes Palladio's Palazzo Thiene in plan: a rectangular block linked by two quadrants with a kitchen and laundry blocks. The rusticated Venetian windows on the outer bays also echo those of the Palazzo Thiene. These bays were originally to have been surmounted by towers derived from Jones's Wilton House, but instead, after Campbell's death, domes designed by Gibbs were substituted. The entrance hall is a 12-metre (40-foot) cube, in imitation of that by Jones in the Queen's House, Greenwich.

Richard Boyle, 3rd Earl of Burlington (1694–1753) and scion of an ancient Yorkshire family, would have been introduced to architecture as one of the 'polite arts' that were studied as a matter of course by the aristocracy. From an early age Boyle was won over by the architectural message of Palladio and was a subscriber to the first volume of *Vitruvius Britannicus*, published in 1715. In 1719 he revisited Italy on a second grand tour, taking with him a copy of the *Quattro Libri*. While in Rome he met William Kent (1685–1748), who was there studying painting. A close friendship developed and Burlington brought Kent

Below: (left) Chiswick Villa, 1725; (middle) Chiswick Villa salon. The apsidal coffering is based on that in the temple of Venus and Rome, in Rome; (right) the octagonal central hall showing coffering and thermal window.

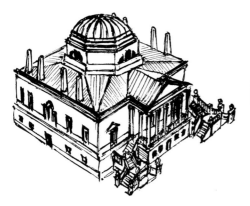

back to England to be installed as designer, first in his London home in Piccadilly, and later at Chiswick. Since the two worked closely together, and Burlington never signed drawings, it is hard to determine to what extent any one idea is his own or that of Kent.

If the overall plan of Chiswick Villa (1725–29) is Burlington's, the interior decoration is Kent's. The building is a free interpretation of Palladio's Villa Rotonda, Scamozzi's Villa Pisani at Lonigo and Serlio's design for a villa in Book VII of his treatise of 1575 and is a square block with a Corinthian portico on one side, raised only on a rusticated basement. The garden front is adorned by triple Venetian windows and the facade is of plaster, scored to simulate stone blocks. Like the Pisani, it has no attic storey but instead a sloping roof rising to an octagonal lantern and saucer dome. Every other bay of the drum is pierced with a thermal window, to admit light to the octagonal hall, and the chimneys are cleverly disguised in the form of obelisks. The disposition of the rooms round the central hall is similar to the Rotonda with proportions relating to the cube and circle. On the garden front the apsidal salon is of double-cube proportion. The gilt coffering echoes that in Palladio's reconstruction of the famous ruins of the Temple of Venus and Rome, also in Rome.

Holkham Hall (1734–64) was another collaboration between Burlington and Kent, built for Thomas Coke, Earl of Leicester. Returning from Italy, Coke had wanted a larger house in which to display his collection of newly-acquired antiquities and paintings. Campbell and Matthew Brettingham were consulted, but the final design is strongly influenced by detail from Burlington's Chiswick

Holkham Hall, Norfolk, 1734–64: the south front with roof pavilions at each corner, a Palladian house feature, and two of the four wing-pavilions.

Basildon Park, Berkshire, 1763–83: like Holkham and Lyme Park, the house is raised over a rusticated basement. However, unlike Holkham, which is in pale yellow brick, here John Carr has used honey-coloured Bath stone.

Villa and by the plan from his Tottenham Park, Wiltshire (1722), in which he first used a central-block plan with four linked wings; this plan in turn derives from Palladio's Villa Mocenigo. Coke wanted Holkham to be a latter-day Roman villa: he even insisted on the use of brick, made on the estate, fired to resemble the yellowish brick of the Tiber Valley. The entrance hall was inspired by Palladio's description of an ancient basilica or Egyptian hall, based on his interpretation of Vitruvius. The hall is flanked by colonnades of alabaster Ionic-ordered columns raised on a podium. At the salon end is an apse, the line of columns continued in front like a screen, as in Palladio's San Giorgio Maggiore, in Venice. The frieze is derived from the temple of Fortuna Virilis and the coffering from the temple of Jupiter (as illustrated by Palladio). As one advances through the hall from the entrance one also notices the continuous lines of antique Greek key and Vitruvian scroll decoration on the podium. While the entrance front is relatively austere, the south or garden front is dominated by a large hexastyle portico. The influence of Holkham's plan and elevation, as well as its pyramidal corner towers, may be seen in Sanderson Miller's Hagley Hall, in Worcestershire (c. 1752); Kent's Horse Guards Building, Whitehall, London (1748–59), and Roger Morris's Lydiard Park, Wiltshire (c. 1740).

Burlington made another excursion into antiquity with his design for the Assembly Rooms at York (1731–32) which, although by necessity fitted into a confined site, were a compromise between the elevation of Palladio's Egyptian hall and an ancient basilica: in consequence the building is six columns wide and 18 columns deep, with an open floor space proportion of 1:3. This was fine for dancing but the space between the columns and wall was too confined for the hooped crinoline dresses of the ladies and was subsequently widened in the 1820s.

Externally, many Palladian houses were extremely austere: for example, at Lydiard Park the entrance is through a simple Doric-ordered doorcase. Other houses, such as Constable Burton Hall, Yorkshire (1768), by John Carr, had a four-columned portico set back from the facade in antis. Carr treated the facade of Basildon Park, Berkshire (1766–83), in the same way. Some buildings have a dignified but subtle elegance that can only be fully appreciated from a distance: for instance, Marble Hill House, Twickenham, built for the Countess of Suffolk by Roger Morris (1695–1749) and the 9th Earl of Pembroke (1693–1750), himself an architect, was not unlike the earl's London house (designed by Colen Campbell), although here there is no portico. Both entrance and garden fronts have a central pediment equal in inclination to the slope of the roof behind. On the centrepiece, the ground or basement storey is rusticated. Above, the piano nobile and upper floor are flanked by giant ordered Ionic pilasters; the bays on either side are of smooth plaster. The door is set within a semi-circular arch with an early example of a fanlight. The pleasing balance of verticality and horizontality is set off on both frontages by a slightly projected horizontal plat-band between basement and piano nobile, and banded entablature beneath the eaves cornice. Two pairs of chimneys rise either side of the pyramidal roof.

Above: York, Mansion House, c. 1730, a civic building in the Palladian style, for sometime attributed to Lord Burlington who designed the nearby Assembly Rooms.

Below: Marble Hill House, Twickenham, west London, 1724–26.

Roger Morris and the Earl of Pembroke also designed the bridge at Wilton, based on unexecuted designs by Palladio. Here, a colonnade is supported over a wide arch linked to pedimented pavilions over narrow arches; the incline on either side is over an outer arch—and all this is just to carry an ornamental pathway. Three other such bridges survive, at Stowe, Prior Park, Bath; and Tsarskoe Selo, near St Petersburg, c. 1776.

As we have seen, the Palladian movement affected church design, from the introduction of the hexastyle portico over the west door at St Martin-in the-Fields to the detailing of the same building's east front. Here Gibbs had introduced an impressive facade, dominated by a central Venetian window beneath a bold entablature and pediment. The central bay is flanked by Corinthian ordered pilasters. Gibb's steeple for St Martin's was to be copied overseas, but it was the east front that would influence the remodelling of provincial parish churches: in Gloucester, all but the medieval tower and steeple of St John's church was rebuilt between 1732–34 by Edward and Thomas Woodward—the east front on Eastgate Street has a pedimented centrepiece that incorporates a Venetian arch but flanked by fluted Doric pilasters supporting the entablature and pediment; further up the Severn in Worcester, the Woodwards also rebuilt St Swithin's between 1734–36—here the east facade has a pedimented centrepiece supported by fluted Doric pilasters and enclosing a Venetian window.

In England, Palladian taste lasted until the last quarter of the 18th century, but in Scotland the Palladian influence was a little more confused. Six years after the publication of *Vitruvius Britannicus* (the manifesto for a return to the orthodox rules of Classicism and a condemnation of the Baroque), William Adam (1689–1748), a staunch Whig, was called on by the Earl of Hopetoun to recast the entrance front to his mansion near Edinburgh, originally designed by Sir William Bruce. Adam dressed the front, between its gracefully curving wings, with giant Corinthian pilasters set on a rusticated basement; above the main entablature, running the length of the frontage, is an attic stage. Reminiscent of Versailles and the Baroque, it is what the Earl wanted of Adam.

At Duff House, Banffshire, William Adam repeats the use of giant
Corinthian pilasters in a more compact, if slightly cramped, house.
Again the attic stage is introduced, along with corner towers which
hark back to Houghton. The curving staircases are Italianate and were
to be repeated by Adam's son Robert in the 1760s, at Kedleston Hall.
Palladian simplicity is almost achieved at Mavisbank House near
Edinburgh for Sir John Clerk of Penicuik. Here the central block is
linked to outer pavilions by curving screens. Perhaps the rusticated
pilasters exert a slight heaviness, and the upper windows are somewhat
cramped with triangular and semicircular pediments; however,
Palladian credentials are added with the windows in the pavilions.

Gradually, Palladian adherence to the *Quattro Libri* and the
requisite 'pilgrimage' to Vicenza was superseded by the Adam
brothers' (primarily Robert and James, both sons of William) new
vocabulary of architectural ornament based on a re-interpretation of
Roman sources—such as Diocletian's palace at Spalato and
excavations at Pompeii and Herculaneum; and later by the austerity
of the Greek revival. Kedleston Hall near Derby, begun by James
Paine and Matthew Brettingham in 1759, and completed by Robert
Adam (1728–92), may be said to mark the division.

14

The Advent of Town Planning

There was no considered or formal town planning in Britain before
the 1630s. Many towns were barely more than one main street of
narrow-fronted jettied buildings with unsanitary side alleys and courts
that received little direct sunlight. The most open and impressive area
would have been the market place, or possibly a space adjacent to the
parish church where either the town hall, perhaps over a colonnade,
or a grammar school linked to the neighbouring parish church, or
perhaps a trade guild would have been located. Nothing in Britain
rivalled the grandeur of a formal continental town centre such as that
of Vicenza in Italy, or Paris, as it was developed in the early 1600s by
Henry IV of France, or the purpose-built planned grid town of
Richelieu. It was the Place Royale (c. 1605, since 1800 known as the
Place des Vosges) that inspired Inigo Jones's layout of Covent Garden
in the 1630s. The opportunity to rebuild London after the Great Fire
to a grid plan by Wren, focusing on St Paul's and the Royal Exchange,
had to be abandoned due to cost. However, speculative development
of terraces of brick and stucco houses had been introduced at Lincoln's
Inn Fields before the fire; this formality was continued in the brick
courts and King's Bench Walk of the Inner and Middle Temple in the
1670s and 80s. In the first formal squares, such as St James's, planned
by Lord St Albans in the 1660s, uniformity of facades was not
adhered to. A greater attempt to do so was made in the first formal
provincial development, that of Queen Square, Bristol (c. 1705).

By 1700 the population of London was growing appreciably, and
ribbon development was spreading eastwards into the Thames-side
hamlets and northwards beyond Piccadilly over land leased by the
dukes of Cavendish and Grosvenor. In addition, successive Acts of
Parliament began to regulate the use of non-combustible materials for

Opposite: King's Bench Walk,
c 1670. This range of lawyers'
chambers is among some of
the earliest post –Fire of
London buildings surviving in
the city. They exhibit beautifully
the use of London mauve-hued
stock bricks contrasting with
the rubbed red-brick dressings
for the windows, which may
originally have been of the
casement type until sash
became more widespread from
about 1700.

Opposite: Bath, interior of the
Assemby Room c. 1775: the
social centre for the upper
town, and the masterpiece
of John Wood the Younger.

building, and there were regulations governing the height and width
of facades and new streets. Unfortunately these regulations were not
binding on provincial building, although disastrous fires, such as those
in Warwick and Blandford, encouraged the rapid adoption of brick in
place of half-timbering.

The Mayfair and Marylebone district of London's West End was
laid out on a semi-grid pattern from about 1720. The street names in
themselves convey a feeling for the events and personalities of the
period: Hanover Street, Harley Street, Audley Street. These streets
were lined with smart but unpretentious brick terraces for people in
the professions, but the open squares were more ostentatious—the
height of fashion, and the residences of the aristocracy. Although
development was speculative and in the hands of a number of
landlords there were increasing attempts to present the whole of a
terrace or side of a square as one facade, as if it were a palace. This
effect might be emphasized by a plaster-covered centrepiece with
pilasters or half pillars and a pediment. Sadly, Mayfair has suffered
from both redevelopment and sometimes unsympathetic restorations
to the original facades, whereas Georgian Bath and Edinburgh each
retain a completeness and sense of scale, and so may be studied for
typical planning features of the 18th and early 19th centuries.

In 1700 Bath was small, and hardly extended beyond its medieval
walls. It had hot mineral springs famed since the Roman era, but
barely more than one good inn to accommodate the needs of
fashionable visitors. By 1800 it had expanded to cross the Avon into
the suburb of Bathwick and also to climb up the narrow sides of the
valley. It now had three major social centres, the Pump Room
adjacent to the hot baths, the Guildhall with a magnificent
banqueting hall, and the Upper Assembly Rooms with a large
ballroom, card room, and tea room, for what was now the fashionable
drink. There was also the General Hospital or Infirmary for rheumatic
diseases. A walk along Grand Parade would follow Sunday morning
worship at the late medieval Abbey Church.

The Georgian creation of Bath was due largely to three
personalities: Richard 'Beau' Nash (1674–1762), who arrived in 1705

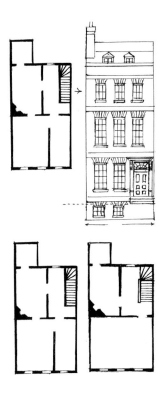

Bath: elevation and plans of a typical Bath terraced house.

to be Master of Ceremonies—a post he also held at Tunbridge Wells; Ralph Allen (1693–1764), who arrived in 1715 and who was to own the nearby stone quarries; and John Wood the Elder (1704–54), who arrived in 1725. Wood had worked for Lord Bingley in Yorkshire and then in London on Grosvenor Square under the builder-architect Edward Shepherd, and also on Cavendish Square for the Duke of Chandos. How Wood became involved at Bath is hard to determine for certain. He may have approached one of the Bath landowners, Robert Gay, with plans he had drawn up, while in Yorkshire, for the speculative development of fields beyond the then city limits. In addition the Duke of Chandos was already proposing development on his own land in Bath.

In 1727 Wood settled in Bath, having taken the risky step of contracting for the building of Queen Square (1729–36). He probably had the financial support of Ralph Allen, who was keen to exploit the virtues of his stone from the Combe Down and Box quarries. Since the development was speculative it was not completed as one project, save for the north side with its stone terrace directly related to the London squares. Raised on a rusticated basement, the upper floors are flanked by giant ordered Corinthian pilasters. At the centre is a projected pedimented centrepiece of six half columns and a projected pavilion of three bays surmounted by an attic storey above the cornice. There is an additional storey in the hipped roof hidden by a parapet. The windows of the main floor or piano nobile are topped by alternating triangular and semicircular pediments.

Wood's ingenuity as an urban architect and planner can be appreciated when one observes the way in which the terraces climb up Gay Street towards the Royal Circus, commencing from the charming bow-fronted house Wood built for himself at the north-east corner of Queen Square and Gay Street. Each house is more or less identical, with a door and two windows on the lower floor, and the upper floors having three windows each. The bow-fronted 21 Gay Street has a fine example of a Venetian window.

The Royal Circus, started in 1754, is Wood the Elder's last and finest work. The buildings surround a circular area of some one

Above: Bath, The Royal Circus started in 1754.

Left: View along Great Pulteney Street c.1780, towards the former Sydney Hotel, c. 1790, now the Holbourne of Menstrie Museum.

hundred metres. They consist of three equal segments, planned so that the axis of each of the three approaching thoroughfares is at the central point of one of the facades. Like all Bath buildings, they are built over a basement with a light well in front, and the three main floors are dressed with paired columns of the Doric, Ionic and Corinthian orders between each window bay; the roof has yet another floor for domestic staff with dormers hidden behind the oval openings of the parapet. The width of each house is marked by the tall chimney stacks rising above each party-wall.

Opposite: Bath, Royal Crescent, 1767–75.

The Royal Crescent (1767–75), the work of Wood's son, John the Younger, is linked to the Circus by the unpretentious Brock Street. It is in the form of a great semi-elliptical block comprising 33 town houses overlooking parkland, and was the first of its kind in Europe. The masonry is ashlar and the ground or entrance floor serves as a base on which a continuous servis of giant ordered Ionic columns is mounted from end to end. The graceful curve is emphasized by the cornice and balustrade. With its utter rejection of ornament (even window cases), it has the mood of neo-Classicism in which each feature must have a structural function. Only the doors at each side have flanking Doric pillars, entablature and pediment. The mid-point of the curve is emphasized by paired columns and a semi-circular headed window.

This was to be the first of many variations on the circus theme. That at Buxton (c. 1780), by John Carr of York, has fluted giant Doric ordered pilasters and a ground floor in the form of an arcade that may derive from the blocks originally surrounding Covent Garden. The Crescent at Clifton (c. 1790) is the widest of all. Soon a crescent became an indispensable feature of the fashionable but formal layout of the new spa towns: for example at Lansdown Crescent, Cheltenham, and others in the seaside resorts of Brighton and Ramsgate. Even in Bath there were later variations, including John Eveleigh's Camden Crescent, employing giant Corinthian ordered pilasters and a rare five-columned centrepiece that is actually well off-centre. Whilst the appearance of Bath is very much one of Classical grace, the new suburb of Bathwick was to be dominated by St John's church, in the Perpendicular Gothic style by the local architect John Pinch the Elder

Below: Buxton, Derbyshire. The Crescent, c 1780, by John Carr of York.

Blackheath, south London: The Paragon c. 1806. Seven brick houses linked by Doric colonnaded wings in the plan of a shallow crescent.

(1770–1827). The body, with prominent pinnacles breaking the line of the parapet, is reminiscent of King's College Chapel, Cambridge.

Since the late 17th century London had been developing fashionable suburbs—initially near to the centre, such as Islington and Piccadilly, but by the end of the next century an hour or more away by coach. Blackheath, for a time famous for its great Palladian mansion of Wricklemarsh, demolished in the 1790s, saw the erection of the Paragon (c. 1806) by Michael Searles (1750–1813), a crescent of seven brick houses with slightly concave facades linked by low wings behind a Doric colonnade.

Elsewhere in the provinces, formal development tended to take place outside the limits of the original settlement. At Cheltenham development stretched outwards on either side of the small medieval town to embrace Lansdown and Pittville. In due course two elegant pump rooms—the Pittville Pump Room (c. 1827), with its strongly Grecian flavour, and the Montpellier Rotunda (c. 1830), with a large coffered dome and lantern derived from John Soane's Bank of England—were built to be the focus of the social scene.

In Edinburgh, neo-Classical building contributed further to the
city's nickname, influenced by its 18th-century intellectual life, as the
'Athens of the North', with the New Town to become the largest
Georgian urban development in Britain. The City hitherto occupied a
narrow ridge on either side of a street running from the ancient
burgh of Holyrood, through the Canongate, High Street and Lawn
Market to the castle perched on a precipitous rock. On either side
of this street tenements rose to six or more storeys and were entered
via dark spiral staircases from narrow alleys or wyndes. These narrow
alleys lined by 'back buildings' ran back on the south side to the
parallel Cowgate. The High Street was interrupted about midway by
St Giles' Kirk and the former Parliament House. The line of these
tenements, broken by the tower and crown of St Giles and the
fortified mass of the castle, remains as one of the most memorable
city skylines in Europe. But during the 18th century the tenements
were unsanitary and disease ridden, leading to calls for radical
rebuilding, or a totally new settlement beyond the North Loch on
fields sloping down to the port of Leith and the Forth. A competition

was held at the instigation of the then dynamic Lord Provost, George Drummond, and won by little-known surveyor James Craig (1744–95). Craig's plan may have been partly inspired by Emmanuel Héré de Corny's plan for Nancy, which consisted of a series of linked squares or open places.

Between 1767 and 1840 a huge area to the north of Princes Street and sloping down towards the Forth was laid out on a grid plan by James Craig. The principal thoroughfare, George Street, containing the Assembly Rooms, links St Andrew's Square in the east with Charlotte Square in the west. In this overall conception of a New Town built as a complete entity, Edinburgh had more in common with the spacious and monumental grandeur of Nancy or Paris during the reign of Louis XV than London, whose West End had been built and developed in a piecemeal and speculative way. During this period a number of celebrated architects, including Sir William Chambers, Robert Adam, Thomas Hamilton, William Playfair and James Gillespie Graham, contributed impressive terraces and individual buildings to Edinburgh, including assembly rooms and schools in the Greek style such as the Royal High and John Watson's.

As a result of the terrain, Edinburgh's streets introduce a variety of ground plans that drop down from level to level, as in Ainsley Place

Edinburgh: Royal High School, c. 1825, the Greek revival at its most austere.

to Moray Place and on to the Royal Circus. Bowed frontages occasionally appear, and wrought-iron balconies are much in evidence, as they are at Cheltenham. Where but in the Athens of the North could you find an attempt to build a national war memorial in the form of a replica of the Parthenon, situated on Calton Hill, Edinburgh's own Acropolis?

Nearby Glasgow was not unaffected by the urge for Classical grandeur and, although undertaken on a very much smaller scale than Edinburgh, George Square was completed by 1787 in a grid-planned extension westwards from the original medieval settlement around the cathedral and Glasgow Green. By the middle of the 19th century the green hills overlooking the narrow River Kelvin were developed by wealthy merchants and industrialists: Park Circus, designed by Charles Wilson (1810–63) and built in 1855–8, was obviously influenced by the Circus in Bath and stands up to comparison very

Edinburgh: Moray Place, c. 1820: one of the most impressive and unspoilt parts of the New Town.

Right: Shrewsbury: a town where the medieval meets the Georgian with timber-framed houses rubbing shoulders with brick terraces and stone civic buildings.

Opposite: Liverpool. Rodney Street with early 19th-century brick terraces built for the wealthy merchants and shipowners on the hill away from the narrow streets of the port.

favourably. Indeed, the effect of the neighbouring Park Terrace rising above the thickly wooded parkland is reminiscent of green slopes below Camden Crescent and Somerset Terrace, in Bath.

By the end of the 18th century many ports and seaside resorts had terraces, squares and crescents. Even that former medieval port on the River Dee, Chester, witnessed the erection of fine rows of brick terraces and the severe Greek Doric Chester Castle by Thomas Harrison. In nearby Liverpool, which saw the greatest growth of any town in the 18th century, elegant brick terraces such as Rodney Street, Canning Street and Abercrombie Square, were laid out. Many had fan lights over doors set into brick arches and flanked by fluted Doric columns. Some have now been restored with sash windows and correctly proportioned glazing bars. The more fashionable houses, such as those in Abercrombie Square, have continuous cast-iron balconies. At the heart of the city the Town Hall (1745–54), by John Wood the Elder of Bath, still stands. The dome was added in c. 1795 by James Wyatt, but the building remains a magnificent example of the Palladian style. Opposite Liverpool, on the south side of the Mersey, is Birkenhead. Here, Hamilton Square was laid from the 1820s by Gillespie Graham as the first stage of a plan to create a

'Merseyside Bath'. In 1847 Sir Joseph Paxton (1801–65) designed Birkenhead Park on the lines of John Nash's Regent's Park in London, to be surrounded by elegant villas; unfortunately this dream of northern elegance was overtaken by the social and economic needs of a rapidly expanding ship-building community.

Another city renowned for its brick Georgian streets and terraces is Dublin—particularly noteworthy are Capel Street and Merrion Square. The stone-built Customs House and Four Courts by James Gandon (1743–1823) overlooking the Liffey owe not a little to Wren's Greenwich Hospital and even St Paul's Cathedral.

In the 18th century the British finally discovered the qualities of sea air, leading to the development of a number of fashionable seaside towns. Scarborough was the first so-called resort and was followed soon after by Margate, the town which popularized the newly invented bathing machine. Margate's Hawley Square and Cecil Square were in plain undistinguished brick (now much altered). A few miles round the Kent coast is Ramsgate, which retains much of its slightly

Tunbridge Wells, Kent, Calverley Crescent, 1829–30. The colonnade is supported by iron pillars.

later Regency charm. Here we see brick and white stucco-fronted terraces with the bow-fronted bay and ornamental balcony above. Entrance is up a flight of steps flanked by railings as a protection from the basement well. Its attraction for all classes was immortalized in W P Frith's famous painting *Ramsgate Sands*. It was at Brighton that seaside town planning reached its apogee with a spaciousness to compare with London's Regent's Park development. If some stucco-fronted terraces might look much like those in Ramsgate or Hastings, few can dismiss the palatial facades of Brunswick Square (c. 1825): bow fronts dressed with pillars in giant orders. Further along the south coast, stucco-fronted terraces added considerable dignity to the popular resorts of Weymouth, Exmouth and Lyme Regis.

Finally, for those who liked to live in an atmosphere of a planned city state but without the feeling of mass housing by the sea, there were the detached villas by Decimus Burton in Calverley Park, Tunbridge Wells. Built of stone, and fronted by cast-iron verandas and long gardens, they offered everything one might desire.

Tunbridge Wells, Kent: villa in Calverley Park, 1829–30.

15

Gothic Survival and Revival

In some respects the Gothic style never really died out in Britain; in fact two great examples, the Anglican cathedrals of Guildford and Liverpool, were only completed in 1966 and 1980 respectively. The latter towers over its surroundings with a force and austerity reminiscent of the walls of Albi Cathedral, in France, while the Lady Chapel has the flavour of a latter-day Saint Chapelle, Paris. As already mentioned, Gothic remained the preferred style for much of the 17th century in Oxford: University College was rebuilt from c. 1634; a hall and chapel were built at Oriel between 1639 and 1640, and a Gothic chapel at Lincoln College in 1681—all in Gothic. Wren added Tom Tower at Christ Church in 1681 to complete the entrance to the large quadrangle, and a few years later in about 1695, William Dickinson, one of Wren's colleagues, produced a design for the reconstruction of the great medieval church of St Mary, Warwick, burnt in the great fire of Warwick in 1694. In about 1715 work began on the Codrington quadrangle at All Souls, to the design of Hawksmoor. Here, a close examination of the detail provides a key to the early 18th-century approach to the style: it is really Gothic under a Classical restraint. For example, the

Opposite: Lacock Abbey, Wiltshire, c. 1760. Interior of the Great hall converted by Sanderson Miller from a Tudor house. It was originally created from the remains of a medieval abbey – appropriate for a manifestation of Gothic Revival.

Below right: Oxford, All Soul's College. The 1715 Codrington Quadrangle by Hawksmoor.

Below left: Oxford, Christ Church, c. 1680. Wren's completion of the Tudor quadrangle.

Greenwich, Vanbrugh Castle, c. 1717. The architect's house of brick ,which he called the 'Bastille'; a romantic evocation of the medieval.

windows of the Library, which are set between boldly projecting pinnacled buttresses, are barely pointed and without tracery; the interior is decorated with Classically ornamented bookcases and a stucco-panelled ceiling, and even a Venetian arch appears between the towers on the east side of the quadrangle.

In London, Hawksmoor designed the two western towers of Westminster Abbey, and the Gothic tower of St Michael, Cornhill (c. 1715) is also attributed to him. A few miles away on Maze Hill, overlooking Greenwich, John Vanbrugh built his Bastille— a romantic evocation of the Middle Ages contrived in brick. Its symmetry and sash windows, as well as the castellated gateposts, give it a somewhat toy-like appearance. Inside, it was contrived for the convenience of an 18th-century gentleman. William Kent, the disciple of Palladianism, also indulged in the revival of Gothic style, or the 'Gothick' as this 18th-century romantic approach to the medieval style is known. At Hampton Court he rebuilt the gatehouse of Clock Court with a plaster vault over the passage, and he was probably responsible for the rebuilt Shobden church, Hereford (c. 1754), in which we see so well the characteristics of Georgian Gothic. The flat coved ceiling immediately proclaims the air of a ballroom turned into a church; the ogee-arched windows look flimsy, and the wooden gallery is decorated with large square panels filled with quatrefoils. At the crossing, clustered shafts rise to support a mere plaster arch, when a crossing tower might be expected.

In Scotland between 1746 and 1749 Roger Morris, the English Palladian architect of that 'perfect villa', Marble Hill, was commissioned by the 3rd Duke of Argyle to design a castellated Gothic mansion set in landscaped grounds. The Duke was a Whig and wished to pledge his support for the Crown as tenant-in-chief immediately after the defeat of the second Jacobite rebellion. Before work started he had the village on the site demolished and rebuilt on the side of Loch Fyne where it would no longer spoil his view. Rectangular in plan, the castle adheres to Classicism in its symmetry, having drum towers capped with spires at each corner. However, its walls are pierced with sash windows set beneath pointed hoods. The entrances are set beneath ogee hoods. Rising above the roof at the centre of the castle is an attic stage pierced with pointed windows filled with intersecting 'strip' tracery so as to appear 'Gothick' from a distance, and adorned with a battlemented parapet.

The Gothic was ideal for the adornment of novelty structures in the grounds of parks and large estates, perhaps inspired by designs in William and John Halfpennys' *Chinese and Gothic Architecture Properly Ornamented* (1752). The Gothic Orangery at Frampton-on-Severn was probably inspired by a design in this book: its symmetrical front, composed of two octagonal drums joined by a narrow entrance bay, is adorned with tall ogee-headed windows and a central door. With its lattice-patterned ironwork in the windows the effect is quite magical as the reflection shimmers in the water of the ornamental canal in front. At Wardour Old Castle, Dorset, the Georgian Banqueting House may be from the same source. Another curiosity is the small Banqueting House at Gibside, near Durham, by Daniel Garrett (c. 1751)—in true early Gothick style this has ogee arches, quatrefoils, battlements and sprouting gables.

Sanderson Miller (1717–80) and Horace Walpole (1717–97) are often seen as the founders of the Gothic Revival style. Miller was a Warwickshire gentleman who turned to architecture as a polite antiquarian interest. He created sham castles and towers, picturesque cottages and Gothic summer houses, but he is best remembered for the new hall at Lacock Abbey, Wiltshire (1753–55), built for the Talbot family. The exterior betrays its period: windows with flimsy tracery beneath the ubiquitous ogee hood, a rose window in the centre like a star, open tracery on the parapet reduced to the delicacy of lace, and the

Frampton Court, Gloucestershire. The *Gothick* Garden House, c. 1760.

Twickenham, west London, Strawberry Hill, Horace Walpole's *Gothick* villa. Developed from two cottages into a gentleman's medieval palace c. 1750–90.

balustrade of the entrance stair pierced with foiled openings.

Walpole was another gentleman of leisure and wealth who turned his mind to architecture and collecting. Son of the prime minister Robert, he is also remembered as having been the greatest correspondent of the period and the author of the first Gothick novel, *The Castle of Otranto*. In 1749 he bought a cottage at Twickenham and over the next 50 years turned it into one of the greatest attractions for visitors to London. Strawberry Hill or, as he called it, 'my bauble', grew over each decade as Walpole sent his 'Committee of Taste' out in search of suitable architectural material to reproduce in his expanding house. Members of his unofficial committee included John Chute, Nicholas Bentley, and Thomas Pitt; better described as enthusiastic antiquarians and amateurs rather than craftsmen with the technical skill and knowledge of, say, James Gibbs. Walpole was however also supported by professional architects including James Essex, Robert Adam and James Wyatt—the latter responsible for the Offices (1790), a detached building at right angles to the main block. The final effect was more important than the means, and so what was made of stone in the original was reproduced in wood and plaster, or picked out in paint on the walls, and of course there was no attempt to reproduce the scale accurately. This particularly upset Pugin when he launched his Gothic manifesto in the nineteenth century. Like Vanbrugh's much smaller house at Greenwich it was created with contemporary comforts with 'plump chairs, couches, and luxury settees covered with linen'.

Inside Strawberry Hill, the rooms exude a 'Gothic gloom', and were given suitably antique titles such as Hall, Long Gallery, Cloister, Great and Little Parlour, Holbein Chamber, Armoury, Library and Breakfast Room. Many are lit through windows filled with 17th - century Flemish glass. The Long Gallery has fan vaulting made of papier-mâché derived from the Henry VII Chapel, Westminster Abbey; the Great Parlour and Library derive from illustrations in William Dugdale's *Old St Paul's*. Fireplaces are set in between niched surrounds and beneath canopies: that in the Holbein Chamber is based on the tomb of Archbishop Warham in Canterbury Cathedral, while the ceiling is based on that of the Queen's Bedchamber at Windsor. The chimney piece in the Library is based on the tomb of John of Eltham in Westminster Abbey. By the time the house was complete it had inadvertently introduced a new mood to architectural design, one that became the keynote of the Picturesque Movement—asymmetry, or what Walpole preferred to call

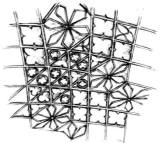

'Sharawaggi' (want of symmetry). This effect was created by the erection of the Round Tower with its stair turret forming a junction with the right-angled, and then detached, Office wing. Walpole described his house as 'pie-crust Gothick' which 'after my death will be blown away in the wind like dust'. Fortunately it has survived, unlike the greatest extravagance of the revival—Fonthill Abbey,

Top: Strawberry Hill, Holbein Chamber.

Above left: Holbein Chamber ceiling.

Above right: *Gothick* window.

Wiltshire (1795–1812), designed by James Wyatt. Both the Abbey and another Wyatt building, Lee Priory, near Canterbury (from about 1790) are no more.

Fonthill Abbey was built for the eccentric millionaire and author of the oriental tale *Vathek*, William Beckford, while Lee Priory was for Walpole's friend, William Barrett. Lee was demolished in the 1950s apart from a stable block and a small fan vaulted parlour (the latter preserved in the Victoria and Albert Museum). It was described by Walpole as 'a child of Strawberry, but prettier than the parent'. Fonthill, on the other hand, simply collapsed. At first Beckford had actually wanted a house that was built to be partly 'ruined', but was persuaded in favour of a habitable design. In plan it was basically a cross with an enormous octagonal tower based on Ely Cathedral's octagon. There was a cloister to one side and each wing introduced elements of castellated and collegiate Gothic. Beckford was impatient and hurried Wyatt, resulting in weak foundations: one day the tower collapsed and Fonthill was no more. Its rambling, picturesque asymmetry is left to us in atmospheric watercolours and engravings. Meanwhile Beckford had 'retired' to Bath where he bought land and two houses on Lansdown Hill. Here—quite undeterred—he commissioned another tower, crowned by a lantern adapted from the monument of Lysicrates in Athens, and still standing today. At Hadlow, near Tonbridge in Kent, there is a Gothic house dating from the 1830s with a tower that, although smaller, is quite obviously inspired by Fonthill.

The second half of the 18th century was a lean period for church building in England, but in 1818, in response to urban expansion, the government passed an Act providing for the expedition of £1 million on new churches. Whilst the Classical style was at first preferred in London, the Gothic was favoured in the provinces. Some churches were very plain as they were built within a restricted budget, yet had to be big enough to seat a large congregation. By the early 19th century Gothic was being used for churches exploiting the new material of cast iron. Appropriately, several of the finest examples are by the man who was first to analyse the development of the style and place it into a meaningful chronology: Thomas Rickman

(1776–84), who in 1812 was elected professor of architecture at the Liverpool Academy. In 1817 his *An Attempt to Discriminate the Styles of English Architecture from the Conquest to the Reformation* was published, and became the cornerstone of the Gothic Revival: it was Thomas Rickman who first put the development of Gothic architecture into a clear stylistic sequence.

In Liverpool, his adopted city, he struck up a friendship with Thomas Cragg, the proprietor of the Mersey Iron Foundry, who was using cast iron for features in cottages, such as fireplaces and door frames. Seeing how cast iron had been used so successfully to span the Severn at Coalbrookdale, in 1770, Rickman was quick to see the possibility of its application in the construction of churches, where space and light were pre-requisites. St George's, Everton was his first church using cast iron and, although clad completely in stone, has an interior of prefabricated columns, arches, vault ribs, panelling and window tracery. The style is Decorated Gothic. His next work, St Michael-the-Hamlet, completed and opened in 1814, again exploits the merits of iron, using it for everything from window tracery to doors and parapets. It was again in the Decorated style but with a clerestory (rarely found before the 15th century in parish churches). In St Philip's, Hardman Street (1816), Rickman adopted the Tudor Perpendicular.

Cambridge, St John's College: the 'Bridge of Sighs', c. 1825.

Rickman's best-known buildings are not in Liverpool, but in Cambridge: St John's College, where in conjunction with his pupil Henry Hutchinson (1800–31) he built the so-called 'Bridge of Sighs' (c. 1825), and New Court in a late Gothic or perpendicular style. At neighbouring Trinity, the Classicist William Wilkins (1778–1839) added the New Court, and at King's built a screen and lodge dividing the Great Court from King's Parade. All of these additions were in the late Perpendicular, which in the case of King's fitted perfectly with the dominating chapel. Indeed the Perpendicular style was in fashion among early revivalists; St Luke's Chelsea (1819-25) by James Savage shows the strong influence of King's College Chapel. The Gothic was also now seen as the style for grammar schools such as King Edward's, Birmingham, designed in the Tudor Perpendicular style by Sir Charles Barry (1795–1860).

16

New Styles and New Materials

Between about 1750 and 1900 the development of British architecture becomes extremely complex. This despite the fact that, at least in the latter part of this period, the Gothic appeared to be the epitome of the Victorian style, applied indiscriminately to everything from railway stations to churches and schools to prisons.

In the 1740s the Chinese style made a brief appearance. Europe had been trading with China from the early 17th century, when the English and Dutch East India companies were founded to bring back trade through the port of Canton. Porcelain, silks, lacquer and tea made a great impact, and the novelty of this far away culture was soon manifest in collections of plates and vases displayed in so-called Chinese houses. Perhaps the earliest example of the fashion is that at Stowe, built on stilts over a lake in 1738, although it has since been removed to Harristown House, County Kildare. The Chinese House at Shugborough, Staffordshire (c.1747), is perhaps the earliest building surviving in England. It was the seat of Thomas Anson whose younger brother, Admiral Anson, had circumnavigated the world between 1740 and 1744, and who had called at Canton en route where he acquired a large collection of porcelain; the Chinese House was built to house this collection. Two years later, in 1749, a Chinese Pavilion was erected at Kew. In 1752 the first five-stage pagoda was built in Shugborough. It was followed in about 1761 by the more famous version at Kew, by William Chambers (1723–1796), who was to become celebrated as one of Britain's finest neo-Classical architects and who had published *Designs for Chinese Buildings* in 1757. While most so-called Chinese buildings were for little more than ornament, the 5th Duke of Bedford commissioned Henry Holland (1712–85) to build a Chinese Dairy at Woburn Abbey. Perched at the side of a lake it is in many respects a

Opposite: Osterley House, west London. Robert Adam's entrance hall, c. 1761, all decorated in stucco except for the black and white marble floor, which echoes the marble design of the ceiling.

compromise between the austerity of Henry Holland's Classicism and a wooden-pillared veranda adorned with filigree Chinese detail. The prevalent enthusiasm for 'chinoiserie' went well with the delicacy of the contemporary fashion for Rococo interiors, a combination perhaps seen at its finest in the Chinese Room at Claydon House, in Buckinghamshire (c. 1770), and popular across Europe at this time.

The 1755 publication of German art historian and archaeologist Johann JoachimWinckelmann's *Reflections on the Painting and Sculpture of the Greeks* led to a fundamental change in the understanding of Classical history. Winckelmann saw the Greeks as the creators of Classical perfection and the Romans as simply copyists, and felt that the spirit of noble simplicity and calm grandeur found in Greek art should be applied to the art of the present. He further reinforced his views on the supremacy of the Greeks in his *History of the Art of the Ancient World* (1764). His writings fuelled the spirit of the neo-Classical movement that affected architectural development throughout Britain and northern Europe from Paris to St Petersburg, and across the Atlantic to New York and Washington. In France this movement was seen as a reaction against the frivolity of the Rococo and the reign of Louis XV, and was to be associated with the moral virtues of the Classical world, subsequently revived by the Revolution, but in Britain it was more archaeologically based. Hitherto, few British architects had studied in Italy, but now this became almost a prerequisite, helped and encouraged by the Royal Academy, which taught architecture from its foundation in 1768. The Society of Antiquaries, founded in 1753, also encouraged the study and examination of Classical remains at first hand.

The second half of the 18th century is dominated by the work of Robert Adam and Sir William Chambers. The two were very different in character: Adam, a master of invention and adaptation, with an eye for ornament, and Chambers, cold and aloof, and a brilliant draughtsman. The latter continued the late-Palladian tradition as in Duddingston House, near Edinburgh, and Lord Bessborough's villa at Roehampton. In his Somerset House (from 1775), between the Strand and the Thames in London, Chambers produced a work that

rises to the grandeur of contemporary buildings in Paris, such as those on the north side of the Place de la Concorde. The broad Thames frontage is raised on a rusticated terrace, pierced with arches reminiscent of those in Piranesi's etchings of imaginary prisons. The main defect of this facade is the want of a larger dome to create a striking centrepiece. Also the dramatic effect of the water lapping the arches of the dark tunnels was subsequently destroyed by the construction of the Victoria Embankment in the 1860s.

Like Chambers, Robert Adam, a Scot, spent some time in Italy, where he immersed himself in a study of the Classical remains. He also crossed the Adriatic to Dalmatia where he made a detailed study of the remains of the Emperor Diocletian's palace at Spalato (Split). He was revolutionary in adapting the vocabulary of ornament found in a Roman palatial building to his own use, although excavations at Herculaneum and Pompeii were beginning to reveal the secrets of the ordinary house and the richness of Roman design and ornament. Adam believed that the Romans had not been rigid in the use of architectural form and proportion, as revealed by his research at Spalato, and that he was therefore free to adapt their precedent to modern circumstances. This earned the derision of Chambers, who kept Adam from membership of the Royal Academy.

Adam was a master of adaptation, particularly in a confined space, and a number of his commissions were for the completion or conversion of existing houses, such as Kedleston (c. 1761), Syon (c. 1763), Osterley (c.1762) and Saltram (c. 1768). Harewood, near Leeds, was his first commission and was completely his own work. In this and his other great houses we see how he used plaster to magnificent advantage on walls and ceilings. Frequently repeated ornament includes anthemions based on the honeysuckle, arabesques, ribbons, paterae or circular flower patterns, candelabra, vases, urns and friezes of linked swags or festoons, or sphinx and putti or repetitive Greek key. Moulded surfaces were often painted white, while flat wall and ceiling surfaces were in pastel shades of pink, blue and green. Where he could not use actual marble he used alabaster and scagliolo, a compound of marble fragments, plaster of Paris, glue and paint.

Opposite: Saltram House, Devon, c. 1780. The Dining Room, a masterpiece of Adam's decorative flair. The colour scheme is pale green relieved by white stucco decoration on the walls, while the ceiling introduces cream. The Axminster carpet, designed by Adam, is almost an exact replica of the ceiling except for the floral designs in place of the ceiling lunettes. The fireplace is of white marble.

Osterley House, west London, c. 1770, the Etruscan Room. One of four rooms by Adam in this idiom. It has a very linear decoration painted in earth colours of browns, red, and black on a pale blue ground.

At Kedleston the Roman is invoked in the Egyptian entrance hall, hardly less grand than that at Holkham by Burlington and Kent in the 1730s, except that it is on one level. Beyond is a circular salon crowned with a coffered dome reminiscent of the Pantheon. The south front is a conscious derivation from the Arch of Constantine in Rome. At Osterley, which is the conversion of a Jacobean mansion enclosing a court, he created a grand entrance in the form of a huge Ionic double portico derived from the Temple of Octavia in Rome. In the sequence of rooms round the four wings he introduced a so-called Etruscan Room, decorated with motifs from what were claimed to be Etruscan artefacts. At the other extreme, his intimate interiors of 20 St James's Square and 20 Portman Square in London combine elegant staircases with rooms of the utmost delicacy.

Adam's Scottish contributions should not be overlooked and include in Edinburgh the University, or 'College', Register House and the north side of Charlotte Square. In the Old Calton burial ground he built a mausoleum to the philosopher David Hume, based on the Mausoleum of Theodoric in Ravenna. In Berwickshire he completed

Above left: Shugborough Hall, Staffordshire, replica of the Athenian Tower of the Winds, c. 1790.

Above: Shugborough Hall, Classical Arch, c. 1790.

Mellerstain House (c. 1768) and converted Culzean Castle, Strathclyde (1777–79) to a battlemented exterior with turrets (yet retaining Classically proportioned sash windows). This romantic structure, dominated by a keep-like central turreted block, seems to hark back to the Elizabethan Wollaton Hall, although the idea of a centralized battlemented block rising above the roof line was introduced to Inveraray Castle, Strathclyde, by Roger Morris (1746–49), albeit with Gothic windows. Adam had a number of less inventive followers including James Wyatt, whose Heaton Hall, Manchester, might pass as a fair imitation.

By the beginning of the 19th century the more austere Greek revival was under way in the hands of a number of notable exponents. The revival may be said to have begun with the designing of the Doric portico for Hagley Hall, Worcestershire (1758), and the Doric temple at Shugborough, Staffordshire (c. 1760), by James 'Athenian' Stuart (1713–88). Between 1751 and 1753 Stuart had been in Greece making measured drawings of Athenian antiquities along with fellow connoisseur Nicholas Revett, which led to the publication in 1762 of the first volume of the *Antiquities of Athens* (subsequently a major source for the reproduction of ancient buildings). A second volume appeared in 1789, shortly after Stuart's death. Shugborough also had a miniature Athenian Tower of the Winds. Thomas Hamilton has been mentioned in connection with Edinburgh, and in Chester his entrance to the Castle is like the contemporary Brandenburg Gate in Berlin, modelled on a reconstruction of the Propylaea (entrance) to the Acropolis in *The Antiquities of Athens*. At Oxford, James Wyatt—who could turn his hand just as well to Gothic—designed the Radcliffe Observatory in 1776, based on the Athenian Tower of the Winds, as illustrated in Stuart and Revett's work. Housing a large room for observation it had to make some concessions to academic use, and the upper octagonal stage is pierced with pedimented windows below a frieze with relief carvings of the winds by John Bacon. The tower has now been incorporated into Green College. The Tower of the Winds appears elsewhere, including as gate lodges to Basildon Park, near Reading.

William Wilkins (1778–1839), who had been a Classical scholar at Cambridge before extensive travels in Italy, Greece and Asia Minor, produced several fine essays in the style. His Grange Park, Hampshire (c. 1808), is a perfect adaptation of the Doric temple style to a country house. At Downing College, Cambridge (1806–20), he designed a series of detached stone blocks round three sides of a large court, using the Ionic order in the large porticoes. His other major academic commissions include the central range of University College, London (1825–25), where the porticoed entrance has ten Corinthian pillars, and the East India Company College (now Haileybury, near Hertford c. 1830), where he repeated his plan of Downing with detached brick-built blocks round a huge court, dominated on its south side by a later domed chapel by Arthur Blomfield. Wilkins also designed the National Gallery, London,(1833–38), in which he re-used the design of the portico from Henry Holland's Carlton House.

Perhaps the most appropriate buildings to be adorned with Greek influences are museums and art galleries, and none more so than the

British Museum in London. Founded in 1753 in Montague House it had by the 1820s become too small and so was totally rebuilt by Sir Robert Smirke (1781–1867), who fronted it with 48 huge Ionic columns—Karl Friedrich Schinkel clad his Altes Museum, Berlin, in Ionic columns at the same time. The two universities were also to rehouse their collections in Classical buildings. At Cambridge, George Basevi created a magnificent frontage on Trumpington Street of twelve Corinthian pillars incorporated a grand pedimented portico for the Fitzwilliam Museum (1837-47). At Oxford the Old Ashmolean Museum, founded in 1683 and claiming to be the oldest public museum in the world, was now too small for the growing collection. As a result of large bequests to the University, including the will of architect Sir Robert Taylor, a building for modern language teaching was to be combined with exhibition galleries for the collections of antiquities. The architect chosen as a result of a competition was Charles Cockerell (1788–1863), whose plan, set on a high podium, faced three sides of an open court on the corner of Beaumont Street and St Giles. His design combined detail from the Greek temple of Apollo at Bassae for the entrance portico with side ranges dressed with detached columns supporting statuary between arches, as on Roman triumphal arches. The two ranges are capped by a bold bracketed cornice reminiscent of a Renaissance palace. Known as the University Galleries and Taylorian Institute respectively, the former was renamed the Ashmolean Museum in 1902. As late as 1882 the museum at Preston, Lancashire, was built in a severe Ionic manner with an Ionic frontage strongly reminiscent of Schinkel's Schauspielhaus in Berlin. In Edinburgh the narrow causeway linking the Mound with Princes Street and the New Town became the site for the Royal Scottish Academy and National Gallery, both in the severe Greek Doric by William Playfair (1759–1823).

A number of public buildings such as banks, town halls, courts, and concert halls adopted the neo-Classical style. Charles Cockerell, architect of the Ashmolean, was appointed architect to the Bank of England in 1833 and designed the branches at Bristol, Liverpool, Manchester and Plymouth, in which he combined the needs of security with austere Classical elegance. In the frontages of rusticated stone he introduced engaged Doric pillars supporting a bold entablature, with an attic stage and pediment above. Entry is through doors set in thick stone cases. Of the many town halls built during the 19th century to express the pride, confidence and economic wealth of a community Leeds Town Hall (1853-58), by Cuthbert Broderick, must take pride of place. Its entrance front is massive with a colonnade of ten Corinthian columns set on a high podium reached by steps. However, this is overshadowed by a huge tower with a peristyled stage well above the roof level. Above this is a concave clock stage flanked by urns and supporting a dome. So while the main body exudes an air of Roman Classical grandeur the tower itself hints at the baroque of Archer and, ultimately, Borromini.

At Liverpool the St George's Hall (1840–54), designed by Harvey
Lonsdale Elmes (1813–1847), is perhaps the grandest neo-Classical
public building of all. Set on an island, it can be viewed from all sides.
Externally its long Corinthian colonnades reveal Elmes's acquaintance
with Schinkel's Altes Museum, Berlin. Its entrances are beneath
pedimented porticos in the east and west facades. Within the building
is a sequence of great chambers for legal proceedings as well as a
magnificent concert hall. Here the feeling is of imperial Roman
grandeur such as the Baths of Caracalla.

Several railway companies adopted the neo-Classical style for
their station buildings. Most famous was the London and Birmingham
Railway's terminus at Euston, with a Doric Screen designed by Philip

New Styles and New Materials **235**

Hardwick (1792–1870) and based on a Greek propylaeum (entrance to a vestibule). Sadly it was demolished in 1962, although Hardwick's terminus building at Birmingham, incorporating the Ionic, still survives—even if it is now marooned, away from any railway tracks. Greek Doric was also used by the London and South Eastern Railway's much more humble Canterbury station (now West, 1846). At Monkwearmouth station, County Durham (1848), the Ionic was used to great effect to create a temple-like entrance to the platform. Although trains still run through, the building is now a museum. On the Great Western Railway I K Brunel (1806–59) used the Classical to grace the western portal of Box Tunnel, opened in 1838—after all, it was near Bath.

Perhaps the most inappropriate usage for the pure Greek temple style is to adapt it to serve as a Christian church. Nevertheless, St Pancras Church in London (1819–22), by H W Inwood (1794–1843) and William Inwood (1771–1843) is modelled on the Erechtheum in Athens. The portico is Ionic, and side vestries reproduce the famous caryatids, one of which had recently arrived in London, courtesy of

Lord Elgin and the Turks. The tower reproduces elements from the Athenian Tower of the Four Winds, which was carefully documented in *The Antiquities of Athens* and which had been reproduced as one of the garden buildings at Shugborough in 1765. In Glasgow, Alexander 'Greek' Thompson (1817–75) built several fine churches in the style. His Caledonian Road Free Church (1856–57) has an Ionic portico set on an enormous podium containing two doors, like entries to the treasury of a temple. To one side stands a dominating tower. A few years later, in 1867, Thomson delivered a paper before the Glasgow Architectural Society condemning the use of Gothic in preference to Classical for the new buildings of Glasgow University.

The underlying feeling of the Romantic Movement swept through both the Greek and Gothic revivals: it embraced landscape gardens and urban parks, and went hand-in-hand with the current interest in landscape painting that was fostered by the admiration for the French Romantic artist Claude and his contemporaries. Some patrons wanted a tame reconstruction of the Roman Campagna in Wiltshire, while others wanted a suggestion of lands far beyond the borders of Europe. Architecturally speaking, perhaps the greatest master was John Nash, whose wide-ranging work encompasses the oriental at Brighton

Below left: Brighton, Sussex. Royal Pavilion, c. 1820.

Below: Gloucestershire. Sezincote, a piece of India in the Cotswolds.

Above: Cronkhill, Shropshire, c. 1820.

Above right: Bristol, Blaise Hamlet, c. 1820.

inspired by Sezincote, in Gloucestershire; Italianate villas in the Welsh marches, such as Cronkhill; Gothic villas in Devon; the cottage ornee at Blaise Hamlet, Bristol; and urban planning to rival Wren's visions. Nash knew the right people, not least the Prince Regent, and had a complete disregard for money—the cause of his eventual downfall.

Nash's greatest work was the layout of Regent's Park and its link through Regent Street to the centre of London. This development was intended for the civil servants and officials who worked in and around Westminster. It was to be serviced by shops and a market fed with produce brought from the Midlands by the newly constructed Grand Union and Regent canals. At its heart was to be a park, now famous for its zoo, to be studded with villas, temples, a palace, barracks and a national valhalla. Fortunately for the landscape, little of this original plan was carried out. Surrounding the park are terraces and villas that when seen through the autumn leaves of Regent's Park, were described by the late John Summerson as 'dream palaces' to rival Wren's Greenwich.

Although not completed on such a lavish scale, Park Crescent (c. 1812) and Cumberland Terrace (c. 1825) have a sense of theatre about them. The grand sweep of cast iron Ionic columns forms a continuous portico to Park Crescent, and the long ranges of austere white stucco with Ionic pavilions and a huge ten-columned portico, linked to each other by miniature triumphal arches forming Cumberland Terrace is breathtaking. Only when one goes around to the back does one see that the gleaming stucco is a sham, and that they are made of brick.

Apart from the plan of Regent Street, little remains of Nash's original design. The curving Doric colonnade lit by gas was pulled down by the 1850s, and by the end of the century most of the buildings had been replaced by shops and offices. Carlton House Terrace in the Mall still survives however, to mark the southern end of Nash's dream. The basement below the terrace is flanked by cast-iron Doric pillars, while the main blocks are of palatial Corinthian. Something of the legacy of Nash's use of stucco lived on for much of the 19th century in the terraces of fashionable Brighton, Hastings, Southsea and Torquay, while his flair for multi-style villas, Gothic or Italianate, is echoed by similar buildings in Malvern, Leamington and Harrogate.

Perhaps Britain's most original architect was Sir John Soane (1753–1837), who is perhaps best described as a 'Romantic Classicist'. A Royal Academy medallist, he travelled extensively in Italy and gazed on the ancient Greek temples at Paestum. Appointed as architect to the Bank of England in 1788, he created a vast area of courtyards, colonnades and vaulted and domed chambers set behind a wall of Portland stone dressed with Corinthian pilasters, and framed at the corners with temple pavilions from Tivoli. His vaulted halls reduced structure and ornament to its simplest, and he virtually created a new grammar of ornament based on grooves and incised lines of Greek key. Soane seemed able to reduce Classical construction to the simplicity advocated by the French neo-Classical theorist, Abbé Laugier. Unfortunately, this ensemble of Piranesian proportion was swept away to be replaced by Sir Herbert Baker's buildings in the 1920s. Something of Soane's imaginative use of

London, Regent's Park. Chester Terrace, c. 1820.

arches, bare brick surfaces, chambers and overhead lighting does survive in Dulwich College Picture Gallery (c. 1814), the first public art gallery to be opened in Britain.

A feature of 19th-century social and intellectual life was the rise of the 'gentleman's club'. The Classical seemed an appropriate style for such buildings, and while Decimus Burton (1809–81) felt the Grecian style appropriate for the Atheneum Club, complete with a frieze based on the Elgin marbles, a few metres away in Pall Mall, Sir Charles Barry was building the Reform Club in the Italianate style, and basing it on the 16th-century Palazzo Farnese in Rome.

As Nash was dreaming up his palaces for Regent's Park and Barry his Italianate contributions to club society, so Britain was going through dramatic social change. The population was expanding rapidly and new centres of commerce and industry were springing up. Cast iron, used so effectively on the bridge across the Severn (c. 1779) at Coalbrookdale, was now utilized as the framework and weight-bearing structure of dockside warehouses and the cloth and woollen mills of the north of England. In London, Thomas Telford (1757–1834) and Philip Hardwick built St Katherine's Dock in the 1820s: the first enclosed dock warehouse system with floors of London clay brick cladding an iron cage, and resting at ground level on immense cast-iron columns. In Liverpool Jesse Hartley (1780–186)–who had trained as a bridge builder in Yorkshire and who had corresponded with Hardwick over the structure of the St Katherine's warehouses–designed a massive enclosed dock of about 3 hectares (7 acres). Opened by Prince Albert in 1845, the huge brick warehouses rise five storeys above a ground-floor colonnade of massive cast-iron Greek Doric columns, broken at intervals by wide elliptical arched bays.

Meanwhile, Britain's technological advance was enough to attract the German Romantic architect, Karl Friedrich Schinkel, to make a tour of Britain from Dover to the Menai Straits, from Liverpool to Leith, and taking in the warehouses of Manchester and the potteries of Stoke on the way.

Below: Coalbrookdale. The Iron Bridge cast by Abraham Darby III in 1779. A remarkable structure demonstrating curved cast iron struts bolted together and anchored into abutments to span a wide space without intermediate supports.

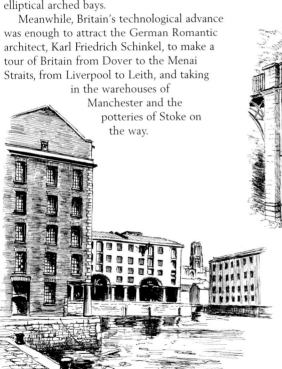

Left: Liverpool, Albert Dock, 1839–45. Brick warehouses over an iron frame.

17

Victorian Gothic and English Vernacular

The year 1836 marked another turning point in the Gothic movement. Sir Charles Barry (1795–1860) won the competition for a design for the new Houses of Parliament, to replace those destroyed by fire in 1834, and A W Pugin (1812–1852), who collaborated with Barry in the design though officially barred because he was a Roman Catholic, published his *Contrasts, or a Parallel between the Noble Edifices of the Fourteenth and Fifteenth Centuries and Similar Buildings of the Present Day* in 1836.

Pugin upheld the virtues of medieval architecture in contrast to the 'self-consciousness' of the prevalent Renaissance style. Although it was generally held that Gothic architecture had developed to a peak of perfection in the late 13th and early 14th centuries, from which it thereafter declined, Pugin on the other hand claimed that it had continued until the 'eleventh hour of the Dissolution' (as he put it). He even depicted what he believed to be the best examples of the gothic style—among them churches, town houses, town halls, gateways, and inns—in contrast to recognizably Classical buildings such as Nash's All Souls Church, Langham Place, John Soane's house in Lincoln Inn Fields and George Dances's frontage of the Guildhall in the City. In the revised edition of his book (1841) he illustrated what he saw as the original grandeur of a medieval town in contrast to that of the present, 'contaminated' by Classicism and industry.

As a Catholic convert Pugin believed the building of Catholic churches to be a religious necessity and saw the revival of Gothic as a moral crusade that he pursued with fanatical zeal. In 1841 he published *The True Principles of Pointed or Christian Architecture*, in which he proclaimed that the Gothic was the only style suitable for a Christian church, and that a successful architect must be a practising

Opposite: London, Houses of Parliament, c. 1840–60. Barry and Pugin's masterpiece provides a magnificent setting for the activities of national government.

Christian. In addition he regarded Gothic as the national style, and therefore advocated a revival of Gothic as interpreted in medieval England—although he had also been much influenced by German Gothic on his first visit to the country, in 1834. He also believed that it was not good enough merely to copy form or ornament, but that medieval structural principles had to be studied and revived (and for this reason he disliked Nash's approach, and the Regency style generally, for what he saw as a misuse of materials, such as stucco to imitate stone). For example, he believed that internal structural supports such as columns and vaulting should not be hidden or disguised by a false covering of painted plaster, or a wooden ceiling.

Sadly Pugin is not always credited with a hand in the design of the Houses of Parliament; while the basic plan, which had to incorporate the surviving medieval Westminster Hall on its west and a symmetrical river frontage on the east, is Barry's, the detail—including the Clock Tower and Victoria Tower—is Pugin's. The style is late 15th-century Perpendicular, to compliment the neighbouring Henry VII Chapel. Pugin attended to all the internal furnishings, even down to the ink wells. Indeed he was also a designer of stained glass, and some of his work even graces windows of medieval churches, for example the west window of 15th-century St John, Beverley. At Scarisbrick Hall, Lancashire (1838), Pugin attempted to create a great house to a medieval pattern and introduced a clock tower with a distinct affinity with that at Westminster.

Although Catholic Emancipation had been granted in 1829, the re-establishment of the Catholic hierarchy did not come until 1851, and Pugin could not rely solely on Catholic patrons, although two, Charles Scarisbrick and the 16th Earl of Shrewsbury, were Catholic. For the latter he built St Giles, Cheadle, Staffordshire (1841–46), a superb expression of Pugin's veneration of 14th century mid-pointed or Decorated style, with a soaring spire sprouting elaborate pinnacles at each corner, adding to the effect of height. The plan has a nave and chancel with flanking aisles, while the highly coloured interior has all the trappings of the medieval Church as Pugin saw it—a screen with holy rood above; a doom painting over the chancel arch; piscina and sedilia in the chancel; nave piers painted with strident chevron patterns; and a Lady Chapel laid with Wedgwood tiles and adorned with brass screens, candelabra and candlesticks. At St Mary's, Derby (1838), he produced a Perpendicular nave, with a clerestory, but with a short eastern apsidal chancel. At St Chad's, Birmingham (1838), he made his last essay, strongly influenced by German Gothic. Another Catholic commission was for St George's, Southwark (c. 1840). It was to have had a western spire above the tower, like Cheadle, but this was never built. Built of brick, perhaps reflecting the limited funds available from Catholic patrons that also curbed Pugin's ambitions for the building, the austere, somewhat 13th-century interior is light and lofty, with a clerestory above the nave arcade.

Although he had even proposed a church for Manchester, with a frontage over 1 metre (4 feet) wider than that of York Minster, Pugin had to be content instead with a number of two-cell plans without aisles, capped with simple bell-cotes and pierced with simple lancets. Fortunately, the impetus given by the foundation of the Cambridge Camden Society in 1839, with its added emphasis on Anglican liturgical requirements, gave Pugin the commissions he needed: in effect this convert to Rome became an ardent disciple of the image, at least, of the Victorian Anglican Church. In the early 1840s his preference for style hinged on the late 13th to early 14th century, with two-cell churches that terminated in a square chancel and were flanked with nave side aisles. The west front was generally adorned with a tower topped by a broach spire or, as at Cheadle, with a spire rising behind a parapet and adorned with pinnacles (Pugin probably had churches in Lincolnshire in mind): St John's, Kirkham, Staffordshire (1842) is a good example.

By the mid 1840s Pugin's outlook had broadened to experiment with other materials such as flint. At Salisbury, the city in which he had been received into the Catholic Church, he designed St Osmund's (1845) for the local Catholic community. Here the west front is flanked on the south by a square bell-tower capped by a low pyramid. His greatest work in flint however was on the cliffs above Ramsgate where he had decided to spend his last years: St

Augustine's (1844) in the '14th-century style', is a mixture of flint and horizontal bands of stone, based on a study of Kentish churches. In plan it has a nave and chancel divided by a tower, which was to have been topped with a spire. To the south is an equally wide aisle and to the east the Lady Chapel. He even has a small cloister on the north, in the Perpendicular style. The interior reflects Pugin's move towards austerity in his last years, although it is decorated with fine tiling and ironwork. Having built his house 'The Grange' adjacent to the church, he intended to spend his remaining years there, watching the ships pass by in the Channel beyond the cliff's edge. Unfortunately his health rapidly declined, and he died exhausted and insane in 1852. He is buried with his four wives in the Pugin Chapel, which projects as a south transept.

One of Pugin's ardent disciples was George Gilbert Scott (1811–78), who said that 'Pugin's articles excited me almost to Fury'. Scott is said to have designed and restored over 400 churches and 39 cathedrals. Like Pugin, he favoured the 14th-century Decorated style, so much so that when commissioned to restore the burnt-out shell of the medieval Perpendicular style Doncaster parish church he insisted on rebuilding it in the Decorated style. Perhaps his most famous building is the Midland Grand Hotel, St Pancras Station (c. 1868–76), essentially a revision of his design for the Foreign Office competition, in which he had only reached third place, largely because the Liberal prime minister, Lord Palmerston, associated the Gothic with High Church Toryism. Of red brick with stone for the hundreds of windows, including the dormers in the steep pitched roofs, the Midland Hotel has a certain north German or Baltic feel about it. From some angles the roof silhouette is one of the most romantically picturesque in London, even if the smoke has now gone. Behind the hotel, a magnificent cast iron roof by the engineer W H Barlow covers the platforms of the restored station.

At the same time as Scott's Midland Grand Hotel was capturing the skyline on London's Caledonian Road, Scott's magnificent new building for the University of Glasgow, founded in 1451, was rising on Gilmore Hill above the Kelvin valley. He was given the commission as

a mark of distinction, rather than it being offered to local architects (including the Classicist, Alexander Thomson). Scott's choice of Gothic, perhaps appropriate in view of the university's antiquity, provoked suspicion of Anglo-Catholic undertones. The result, with its 91-metre (300-foot) tower and open-tracery spire is truly grand, indeed grander than any 19th century addition to Oxbridge. With a facade over 198 metres (650 feet) wide it encloses two quadrangles divided by a large hall. The detail is a deft mixture of 14th-century Gothic laced with a dash of Scottish baronial turrets and stepped gables. To retain the university's academic pedigree, Pearce Lodge and the Lion and Unicorn Staircase, part of the 'Old College', were moved stone by stone to the new site.

   Hardly less impressive, though smaller, is Scott's new chapel for St. John's College, Cambridge (1866–69). It dominates the front court with its T-shaped plan and its crossing tower based on Pershore Abbey. The style is 13th-century French, with a long apsidal choir. For

London: St Pancras Station, Midland Hotel, c. 1868. A fitting entry to London for passengers in the railway age.

Above: Oxford: Exeter College Chapel, c. 1857.

Above right: London: All Saint's Margaret Street, 1850–59.

Exeter College, Oxford he also designed a new chapel, but on a much smaller scale, although its steep-pitched roof and fleche (slender spire) towers over the surrounding buildings of what was then the most populous college in Oxford, and quite obviously owes much to the early 13th-century Sainte Chapelle in Paris.

Among the other leading revivalists was William Butterfield (1814–1900), who exploited the multicoloured qualities of brick and stone, so-called 'constructional polychromy'. He also came under the influence of the Cambridge Camden Society and its president Alexander J Beresford-Hope, and through him was commissioned to restore St Augustine's Abbey, Canterbury, as a college. By later standards this is reasonably conventional, and the rebuilt Abbot's Guest Hall, to be used as the library, was modelled on the Hall of Mayfield Manor, Sussex.

Butterfield's All Saints', Margaret Street, Westminster, (1849–59) was built as the model church of the Ecclesiological Society (as the Cambridge Camden Society had now become). On a restricted site it incorporates accommodation for the clergy on either side of a courtyard. The interior has a blaze of colour across every wall surface, and marble shafts gleam—as do the wrought-iron screen and floor tiles. Decorated the church may be, but its simple forms and window tracery recall the 13th rather than he 14th century.

Although a disciple of Pugin, Butterfield was not always prepared to be tied to the former's rules of taste or design; some regarded Butterfield's polychromatic surfaces as distasteful. In academic buildings he introduced a mixture of red brick and creamish stone in horizontal bands and chequer and diamond patterns. His masterpieces in this vein are Keble College, Oxford (c. 1870) and Rugby School Chapel. At Keble, founded initially for students of limited means to train for the Anglican ministry, he broke with Oxford tradition by designing ranges in bands of red brick interspersed with black-brick chequer-work, creating a Tudor flavour round the large quadrangle. These ranges broke with then Oxbridge convention, having its rooms arranged along corridors rather than on individual staircases. The chapel, raised on an undercroft, dazzles the

Oxford: Keble College Chapel, c. 1870. The finest example of Butterfield's polychromatic surfaces.

London: the Law Courts in the Strand, 1866–81. Here G E Street adapts the features of a French 13th-century cathedral for a major public building.

eye with its chequer-work pattern of white brick set amid red. Essentially rectangular in plan, it is broken by a short transept on its south side facing into the quadrangle. The windows are 13th-century geometrical in bays divided by boldly projecting buttresses that sprout stone pinnacles rising against the steep-pitched roof. Inside it is richly coloured beneath a polychrome stone vaulting. The windows are set above a band of mosaic panels depicting scenes from the Old Testament. The altar stands on marble steps in front of an alabaster reredos. Again Butterfield broke Oxford convention by placing the seating in rows facing forward to the sanctuary like a parish church.

City of London: a surviving Victorian 'Venetian Gothic' office block.

George Edmund Street (1824–81), who trained in Scott's office, was a prolific architect and as an active member of the Ecclesiological Society was responsible for some outstanding churches. His St James the Less, Pimlico, London (1860), is an excellent example in which he assimilated continental Gothic elements. He was also responsible for some outstanding domestic commissions, and the latter part of his life was taken up with building the Law Courts (1866–81) in the Strand. Here he was strongly drawn to the French 13th-century style with lancets, blind arcading and turrets. The stone-vaulted great hall is a masterpiece.

Another revivalist drawn to the French 13th-century Gothic was John Pearson (1817–97). His earlier works included picturesque small castles and manors such as Treberfydd, Breconshire (1848), but his outstanding work is Truro Cathedral, begun in 1880. It looms over the small city in its golden-grey granite. Cruciform in plan, it has a distinct flavour of 13th-century Chartres. Only the introduction of a bold crossing tower is untypical, since the French had largely

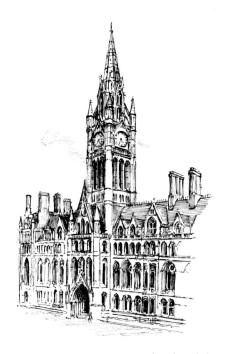

Above: Manchester Town Hall, c.1867. Perhaps the grandest of all the grand Victorian Gothic civic halls.

Above right: City of London. The Prudential Assurance Building in Holborn, c. 1879.

abandoned these in cathedrals by then.

The writer and critic John Ruskin was drawn further afield in his admiration of continental Gothic, and his *Stones of Venice* (1851–53) advocated its ornament as appropriate for English building. His words were immediately felt by Thomas Deane and Benjamin Woodward in their University Museum, Oxford (1855), and in the 1870s numerous Venetian Gothic office blocks and even warehouses sprouted throughout Britain's rapidly developing cities.

Alfred Waterhouse (1830–1905) was another outstanding and prolific exponent of the movement. More eclectic in taste, due to his extensive European travel, one of his first works was the now demolished Assize Courts, Manchester (1859), in which he used

Venetian Gothic. His most memorable building, indeed perhaps the most memorable of the whole Victorian era, is Manchester Town Hall (1867). It stands solid on an irregular site, its main facade dominated by a splendid tower, asserting Manchester's place as the second city of the empire. However, Waterhouse's vision extended back in time to the Romanesque buildings that he had seen, especially in Germany. His finest work in this style is the terracotta-banded Natural History Museum, in London's South Kensington (1873–81). The deeply recessed portal and tall flanking towers suggest a middle Rhineland cathedral. The capital carving on the jamb shafts of the entrance depicts a wide variety of animals and plants. More northern German is his striking red brick and tiled Prudential Assurance Building, in Holborn (1879).

By the late 1870s the fanatical enthusiasm for Gothic had begun to wane, and other periods and styles were creeping in. For example, Gothic was no longer seen as the only style suitable for academic buildings: near Egham, in Surrey, W H Crossland built the most remarkable university building of all, Royal Holloway College (1879–87), a vast 16th-century chateau in red brick and white stone, in the style of the Loire chateaux of François I. Even at Cambridge, that bastion of ecclesiology, Basil Chapney's Classical design for the Divinity School was chosen in preference to the Gothic.

Besides expansion of the two ancient English and four Scottish universities during the reign of Victoria it was the age of the public school. In many cases the old grammar schools were transforming into a new breed of institution, to sit alongside new schools founded, not by monarchs or archbishops, as previously, but by wealthy merchants, successful scholars and Anglican clergy. These new schools were built in Gothic: it was after all, the 'Christian style', according to Pugin. Some of the venerable schools were virtually rebuilt in the 19th century: both Rugby, founded 1567, and Tonbridge, founded in 1553. A few new schools, like Uppingham in its mellow ochre stone, could be mistaken for an Oxford college. Cheltenham College is in what may be termed 'public school Gothic' and with a chapel that looks like a miniature version of King's College Chapel, Cambridge. A similar chapel is to be

found at Radley, designed by Thomas Jackson (1835–1924)—who has the distinction of having designed more buildings in neighbouring Oxford than any other architect. Many schools were buried deep in the countryside and hidden from public gaze by trees and high walls. Not so Lancing, one of the so-called Woodard Schools founded by Nathaniel Woodard, curate of Shoreham, for the Christian education of the children of the middle class. Its chapel by R C Carpenter stands proudly on a hill overlooking the Adur valley, and from certain angles looks like the severed choir of a 13th-century French cathedral, with massive flying buttresses over the side aisles and apsidal east end. The school buildings are in the local flint, dressed with stone. At Birmingham the new buildings for King Edward's Grammar School were designed in the Tudor Perpendicular by Sir Charles Barry.

Not all schools chose Gothic, however. Wellington, founded in 1853 by public subscription to honour the hero of Waterloo, was in the William and Mary red-brick Classical style, by John Shaw junior (1803–70). Nevertheless, the first Master, Edward Benson, insisted on a chapel in the Gothic, so George Gilbert Scott was commissioned to design one. At Dulwich College, south London (1866–70), by Charles Barry junior (1823–1900), a form of Italianate Romanesque reappears, intermingled with Gothic (with the additional influence of the German Bogenstil—or round arch—fashion, and decorated with terracotta panels). At Marlborough College, Wiltshire, the early 18th-century Queen Anne style was used to harmonize with the town buildings

The Gothic was, like the Classical, deemed suitable for everything from villas to country railway stations, and other buildings such as the portals of railway tunnels—these perhaps ideal to aid the atmosphere of 'Gothic horror' as one entered the darkness in the dim oil-lit train carriages. The most celebrated portals are perhaps the northern portal of Bramhope, in Yorkshire, and the northern portal of Clayton, in Sussex. Villas sprouted up in Gothic style, behind appropriately styled gate-posts or lodges, while in the Scottish Highlands there was so-called 'baronial Gothic', in imitation of Balmoral Castle. However, if there must be one Gothic revivalist who beats all others in terms of his romantic approach to the Middle Ages, as if his creations were from the background to a Pre-Raphaelite painting or a manuscript of the Duc de Berry, it is William Burges (1827–81). He had the good fortune to come under the patronage of the Marquis of Bute, whose wealth was partly built on Welsh coal and Cardiff docks. Burges had studied French medieval castles, through the *Dictionnaire raisonné de l'architecture française du XIe au XVIe siècle* (*Dictionary of French Architecture from the 11th to the 16th Century*) by architect and theorist Viollet-le-Duc, published in several volumes between 1854 and 1868. This made him the ideal architect to turn the remains of the Norman fortification of Cardiff into a latter-day Carnaervon, and even more romantic at that. Its walls are tall, machicolated and sprouting numerous towers, some with turrets and spires. The interior is ablaze with marble, coloured floor tiles and wall paintings of Arthurian legend that in their use of complex symbolism demonstrate Burges's great scholarship.

Bristol: Welsh Back, granary for Messrs Wait and James, 1869–71. The finest surviving example of Bristol's so-called Byzantine Romanesque.

About eight miles north of Cardiff is yet another work by Burges, Castell Coch—it has an air of Camelot. Externally austere, inside it is such a riot of colour and exuberance that one is almost convinced that life was much better in the Middle Ages: Lady Bute's bedroom is crowned by a dome, and even her washstand is flanked by battlemented towers.

True disciples of ecclesiology viewed the principles of Gothic as a sacred text that would bring Christian strength to the new working-class suburbs of the fast-growing industrialized cities as their skyline was punctuated by spires and pinnacles, but industrialists were more imaginative in their patronage of styles for their buildings, and often favoured a touch of the exotic. Bristol, Leeds and Glasgow have some remarkable industrial buildings. At Bristol, Welsh Back is still dominated by the huge granary for Messrs Wait and James, built in 1871 in Byzantine Romanesque style. Its polychromatic brick surfaces are punched with deeply recessed arches containing ten floors. The openings within the arches are not glazed but acted like a ventilation sieve with the air circulating to protect the corn inside from mildew. The ground stage of pointed arches is surmounted by ogee-pointed drip stones, while those above have fan-patterned arch surrounds. The height is broken by four cornice levels, and the summit is crowned by a boldly projecting machicolated parapet sprouting swallow-tail battlements. The sight of the building's shimmering reflection in the waters below is worthy of the Grand Canal. Also in Bristol is the Stokecroft carriage and harness warehouse for John Berry and Sons, built in 1862, which with three tiers of polychromatic stone and slightly pointed arches beneath a boldly projecting cornice is reminiscent of a Florentine 13th-century palace.

If the Stokecroft warehouse might lack true conviction as a Florentine palazzo, due to the size of the arcading necessary to its total height and width, the eye might be totally deceived on first sighting the towers of the Tower Pin Works, from 1864, on the banks of the Leeds and Liverpool Canal. One tower is indeed a smaller version in brick of Giotto's Florentine campanile while another seems to have been borrowed from Italy's 'city of towers', San Gimignano. Leeds has other gems reflecting the diversity of Victorian industrial taste: Temple Mill (1838-40), forming the last part of the large flax spinning development set up by John Marshall was designed by Joseph Bonomi the Younger (1796–1878) in the Egyptian style. He had travelled in Egypt and based

Leeds: the stone–built office of the Leeds and Liverpool Canal Company, c. 1780, with the Italianate towers of the Tower Pin Works, based on the campanile of Florence Cathedral, c. 1864.

his building on the temple at Edfu. It is a remarkably original building constructed from large blocks of granite. The frontage to the office is adorned with six columns surmounted by papyrus-motif capitals supporting a lintel and coved cornice. The single-storey factory on the left of the office block has a huge working area beneath a flat roof supported by rows of cast iron columns and pierced by sixty-five conical rooflights. There was even a heating system introduced beneath the floor, with warm air forced through ducts and controlled with water to maintain strict temperature and humidity levels. The roof above was covered with turf so that sheep could graze in the heart of Leeds. This faux Egyptian style also made a brief appearance in the so-called Egyptian House at Penzance, 1840, and the Synagogue at Canterbury, 1843.

Leeds: Marshall's Mill, 1838–40. Surely one of the greatest surprises in any British city? The Egyptian detailing on the capitals and fluted entablature is exquisite.

A few hundred feet from the Classical splendour of Cuthbert Broderick's famous design for Leeds' Town Hall (1853) is another industrial gem, the St Paul's Warehouse, built in the Moorish style overlooking Park Square. It was designed by Thomas Ambler (1838–1920) for the clothing magnate John Barron and built in 1878–79. Internally it was constructed of cast iron with stone flagging for floors and stairs, to protect against the risk of fire. The exterior is divided into three stages of soft pinkish brick with cream stone cornices. The battlements are Moorish, and the corners are adorned with intricately decorated terracotta minarets. Glazed tiles and intricate terracotta moulding surround the main

Above: Leeds, St Paul's Warehouse, 1878–79. Another remarkable legacy of the city's industrial past.

Above centre: St Paul's Warehouse. One of the remarkable Moorish-style entrances in glazed tile and intricate terracotta moulding.

Above right: Birkenhead, Alfred Dock, hydraulic tower, 1863. A superb example of 'Merseyside Tuscan'.

entrance of a building that can, if the sky above is blue enough, transport one, in mind at least, to Seville or Cordoba. In Birkenhead, John Hartley's (1819–96) 'Merseyside Tuscan' hydraulic tower at Alfred Dock, 1863, is a wonderful fusion in miniature of the Palazzo Vecchio, Florence, and Siena Town Hall, it's air of antiquity today helped by exposure to a century and half of Merseyside smoke.

If Glasgow University dominates the west end of the city as a remarkable monument to the Gothic revival, then the east end and Glasgow Green is dominated by an equally remarkable building, the former Templeton's Carpet factory with perhaps the finest display of polychromatic brickwork in Britain. Designed by William Leiper (1839–1916) in 1889 its red and cream brickwork brings the flavour of Venice to Clydebank. The City Corporation had asked for a building based on the Doges Palace, and got it: rising through four floors, the ground floor has windows set into semi-circular arches with two stages above of Gothic twin and treble-light windows, while the intervening spiral colums add a Moorish flavour; the top floor is marked by a row of sexfoil roundels and lancets set beneath bands of chevron-patterned brickwork.; the parapet has swallow-tail battlements and the corners of the facade have polygonal towers topped by pinnacles supported on open Gothic arches. Fortunately the building has recently been converted to flats and so is saved from the fate of the Lambeth Pottery, London, with its huge chimney based on the Palazzo Vecchio in Florence, demolished in the 1970s.

In the professional middle-class suburbs, well away from the smoke, detached villas might feature pointed doorways, Gothic turrets and battlemented towers, and perhaps with a growing preference for Tudor, wide mullioned and transomed stone windows set into chequer-patterned red-brick walls. Rooms were high, and there were sufficient to provide for a parlour, library, nursery and accommodation for a servant. A basement might provide space for servants' quarters, a laundry, or a wine cellar. A wall and front lawn would set the house well back from the street, and behind the house the garden might extend for 30 metres (100 feet) or more. Some of the best examples are still to be found in North Oxford, sometimes described as the finest surviving upper-middle-class Victorian suburb. But they are also to be found in Bristol and Bolton, Leeds and Liverpool, and many other cities and large towns throughout Britain. This kind of urban ostentation was given increasing encouragement by the so-called 'Arts and Crafts Movement', which looked back to an idealized Middle Ages and had a reverence for the work of the medieval craftsman and

Glasgow: The former Templeton's Carpet Factory c. 1890 is perhaps the most remarkable display of polychromatic brickwork in Britain. It is scheduled for preservation and conversion into flats.

Above: Oxford, Norham Gardens. Victorian Gothic villas for the academic community of dons and their families, c. 1870.

building in local and traditional materials using traditional methods (an architectural preoccupation referred to as Vernacular style). There was also an interest in regional vernacular style, branching out beyond the Gothic and through the Tudor to the revival 'Queen Anne' style characteristic of much late Victorian architecture and design. But it was in south-east London's Bexleyheath rather than Oxford's Woodstock Road that the Art and Crafts Movement may be said to have been born, with Philip Webb's (1831–1915) Red House, for William Morris (1859-61). Here Morris wanted something 'very medieval in Spirit', and the result is a mixture of vernacular country rectory and farm or, as Morris's friend and colleague, the painter Dante Gabriel Rossetti described it, 'more a poem than a house'. Webb was particular in his use of local materials, so that buildings would fit in with their setting. The building's red brick, now with a patina of a century and a half, hints at the Gothic, with a pointed arch over the porch and windows set within pointed recessed bays but is certainly 'un-Gothic' in its row of circular windows that light a corridor within. The steep-pitched roofs are of blackish tile, crowned by bright red ridges. Dormer windows project, as in a cottage, and the roof line is broken by tall chimneys. At the junction of the L-shaped plan is a well, covered by a steep-pitched gable of bands of coloured tiling.

At Standen, Sussex, Philip Webb produced another remarkable essay in the Arts and Crafts vernacular for James Beale, a wealthy solicitor. Built between 1892–94, it perfectly encapsulates the spirit of Sussex vernacular as it sits on the hillside looking over the Weald. Like the Red House it is roughly L-shape in plan. It has everything: brick and stone, gables, pitched roofs, dormers, tile-hung surfaces, weatherboarding, 'Queen Anne' sash windows and tall chimney stacks of two-tone brickwork. Webb's one break with tradition is the square white tower, with a balcony that might be more at home on the Mediterranean.

Richard Norman Shaw (1831–1912) was equally inventive as Webb, as seen at Cragside, Northumberland where from 1870 he

Bexleyheath, Kent: the Red House by Philip Webb for his friend William Morris, 1859–61.

designed a magnificent 'castle' for the armaments manufacturer William Armstrong, and grand enough to entertain the Prince of Wales. Relatively close to Tyneside, yet in a rugged setting of pine woods and wild hills that feels remote, it rises like a Hollywood stage set and creates a perfect element of surprise since it only comes into view after a long curving, uphill drive. While its style ranged from Surrey half-timbered early Tudor, slightly inappropriate for its locality, to huge mullion-windowed Elizabethan and Jacobean gables, stone crenellation and tall stone chimney stacks, inside it was far from 16th-century in its comforts: it was lit by electric light and had central heating in the bath rooms. The service rooms were placed in a court

behind the main house so as to leave the main rooms of the house with unimpeded views. Norman Shaw had an inventive, theatrical flair and could adapt his talents to any setting while catching something of the architectural mood of the area. If London suburbia required something more formal than the whimsy of the English country cottage, he could rise to early 18th-century Queen Anne, as at the Bedford Park Estate, Turnham Green. But the Arts and Crafts vernacular was here to stay for a long time. Both Webb and Shaw had their successors, such as C A Voysey, Walter Crane, Edwin Lutyens and Herbert Ellis. Their work ranged from the wealthy west London suburbs to the shores of Windermere, and to the Cadbury estate at Bournville, Birmingham, built for industrial workers.

Meanwhile, back in the ever-expanding suburbs there were the miles and miles of 'two-up, two-down' working-class streets, lined with flat-fronted terraced houses that had neither a bath nor an indoor toilet. Architecture had to be basic and functional, and the only visual break would come at the end of a street with a corner shop, or perhaps a public house that might offer a little decorative—and social—relief. All this was remote from the visions of Pugin and Ruskin, the colourful ritualistic world of the ecclesiologists or those seeking to recapture a rustic world of Tudor gables and tile hung villas.

18

From the Forth Bridge to the Festival of Britain: the First Half of the 20th Century

By the last decade of the 19th century architecture had moved into the realm of engineering, and a lively debate started as to the aesthetics of what some saw as the products of the machine age. In 1777–79 Abraham Darby had spanned the Severn with his magnificent cast iron arched bridge, seen by many as having an 'acquired beauty'. However, similar magnificence on a far grander scale was first seen in the Forth Bridge, built between 1883 and 1890.

Designed by Sir John Fowler (1817–1898) and Sir Benjamin Baker (1840–1907), the Forth Bridge consists of three huge cantilevered towers linked by side spans to each other and to approach viaducts on each side of the Forth—at its narrowest point, but too deep to be bridged by a conventional viaduct. In any case the North British Railway Company could not risk another Tay Bridge disaster, when in 1879 cast iron columns collapsed and the central section was blown down, killing many. The Forth Bridge was built of steel which, unlike iron, would expand and contract under pressure rather than snap. Fowler and Baker applied the laws of physics to the structure: for instance, to allow for the vibration of passing trains, the linking sections of the central cantilever are laid against, but not fixed to, the outer cantilevers; this also applies to the track sections from the outer cantilevers to the approach viaducts. Allowance was also made for the fact that the east side would warm up in the morning sun and the west in the afternoon, so producing continuous expansion and contraction of the girders and tubular steel towers. Since its opening in 1890 the Forth Bridge has earned a place in the affection of the British nation even if it does keep open the debate as to whether it is architecture or engineering, or both. It also needs continuous

Opposite: Queensferry, Midlothian. The Forth Bridge, 1883–90.

London: Abbey Pumping Mills c. 1862–68. The exterior is Gothic but the interior exploits cast-iron. It is rightly called the 'cathedral of the London sewage system'.

maintenance, giving rise to the colloquial term 'like painting the Forth Bridge' for a never-ending task.

Just four years later, in 1894, Tower Bridge designed by Sir Horace Jones (1819–1897), who had been architect to the Corporation of the City of London from 1864 to 1887, was opened across the Thames: two cast iron towers clad in an elaborate stone skin of Gothic detail. In the centre two huge bascules rise to allow the passage of ships. A master-stroke; it seemed the perfect entrance to the Capital of the Empire.

By the end of the century architecture had become a fully chartered profession. The Royal Institute of British Architects was founded in 1834. Although still taught at the Royal Academy, it was now joined by courses at Regent Street Polytechnic and a college at Liverpool, later incorporated into the university in about 1895. The system of architectural apprenticeship, or pupillage, continued, but a formal prescribed academic training increasingly became the norm for future designers. The profession was given a further label of distinction by the magazine the *Builder*, founded in 1842, and by the end-of-the-century *Architectural Review*.

The flourish of the Baroque revival style seemed to exude the right élan for Britain, as the country sailed into the ironclad era immediately preceding the First World War. A mixture of Wren and Vanbrugh, embellished with a flavour of Charles Garnier's (1825–1898) Paris Opera House, the Baroque was particularly applicable to the new theatres and music halls, which certainly did their best to capture a little of contemporary Paris and Vienna in their ornate interiors.

Of civic buildings, Cardiff City Hall and Law Courts by H Lanchester and Edwin Richards (built 1896–1906) attempted to celebrate Cardiff's rise as the most important coal-exporting port of the empire. Another work of theirs is Deptford Town Hall, London (1903–5), which although much smaller celebrates the borough's naval connection with statues of naval heroes set into canopied niches in a grand baroque frontage. Other notable London Baroque town halls include nearby Woolwich and Lambeth, the latter with a tower that looks distinctly similar to Wren and Borromini. There was also a vogue for domes at this time, most notably on the Wesleyan Central Hall, Westminster (1905–11). While the outer dome is of lead, the inner over the central hall is of reinforced concrete, developed in France by Auguste Perret. The dome on the Old Bailey, or Central Criminal Court (1900–06), echoes the architecture of Wren. At Stockport, Cheshire, the town hall is covered by a dome. On the south bank of the Thames, almost opposite Barry and Pugin's Gothic Houses of Parliament, County Hall (to become the headquarters of the London County Council) by Ralph Knott (1878–1929) arose between about 1905 and 1922 with a breathtaking central concavity of Bernini proportions. An additional ruggedness is given by the arched bays of rusticated stonework, a quality akin to Vanbrugh.

It was the lift (American elevator) developed by Elisha G Otis in New York in the 1850s that really transformed the size of buildings, not only in the United States with the steel-framed skyscrapers of New York and Chicago, but in the hotels, stores and office blocks of British cities. The large shop or department store was really a Parisian invention of the late 19th-century, with the Magasin au Bon Marché of 1876 and Le Printemps, c. 1880, while in England the Marshall and Snelgrove shop in Oxford Street, London was the earliest, dating from c. 1876. By 1900 department stores were rising fast: in London, Harrod's in Brompton Road in Baroque yellow terracotta tiles (c. 1897–1905) still exudes Edwardian opulence, while Selfridges in Oxford Street (1910) is in the High Renaissance style with giant ordered half pillars of white stone.

Hotels were built to cater for the increasing tourism encouraged by a developed railway system, although there were clear social divisions between those who stayed in cheap seaside lodgings and those who stayed at a resort, spa or city. For the rich the 'grand hotel' was born, and the Grand Hotel, Scarborough (1863–67) was one of the first, conveying a distinct flavour of the French Second Empire style of Napoleon III. The Grosvenor Hotel, London, adjacent to Grosvenor Place, is another major example in this style. By the early years of the 20th-century, ostentation tended to be reserved

London: Selfridges, c. 1910. The perfect classical department store, stone over a metal frame.

increasingly for interiors, and a formal Classicism prevailed in some of the major London hotels. Norman Shaw's Piccadilly Hotel (1905–08) has a ground colonnade filled by shops while, above, two pavilions are linked by a long free-standing Ionic colonnade. The Ritz Hotel, again in Piccadilly, by Charles Mew and Arthur Davis (built 1903–06), also has a ground floor arcade. Above, the windows are divided by vertical rusticated strips, and the main floors are divided from the attic stages and roof by an unbroken cornice.

Although Britain was not affected by the Art Nouveau Movement to the extent of the continent (for example the Barcelona of Gaudi or Brussels of Horta) there was one major British exponent of the style: Charles Rennie Mackintosh (1868–1928), whose greatest work is the Glasgow School of Art. Built of granite and set on a steep slope, it is angular and restrained in its use of curves; the main link with the continent is the curving ironwork and ornamental projections from the windows. For curve and flow and use of coloured tiles, the quintessential elements of the style, the entrance to the former Turkey Café in Leicester (1900–1), designed by Arthur Wakerley (1862–1931), is an excellent example.

The Victorian age had witnessed the transformation of Britain from a land of country to town dwellers. The population settled where industry developed, with all the resulting social consequences. Few thought of the health of the people growing up and living under a constant pall of smoke. Industrialist and benefactor Sir Titus Salt (1803–76) was an exception in the 1850s, with his model town of Saltaire, near Bradford. Here he built homes for his employees, a hospital, chapel, high school and a school of art. This was followed towards the end of the century by Lord Lever's (1851–1925) Port Sunlight near Liverpool. Here we find Tudor-style terraces inspired by Cheshire's half-timbered houses, fronted by lawns and tree-lined streets. At its heart stands an art gallery providing cultural refreshment and renewal for residents. The Quaker George Cadbury (1839–1922) set up a similar, but at first less ambitious, development at Bournville, Birmingham, in 1893 for employees of his chocolate manufactory. Besides rows of terraced houses with Tudor gables, there were a school complete with a bell-tower, continuation-education college, health centre, concert hall, shops and sports fields. By 1914, the advantages of a carefully planned living environment for workers was proven, with the mortality rate at Bourneville half that of the rest of Birmingham. At 1902 another Quaker, Joseph Rowntree (1836–1925), founded Elswick Model Village in a suburb of York for employees of his chocolate factory.

In the west of London the Bedford Park estate was created as a garden suburb for the 'middle class' (intended to be artists and intellectuals, rather than factory workers) by Jonathan Carr in 1875. Carr initially commissioned E W Goodwin to produce designs for the houses, but Norman Shaw was invited to contribute designs including one for a church and a public house. The architectural flavour is eclectic, encompassing Tudor; Jacobean with Flemish gables; Queen Anne in orange brick with pedimented dormers; Georgian with the occasional Palladian window; and finally mid-Victorian rectory style—with tile-hung gables, red brick walls inset with terracotta panels and porches filled with coloured glass that would look more at home in the Kentish Weald. The rooflines are broken with tall brick chimney stacks. Further elegance, and indeed a unique identity, was created by the introduction of balconies with white painted wooden balustrades. Front gardens were also set behind low red brick walls adorned with white painted railings. Bedford Park became a model for many housing developments elsewhere, although few attracted such attention. However, out of this was born the Garden City Association, in response to an influential proposal by urban planner Ebenezer Howard (1850–1928) in his *Garden Cities of Tomorrow* (1902).

Howard's ideas differed from those of Lever or Cadbury in that he believed the ideal town would be created around a number of industries rather than a specific industry or firm. Each town would be a fully contained unit, separated from a major city or conurbation by a protected belt of open country, but linked to it by a reliable system of rail communications. Towns would have educational facilities, to include both schools for children and a literary institute for adults, medical facilities (including an infirmary) and shops. Most important

for the health of the inhabitants, there would be a generous provision of parks. The first of these new towns, Letchworth, Hertfordshire, was begun in 1903, and in 1907 land was acquired near Golders Green, where over the next decade Hampstead Garden Suburb was laid out to the design of Sir Edwin Lutyens (1869–1944). The third garden suburb was Welwyn Garden City, in 1919. The style used was a vernacular country-cottage type with prominent gabled wings. This country vernacular is also to be found in the Well Hall Garden City (now Progress Estate), Eltham, built by government between 1915 and 1917 for the wartime workers at the Royal Arsenal, in nearby Woolwich; however, it lacked that most important facility, a public house.

After World War I further radical changes affected the growth of towns and the ordinary domestic house. The widespread employment of women and girls in the hitherto male-dominated professions and trades led to two or more wage earners in the family, which led to higher social aspirations. Now those who wanted to could leave the inner suburban terraced streets and live in the fresh air of the outer suburb; so the three or four bedroomed semi-detached house was born, often in Tudor style brick, and on a slightly less grand scale than

the middle-class 'Queen Anne' or 'neo-Georgian' mansions of Bedford Park and Hampstead Garden Suburb. In spite of mockery of the 'Tudoresque', by such critics and writers as Evelyn Waugh, the style spread quickly, as did the Southern Railway electric tracks to service estates that were now covering the fields of rural Sidcup, Petts Wood and Orpington. Rural Middlesex became the territory of the Metropolitan Railway to Harrow and Pinner: the 'Metroland' of John Betjeman. In north-west England the Mersey electric railway served the new estates on the Wirral and Southport. Villages became absorbed into towns, and towns built bypass roads to encourage the motorist to circumnavigate them. Notable examples are the Kingston bypass (c. 1930) and the Oxford northern bypass (c. 1938).

As regards country houses, Norman Shaw was one of the finest exponents of the art of building for those who desired a new seat in the style of the 17th or 18th century. His Smeaton Manor, Yorkshire,

Opposite: Worksop, interior sitting room c. 1900–20.

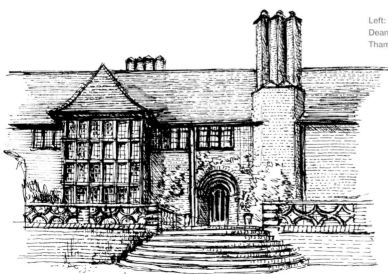

Left: Sonning, Berkshire. The Deanery, Lutyens essay in Thames valley Tudor, c. 1900.

Liverpool: Roman Catholic
Cathedral (unrealised project),
c. 1930.

for example (1892–94), has the feel of a Restoration house, while at Bryanston, in Dorset, he built a Queen Anne styled mansion (1890–93) for the Duke of Portland.

Sir Edwin Lutyens is usually seen as the last of Britain's traditional architects, able to merge the simply practical with a sense of the picturesque. He could design in the Surrey vernacular with steep-pitched brick gables and tall chimneys spreading round a cloistered court as at 'Orchards' near Guildford (1907), or Munstead Wood (1896), and was also a master of spatial design comparable to Robert Adam. Lutyens liked to exploit local materials, whether it be soft clunch stone as at Marsh Court, Hampshire (1901), in which he invokes the Elizabethan style; the Deanery, Sonning, Berkshire (1899), exploiting the warm brickwork of the Thames Valley, or granite at Castle Drogo, Devon (1910–30). At Heathcote, near Ilkley (1906), he uses Classical symmetry to reinforce his use of the Doric order on the ground floor, while at nearby Gledstone Hall he pays homage to Palladio. This very personal use of Classicism can be seen on a grand scale in his work at New Delhi, where he designed the Viceroy's House. Unfortunately, Lutyens's great plan for Liverpool Roman Catholic Cathedral got no further than the cavernous crypt. World War II intervened and there was insufficient money to build what would have rivalled Wren's St Paul's, with an even taller dome set over a massive body of pinkish brick interspersed with bands of granite. The west front was to be pierced by a huge central arch harking back to that on the Norman front of Lincoln Cathedral, but also invoking the power of a Classical triumphal arch.

World War I also marked the end of major country house building in Britain, partly due to size, cost of upkeep, and the drifting away from domestic employment of those who had been traditionally 'below stairs' for generations. The first two decades or so of the 20th century seem to continue the process of stylistic revivals, but from the late 1920s the International Modern Movement began to appear. This movement, with its concern for art as a means of social renewal and, ultimately, political change had a dramatic impact on art and design throughout Europe (and especially Germany with the work of the Bauhaus), and was further helped in the 1930s by the influx of architects and scholars seeking refuge from the rise of Communism and Nazism on the continent. In Britain its introduction was greeted with some suspicion by the establishment: at first to many it seemed more an intellectual endeavour than a move for mass architecture. To advance its ideas into more practical realization in Britain, the Modern Architecture Research Group (MARS) was founded in 1933. Founding members included Berthold Lubetkin (1901–1990), a Russian; Ove Arup (1895–1988), an Anglo-Dane, and Welles Coates (1895–1958), a Canadian. Lubetkin was to achieve fame with his Penguin Pool at Regent's Park Zoo (1934) with its intersecting spiral ramps of reinforced concrete. Lubetkin was also a founding member of Tecton, in 1932, a group of architects that pledged to further modernism, also known as International Style, in Britain.

The first building to show the characteristics of continental modernism—plain white surfaces, windows set in steel frames and a flat roof—had however been built a few years earlier in 1925: 'New Ways', Northampton, by the German architect Peter Behrens (1868–1940), for the model railway manufacturer J Bassett-Lowke. Behrens's influence here was his former pupil, Le Corbusier (1887–1965), whose Maison Citrohan project had been exhibited at the Paris Salon in 1922. Right angles and flat roofs, features of Cubism, now seem to predominate, and this white faced cube sat awkwardly between the tall gabled tile-clad houses of an earlier decade. In 1929 the first British-designed house in the International style suddenly appeared on a hill above Amersham, 'High and Over' by Bernard Ashmole (1894–1988) and Amyas Connell (1901–1980). Both its bare gleaming white walls, pierced with continuous window strips, and a wide balcony beneath a roof supported on stilts reduced its appearance to simple functionalism. At first, it was almost too much for the citizens of the 'Chiltern Hundreds'.

Northampton: New Ways, 1925.

The writings of Le Corbusier, first published in English in 1927, now claimed serious attention from some planners who felt that his suggestion, of replacing the centre of Paris with 18 immense skyscrapers, could possibly solve similar population problems in British cities. Providing their foundations were secure, the buildings could stand on thin pilotis (pillars) and rise hundreds of feet into the sky. The first block constructed on this principle in Britain was High Point I, in London's Highgate (1933–35), by Berthold Lubetkin: it has all the ingredients of the cubist vision in its clean lines, floors of steel-framed studio windows and projected balconies. Just across Hampstead Heath, fellow Mars group member Wells Coates designed the Lawn Road flats (1933), a slender white concrete block with three continuous balcony fronts fed by enclosed stairs and a lift (elevator) at one end. At 2 Willow Road, Hampstead, the Hungarian

Opposite: Highgate, London.
High Point, 1933–35.

Left: Hampstead, London.
2 Willow Road, 1939.

architect, Ernö Goldfinger built his own house (1939), which was a rectangular terrace block of three flats. Its utilization of the maximum space, with an integral garage on the ground floor was then novel; upstairs, the split-level rooms are lit by wall-to-wall studio windows.

While High Point I and its successor Highpoint II (1936–38) were rising in their all-white magnificence to accommodate the wealthy, elsewhere the London County Council was engaged in large-scale slum clearance. As early as 1864 this had been attempted by the Peabody Trust, a benevolent trust set up by George Peabody, an American philanthropist, to provide communal housing for the lower working class in London. Many of the estates were built in a square with an inner court so they were secure from the outside world. Some, built of yellow London stock brick, rose to four or more floors with outside connecting balconies. Today, examples survive as listed buildings in Islington, Westminster and Southwark. By the 1930s the LCC was mindful of new trends in mass housing, including the 'Siedlungen' projects in German cities such as Berlin, Frankfurt and Stuttgart, which tended to be relatively low and horizontal and set amid green spaces. In London, as in other cities, open space was at a premium, and so new estates were built in blocks of up to five or more storeys, set facing each other across courts that were wide enough to let the sun penetrate, even in the depths of winter. Many were built of red brick with external balconies on each floor linking enclosed stair wells, and in some cases lifts (elevators). A fine example is the Ebury Bridge Estate, Pimlico, begun in 1936: the blocks were constructed in various hues of red and mauve brick and have undergone recent renovation, retaining a community feeling absent from post-war high-rise developments. Elsewhere, good ideas were not always as successful in realization: at Quarry Hill, Leeds, the then largest estate in Britain was built in the late 1930s with steel-framed blocks clad in concrete and with rounded entrance facades bringing a hint of the Art Deco; even if designed as a conscious attempt to copy the Karl Marx Hof, a working-class estate in Vienna with huge arches connecting each court, and each flat (apartment) having a solid fuel range, the whole scheme was just too big. The vast surfaces of

Above: Eltham, south London. Eltham Palace, Courtauld wing, Art Deco entrance hall, 1933–36. The source of natural light is the concrete dome inset with circular glazed panels.

Opposite: Hampstead, London. 2 Willow Road, 1939, split level studio and sitting room.

concrete wore badly, exacerbated by the industrial atmosphere, and the estate was demolished in 1974.

Councils not only built high-rises but also the alternative, low-level estates encroaching on to the ever-shrinking countryside. This led to the creation of designated green-belts round large cities, as well as tension between those who occupied red brick 'semis' set behind a fence, and Council terrace occupants. The needs of the new suburban consumer class who now owned their own home and perhaps also had a small motor car had to be met with large stores and streets that became 'shopping districts'. Towns now advertised themselves as resorts for shopping, even if catering on a slightly lower level than London's Piccadilly or Brompton Road, and the railway companies obliged with cheap 'shoppers' excursion tickets to London and the major provinces. In London, the early 20th-century stores such as Selfridges in Oxford Street had favoured a Classical appearance, while Liberty's had opted for Tudor and half-timbered gables. A dramatic breath of modernism was introduced with William Crabtree's glass-clad facade for Peter Jones in Sloane Square, (1936–39). Its graceful facade echoes the elegant curve of the superstructure of contemporary Atlantic liners. Its six floors form a continuous sequence of rectangular panels along the two entrance facades and became a model for post-war department stores.

In the provinces, authorities tried to create a town's new image with a large store reflecting the latest architectural fashion, especially Art Deco with its sharp angular surfaces in light stone and roofing with pleated patterns of green or red tiling. Decoration was restricted to shallow horizontal and vertical bands and abstract curved reliefs with radiating lines, like a sun. An excellent example is the Granby Corner store in Leicester (1932).

If these new stores became the consumers banqueting table, the factory was the kitchen where the food was prepared. Except that now it was not only food but everything from razor blades, bakelite radios, gramophone records and vacuum cleaners to breakfast cereals and the popular hot drink, Ovaltine. The arterial roads, such as the Great West Road out of London (known unofficially as the 'Golden

Left: Highgate, London. Private flats of brick, c. 1935. The balconies of re-inforced concrete provide panoramic views. The windows are of steel frames painted white.

Below: Sloane Square, London. Peter Jones department store, c. 1936–39. A fine example of a façade of glass held within a cage of steel. The roof terrace resembles the deck of an ocean liner.

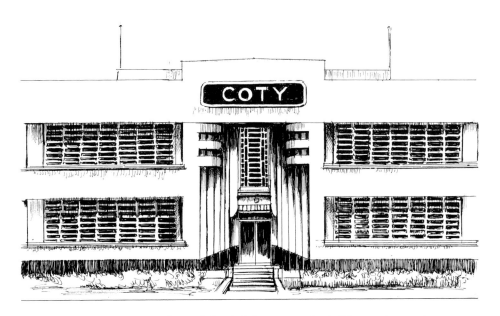

Heston, west London: Coty Factory, 1933, on the Great West Road. The entrance in gleaming white façade is a superb example of the staggered surfaces beloved of Art Deco designers.

Mile') and the slightly more northerly Western Avenue, became a showcase of new factories. The first to be completed in 1927 was for Smith's Potato Crisps and was followed rapidly by factories for Firestone Tyres, Curry's Cycles and Gillette Razor Blades. If any factory can make claims to being the 'cathedral of modernism' it is the Hoover factory, by Wallis, Gilbert and Partners, built in 1931 on Western Avenue. The building is a beautiful balance between simple vertical and horizontal lines. Staggered-surfaced white cement piers, curved at the base above courses of black tiles, rise through three stages of steel-framed windows to a simple lintel that is decorated at its summit with a shallow line of fluting. The entrance doors seem at first sight to be set back in a recess but this is an illusion created by U-shaped lines in the flanking wall. Above them is a canopy with an incised tassel pattern, and in the space between the canopy and lintel there is a ray-shaped motif. Sadly another industrial masterpiece by

Wallis and Gilbert, the Firestone Tyre and Rubber Company Factory from 1928, has been destroyed.

At Beeston, on the southern approach to Nottingham, is the Boots Pharmaceutical Factory by Sir Owen Williams (1931–32). Then one of the largest reinforced concrete buildings in the world, it consists of an enormous rectangular hall whose length is broken on the south side with the projection of a series of glass-faced blocks, cantilevered over the loading bay on the ground floor. The interior is open from the production floor to the ceiling, pierced with thousands of glass roundels in the reinforced concrete. Surrounding the production floor are galleries, or floors, to which packages are lifted for storage by conveyor belts at the sides. Externally, each floor is clearly defined by a thin unbroken band of concrete in the glass screen. Each of the four blocks are angled at the corners which greatly softens the overall effect of the extreme length.

Perivale, west London: the former Hoover Factory on the Western Avenue, 1932, a cathedral of Art Deco.

Above: Beeston, Nottingham: Boots Pharmaceutical Factory, 1930–32.

Above right: Boots, interior with vast open-plan atrium. Production takes place on the ground floor with the upper floors used for storage. Packages are lifted by the conveyor belts at the sides. Light is admitted through thousands of glass panes set into concrete panels resting on steel trusses.

Opposite: London, Battersea Power Station, c. 1931–55: Giles Gilbert Scott's brick masterpiece sadly lying derelict and awaiting a new use.

If industrial architecture is not, for most people, as attractive as a stately mansion, Giles Gilbert Scott (1880–1960), son of George Gilbert Scott (junior), proved it possible to design a masterpiece of elegance in industrial terms when he created his Battersea Power Station (1931), in London. It is essentially a huge turbine hall encased in a shell of pinkish-brown brick, with enormous square bastions at each corner, acting as supports for the four white brick chimneys. To emphasize the fluting on the chimneys the surface of these bastions is incised with deep fluted channels in the brickwork. If the interior was a magnificent cathedral dedicated to electric power then, fulfilling this ecclesiastical analogy it was decorated with tall fluted piers of glazed tile and the control room, entered through bronze doors, was clad in Italian marble. Also in London, Scott's masterly use of brick in an industrial building is again seen in his Bankside Power Station (1955–57), now home to the Tate Modern museum of modern art, with the wide facade and single square chimney at mid-point adorned with projected vertical strips of brickwork.

Due to the worsening political situation in Central Europe during the 1930s there was an increasing influx to Britain of emigree artists and architects, whose influence was to last well after many had left British shores for America. They included the German refugees Erich

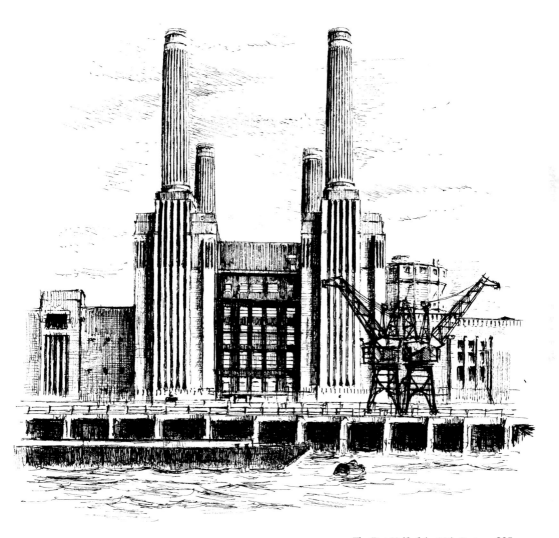

Mendelsohn (1887–1953) and Walter Gropius (1883–1969), leading figures of the Bauhaus school closed by the Nazis in 1933. Mendelsohn designed the De La Warr Pavilion at Bexhill (1935–7), in which he introduced a semi-circular glazed stair tower with similar features to those in his Schocken Department Store, Stuttgart, 1927. Gropius collaborated with Maxwell Fry (1899–1987) on the Impingham Village College near Cambridge (1935–7), which became the inspiration for much post-war school building. Unfortunately the style was largely limited to the southern counties, where several hospitals also came under the influence of the modernist International Movement. An excellent example is the Kent and Canterbury (c. 1935–7). Its emphasis on long corridors and wards with large steel-framed windows is far removed from the heaviness and gloom of a Victorian infirmary. In London the Finsbury Health Centre by Tecton (1935–8) created an informal environment of light and space that encouraged the local citizens to regard visits to a doctor and nurse as a normal part of modern life. It was even fronted by lawns and flower beds for additional informality.

Bexhill-on-Sea, Sussex: De La Warr Pavilion, 1935–37. Eric Mendelsohn brought the influence of the Bauhaus to bear in this wonderful building. The re-inforced concrete structure is reduced to the minimum to provide as much light to the interior as possible.

In a small way, the modernization of the railways and the expansion of the underground train system (or tube) into the London suburbs saw the use of modern materials and design. Some stations, such as Richmond, were rebuilt with platform roofing of concrete and glass. At Ramsgate, Kent, the station was rebuilt with a large and light booking hall covered by a barrel vaulted ceiling and windows with steel frames obviously inspired by antique Roman thermal windows. Concrete also featured in the roofing of London's underground station platforms such as those on the Piccadilly, Central and Northern Line extensions. Arnos Grove (1932) has a huge circular booking hall of brick lit by large steel-framed windows, part of a programme of modern station building on the London Underground under the inspired guidance of Sir Charles Holden (1875–1960). It is remarkably similar to the booking hall in Berlin's Feuerbachstrasse Station (1931) on the then newly-electrified suburban railway. While for many people the image of Arnos Grove is of the perfect 1930s underground station, a lesser known and very similar circular hall is found at Southfields Library, in a suburb

North London: Arnos Grove underground station, 1934. The booking hall is within a tall brick drum pierced with large steel-framed windows.

of Leicester, designed by Symington, Prince and Pike, and built in 1939.

Another outstanding Piccadilly Line station by Holden is Southgate, which incorporates a bus station and shopping centre. At Wood Green station Holden exploited a curving surface of bare brick above a broad band of windows. At night these stations would look like lighthouses piercing the suburban gloom. East Finchley (1939) brings the 'lighthouse effect' to platform level with the stair shafts from the booking hall enclosed in a circular screen of glass. Here Holden, and his associate H Bucknell, must have been inspired by Mendelsohn's modernist De La Warr Pavilion at Bexhill, in Sussex. At the other end of the Piccadilly line is Hounslow West, which has a polygonal booking hall clad in Portland stone with virtually wall-to-wall windows at attic level. The interior has a glazed tile frieze by Basil Ionedes, a noted theatrical designer.

No less striking is the headquarters for London Transport built above St James's Park Station in 1929–30. Designed by Holden and built on a triangular site it is composed of two intersecting blocks of nine floors in receding stages and is clad in Portland stone. At the 'crossing' is a squat tower, making it one of the highest office blocks in its day. The building exploits the beauty of the white stone pierced by uniform ranks of steel-framed windows. A relief to this austerity is provided by the bas-relief figure sculptures by such well known contemporary artists as Henry Moore, Jacob Epstein and Eric Gill.

As the 1930s drew to a close another war became inevitable, and with the development of aircraft as a strategic weapon serious damage or destruction of buildings through bombing seemed likely—as was amply demonstrated by the destruction of Guernica in 1937, during the Spanish Civil War. Unlike paintings, which can be removed from gallery walls, buildings cannot be moved. Where possible, ancient glass and small furnishings were removed from churches and treasures were removed from public buildings. Plans were drawn up for the compulsory requisition of country mansions for military occupation, or to take schools evacuated from large towns: Chatsworth and Castle Howard both took evacuees. Sand bags were placed against the walls of vital buildings, and at Canterbury Cathedral it was even considered expedient to cover the nave floor with earth to stop blast damage. Civilians not called up for military service were organised for fire watching, and this undoubtedly saved many buildings—including St Paul's Cathedral in London.

The bombing campaign against British civilian targets began in August 1940 and lasted until March 1945 with the explosion of the last V2 rocket. Damage was serious but not as bad as expected, though there were grievous losses to historic town centres and individual buildings. In the 1940–41 'blitz' the City of London lost many Wren churches and public buildings, including the Guildhall and those of the city livery companies. St Paul's was damaged with a bomb destroying the Victorian high altar and another seriously damaging the north transept, though this news was kept from the public for security reasons. In the provinces, the heart of the cities of Coventry and Bristol was burnt out, including Coventry's medieval cathedral. At Bristol a number of churches were destroyed as well as half-timbered buildings such as the four-storey Old Dutch House. Plymouth and Liverpool were devastated with the loss of many historical buildings. In 1942 the so-called Baedeker raids were launched against specific towns of historical interest: Bath, Canterbury, Exeter, Norwich and York. Much of the centre of Exeter was destroyed beyond recognition, although the cathedral received only superficial damage. At Canterbury, devastation was largely confined to the southern side of the city, and here again, the cathedral escaped with superficial damage. Bath lost a number of 18th-century buildings, including those on the south side of Queen Square. At Norwich and York the damage was more sporadic but some streets lost their historic character forever. Fortunately such architectural jewels as Oxford, Cambridge, Stratford-on-Avon, Warwick, Chichester, Chester, Lincoln, Durham and Edinburgh survived virtually unscathed. The question then confronting town planners and architects in 1945 was whether to restore to the original appearance or rebuild in the contemporary style. However, it was not until after 1951 and the Festival of Britain that an architectural revival truly began.

19

Towards Canary Wharf and Beyond

The economic strictures that followed World War II held up
architectural progress in Britain until the 1950s. The Festival of
Britain was really an exception, and allowed up and coming
architects, artists and designers to show their mettle after the drab
war years; moreover, it was billed as a 'tonic to the nation'. Conceived
in 1948 during a period of austerity and increased rationing it was
designed to take place in 1951, commemorating the 100th
anniversary of the Great Exhibition, held in Hyde Park in 1851. The
main site for the festival was partially derelict land on London's South
Bank, between Waterloo Bridge and the railway bridge from Charing
Cross. A secondary site was created in Battersea Park, with attractions
for children, and another in the East End was developed as a model
housing estate. Opened by King George VI in May 1951 the festival's
buildings exploited new materials, such as the aluminium featured in
the Dome of Discovery and the remarkably futuristic Skylon,
shooting 91 metres (300 feet) into the sky.

Unfortunately the incoming Conservative government under
Churchill saw the Festival of Britain as a vast socialist waste of money
and ordered its demolition as soon as it closed at the end of
September. The time was not yet ready for such adventures into the
realms of avant-garde design. But, like the Paris International
Exhibition of 1889, the festival left one permanent and well-known
building, the Festival Hall (now the Royal Festival Hall) by Robert
Matthew (1906–1975) and Sir Leslie Martin (1908–1999). The
exterior was remodelled in the 1960s, but the interior introduced a
magnificent spatial flow of galleries, landings and open-air restaurants
with linking stairways. The ceiling above is supported by slender steel
stanchions embedded in concrete. A recent major rebuilding and

Opposite: Canary Wharf,
London under construction,
2001

London: Royal Festival Hall, 1951.

renovation project has however entirely transformed the whole of the South Bank area.

Unfortunately there was much to be rebuilt or replaced, in London especially, as a result of war damage. Prefabricated single storey houses erected in several days on a concrete foundation had fulfilled the immediate need and were meant to be only temporary.

Many however remained until the 1960s, and the few survivors are now listed buildings. Extensive plans for mass housing inspired by Le Corbusier's Unite d'Habitation in Marseilles (1946–52) seemed the answer. One of the first was the Roehampton Estate (1955), which saw the LCC trying to bring the benefits of a green environment to the urban population. The blocks are not as large and nor did they have the generous circulation areas and communal spaces of the French model. At the same time, plans were afoot for the creation of satellite towns outside the large conurbations: Crawley, Harlow, Basildon, Kirby and Cumbernauld and, in the 1970s Milton Keynes, Runcorn, and Peterlee. In terms of road communications Britain finally caught up with Germany in 1958 with the opening of the first section of motorway, the Preston bypass, followed shortly after by the first section of the M1 between London and Birmingham. The motorways produced a new kind of architecture in service stations, restaurants and bridges. New airports were developed or expanded at Heathrow, Gatwick and Stansted, with huge terminal buildings spanned by roofs of reinforced steel, long walkways and concrete balconies.

A few years after the creation of the Festival Hall came the controversial rebuilding of Coventry Cathedral in a modern style that exploited the beauty of bare brick as well as modern stained glass. Designed by Sir Basil Spence (1907–1976), the walls are staggered with alternating bays of brick and windows from floor to ceiling. The glass is by John Piper and Patrick Reyntiens. Few can deny that the sun shining through the coloured glass in dappled patches across the Bethlehem font and floor is a memorable sight. In the 1960s Liverpool Roman Catholic Cathedral was finally finished over Lutyens's crypt though, designed by Frederick Gibberd (1908–1984),

Liverpool: Roman Catholic Cathedral, c. 1960–67, a return to the circular planned church.

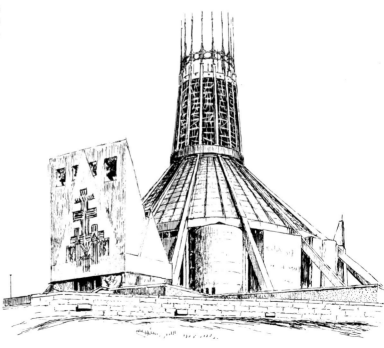

it is circular in plan and so bears no allegiance to Lutyens's intended design. The altar is set centrally beneath a huge glass lantern in keeping with then current liturgical thinking.

In the field of higher education there have been some impressive as well as controversial developments reflecting new ideas of higher education. The first post-war university was at Keele, in north Staffordshire, founded in 1948 round the nucleus of an 18th-century mansion. The next university to be founded was Sussex in 1960. It was sited at Falmer, a few miles from Brighton, in open country. Sir Basil Spence surrounded a main court with ranges of brick pierced by large windows, over arched galleries of concrete and linking bridges, thus integrating the buildings with the countryside. For Leicester, James Stirling (1926–) designed the tall glass-clad Engineering Building, with its frame of vertical bars and horizontal bands of red brick dividing each stage, its formality softened by the angled corners.

Owing to the dramatic expansion of university education in the 60s, campus universities were founded at Canterbury, Colchester, Lancaster, Norwich, Warwick, York and Stirling. These were prize commissions for the most distinguished architects, the emphasis being increasingly on light. Considerable care was also taken to integrate the buildings with the landscape, especially at Canterbury, Colchester and York. However, while individual blocks or colleges could introduce interesting shapes and facades, there were often too many bare concrete surfaces and windswept balconies, leading to a feeling of bleakness. Also, interiors sometimes became monotonous and confusing, with endless bare, brick-lined corridors.In many respects it was easier to introduce modern university buildings to a totally new site than to try to integrate them with existing buildings in the traditional Oxbridge style. However, there have been some successful additions, such as St John's, Oxford, which led the way in 1958–60 with the so-called Beehive Block in the North Quadrangle, by Michael Powers of Architects Co-Partnership, chosen in preference to a Tudor Gothic plan. The serrated structure of broad expanses of Portland stone encloses hexagonal study-bedrooms lit by wall-to-wall windows. The three staircase wells are lit from above by lanterns that rise above the roof and are surmounted by pyramids. Ten years later came the L-shaped Sir Thomas White Building by Philip Dowson , using a concrete frame enclosing rectangular boxes for the students' rooms. The ancient rubble stone college boundary wall was preserved by building the new block on stilts over it. At Cambridge, Christ's and St John's led the way, the latter with the Cripps Building (c.1970) blending happily with the setting of the Backs.

Colleges founded on new sites included Churchill in 1959, described by Pevsner as 'an outstanding concept, the best of the new', and New Hall, built in 1964 by Chamberlain, Powell and Bon. Here, for once, concrete is exploited in a very attractive manner; the sunken court fringed with watercourses is dominated by a tall, domed dining hall recalling a Byzantine church.

It was not only in the field of higher education that dramatic architectural progress was made. With the Education Act of 1944 proposing free primary and secondary education for all children between the ages of five and fifteen, and an expanded curriculum to meet a variety of academic needs, more schools were needed. These were far removed from the often forbidding 'school board' structures characteristic of the 1880s, flanked by lead-capped pyramid towers and set within a high-walled asphalt playground. A pioneering work, mentioned earlier, was in fact Impingham Village College, Cambridgeshire (1936), by Walter Gropius. Set amid green lawns and a large play area, it was a single storey building with classrooms entered from a long corridor and lit by wall-to-wall windows. Its basic steel frame with glass infill pointed the way to the post-war school building programme of pre-fabricated assembly. Peter and Alison Smithson's Hunstanton Secondary School, Norfolk (1949) is a fine example of a simple cube structure of exposed steel joists, duplicated to enclose a wall of rectangular glass panes. Even the electrical conduits and other services are left exposed. The result heralded what became known as 'New Brutalism'. Some may call the result characterless, others regard it as clean, rational style where, as the Smithsons's architectural hero Mies van de Rohe once said of Modernism, 'less is more'.

It is in the realm of post-war housing that we find the most controversy. By the late 1950s the prefab was almost a thing of the past as cities and town centres were to undergo comprehensive redevelopment that, in some cases, swept away what the bombing had left. The image of the back-to-backs of Manchester's Coronation Street was about to change. In their place, large areas were transformed into inhuman 'concrete jungles', such as Birmingham's Bullring. What was not designated for urban motorway was given over to high-rise flats (apartments) reaching ever-increasing heights as the decades passed. These were not luxury constructions like High Point but public housing projects funded by local councils, and often built of inferior materials in order to cut costs. In West Ham, east London, the collapse of Ronan Point due to a gas explosion in 1968, which killed several people and happened very shortly after its opening, marked the turning point in high-rise thinking and led to changes in building codes to prevent this kind of disaster occurring again. In addition, few 'council blocks' had any social infrastructure, such as shops; damp was endemic due to poor construction, and lifts (elevators) regularly broke down or were vandalized, leaving occupants trapped. Since the late 1970s there has been more concern with establishing a sense of community in public housing, through the development of low-rise buildings, and some of the older tower blocks have been demolished. Some of the better examples of ex-council housing have since become very desirable. There has, however, also been a recent resurgence in residential high-rise buildings, now for a 'high-end' market wanting luxury living.

In 1961 London witnessed the completion of the Shell Centre by Sir Howard Robertson (1888–1963)—not to be confused with the Art Deco Shell Mex House, dating from the 1930s—as the giant headquarters of Shell Petroleum, and the age of the skyscraper office block had begun. The Vickers Tower (now Millbank Tower), also completed in 1961, was 118 metres (387 feet) high, and the first structure to exceed the height of St Paul's, although many have surpassed it since. Unlike the Shell offices, which are simply a rectangular block of steel clad in stone, the Vickers Tower is largely

London: Centrepoint 1962–65. As a tower block it has considerable beauty but with its height it would be more at home dominating a new Spanish coastal resort rather than the locality of St Giles Circus, with its narrow streets and mixture of surviving 18th- and 19th-century buildings. In the foreground, St Giles-in-the-Fields by Henry Flitcroft, 1731–33, provides a striking contrast in scale.

glazed, and angled to reflect the sun. Completed in 1963, Centre Point by Richard Seifert (1910–2001) arose at the junction of Oxford Street and Charing Cross Road. Although provoking controversy at the time of its construction and for some years afterwards, it has a subtle curve and ripple effect created by the concrete divisions of each floor. Built around the same time, the nearby Post Office Tower (now the BT Tower), a slender cylinder of steel and glass with the primary purpose of supporting the microwave aerials which, at that

Above: London. The Post Office Tower c. 1964.

Left: Old Broad Street, London, former Nat West Tower, now Tower 42, c. 1970–80, the first building in Britain to rise above 200 metres. Its close frame of steel creates a marvellous soaring effect, enhanced by the curved plan of the building.

City of London: Lloyds
Insurance Building, c. 1978–86.

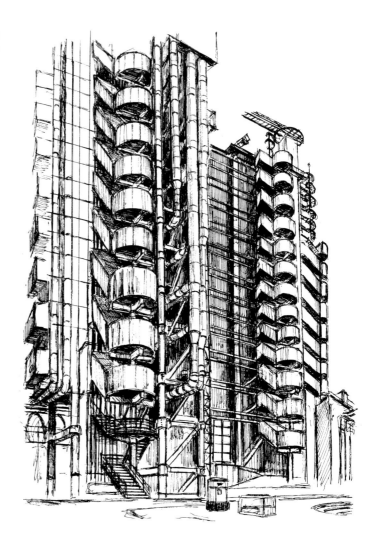

time, were used to carry telecommunications traffic, proved that functional technology could also be elegant.

In the City of London, Richard Rogers's (1933–) Lloyd's Building (1979–84) is the corporate headquarters for the Lloyds insurance company. A huge glass cavern with a semi-circular roof, the structure is unique in having its services, such as staircases, power conduits and water pipes, visible on the outside—this included glass lifts (elevators), which were unique at the time. Some believe that it is altogether a more successful work than Rogers' and Renzo Piano's earlier Pompidou Centre, Paris.

In terms of size, Canary Wharf in London's Docklands outstrips anything in the City of London. One Canada Square (Canary Wharf Tower), by Skidmore, Owings and Merrill, dominates this vast development, at 235 metres (771 feet), and was briefly the tallest office tower in Europe. Designed by Cesar Pelli (1926–) and completed in 1991, it rises almost sheer to its pyramid roof. To some it appeared as a re-incarnation of a Pelli tower seen in several American locations, including Manhattan.

By the late 1980s the terminal railway station had come to be seen as a piece of architecture that could be inconspicuously hidden from view—after all, with electricity having replaced steam traction there was no need for the huge cast iron roofs above the platforms, and the space could be used instead for offices. Certainly, after the spaciousness of the steam-age station, the enclosed replacements, such as that at Charing Cross (built 1987–90) by Terry Farrell and Co. can feel claustrophobic. However, from the outer ends of the platforms at Charing Cross one can see the imaginative incorporation of office floors between the tracks and the curving roof, while the station's front, when floodlit, seems rather like a Broadway stage backdrop. It is beautifully tied together with horizontal and diagonal rods of steel, and supported above the platforms on stout fluted Doric columns.

If the ghosts of the Victorian station builders are writhing at the transformation of Charing Cross and Liverpool Street, or Cannon Street and Euston, they would surely enjoy the work of Farrell's former colleague, Nicholas Grimshaw (1939–). His company built

Above: London, Charing Cross Station, 1987–90, one of a number of London railway termini to be covered over by office development. In this case the result is spectacular.

Above right: London, Waterloo, International Terminus for Eurostar, 1991–93.

the Waterloo International station (1991–93) with its continuous roof of glass, supported on a procession of steel arches, that gracefully curves to the plan of the platforms below. The feeling of lightness is perhaps in keeping with a new age of high speed travel.

Well into the early 21st century, perhaps we can look back at the last decades and consider which of the more recent buildings make a positive statement of the achievements and direction of British architecture. The new British Library building on London's Euston Road, designed by Colin St John Wilson (1922–), opened in 1998 after years of delay. It needed to be large and secure, but its broad brick surfaces, appropriately broken at intervals, and the sunken entrance piazza of patterned tiles are welcoming. Security is also paramount at the Ruskin Library in Lancaster (1998), yet the result is refreshing and appealing with its sparkling glazed concrete bands on shell-like walls. The curved surfaces and tall strips of glazing at each end provide a sense of welcome, absent in many university buildings.

In Edinburgh, the new Museum of Scotland, by Benson and Forsyth (1999) is also, of necessity, solid, but its colour and visual authority are impressive. Indeed, its very outward solidity masks the inner space and transparency created by overhead and high wall glazing. Its external wall surfaces have subtle patterns of coursing which exploit the natural colour and texture of the Clashach sandstone.

Above: Lancaster University.
The Ruskin Library, 1998.

Left: Edinburgh, Museum of
Scotland, 1999.

Also in Edinburgh, controversy surrounded the building of the Scottish Parliament almost from the day the proposal for a separate national assembly was announced, and increased as costs mounted and opening dates were postponed. The building's situation, at the bottom of the Royal Mile and opposite Holyrood Palace, was a sensitive one, and any structure created to represent the contemporary spirit, perhaps of architectural independence as well as political, was likely to sit badly alongside so many historic buildings. Designed by Enric Moralles (1955–2000), who died only a year after construction commenced, the building was inspired by the location below Arthur's Seat: Miralles stated that he wanted the building to be 'sitting in and growing out of the landscape'. After finally opening in 2004, the building has won a number of awards. From the air the true originality of the design is revealed, with the white roof complex reminiscent of a group of boats moored together, their bows abutting a quayside, and a complex of leaf-shaped stainless steel and glass roof-lights providing reflected 'ripples' of light. The walls are made from various materials, including Aberdeenshire granite, and are given a highly imaginative treatment with abstract patterned slabs of ochre- and purple-painted mortar incorporating the windows. The public entrance opposite Holyrood Palace is supported on cantilevered piers supporting a projected pergola of solid oak lattice poles. Oak poles also frame some of the windows, and Miralles interest in natural objects led him to reproduce poles in concrete along the boundary wall. Along the side of Canongate is a concrete wall by Sora Smithson, embedded with a representative collection of Scottish stone. The rear of the complex is perhaps the least successful aspect, with concrete security walls somewhat resembling the entrance to a prison.

Several recent glass-clad buildings exploit the attraction of this material. The Roy Castle Building (completed 1997), home of the University of Liverpool Cancer Research Centre, soars gracefully to a tower at one end. Roughly oval in plan, its curved lines recall the sides of a ship's hull closing to an aluminium prow. The curving roof recalls the deck of a ship as its weight is taken by the aluminium strips below. Fittingly, the National Glass Centre in Sunderland

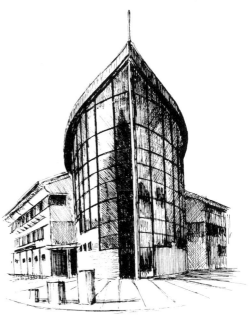

(1998), by Gollifer Associates, is a spectacular glass-covered building that exploits its subject at every opportunity within a reinforced cage of steel. Even the roof has become a transparent viewing platform through which visitors are invited to view the mysterious process of glass production. The building was the first major building to open in Britain that was funded by a Capital Arts Lottery award, a source of funding for many new buildings at the turn of the millennium.

New building has provided a means of regeneration, especially in former industrial areas such as Tyneside, Clydebank, east London, and Cardiff Bay. In Glasgow, both the Clyde Auditorium and the Glasgow Science Centre illustrate the determination of Glasgow to rejuvenate the derelict areas of Clydeside, once the greatest shipbuilding centre in the world. The Clyde Auditorium (1997), added to the Scottish Exhibition and Conference Centre, is a stunning building known

familiarly as 'the Armadillo'. Set on the site of the Queen's Dock in Finnieston it has eight overlapping plates of gleaming aluminium that curve across the roof to become the sides of the structure, shimmering in sunlight. Because of its shape, it is sometimes seen as Scotland's answer to the Sydney Opera House, although no comparison was intended. Nearby and equally memorable is the Glasgow Science Centre, built on the former Prince's Dock in Govan. Its three buildings are an exhibition hall and planetarium clad in gleaming titanium; a shiny pod like a huge rugby ball housing an Imax theatre; and a tower nearly 152 metres (500 feet) high with a 360-degree observation platform.

In London, the Millennium Dome (now officially renamed the O2 building, although few people call it this) on the East Greenwich peninsula may be seen as a building that opens outwards rather than in, exploiting tensioned steel wire holding a taut surface of fabric panels, and a visible 'exoskeleton' of yellow pylons. From a distance it almost seems to hover, as if a giant spaceship were landing on the tip of the peninsula. Fraught with controversy, ever since its completion in 1999 and its subsequent financial failure as an exhibition space, it has been a venue for a variety of entertainment and exhibition events since 2001. What must be one of the most ambitious and exciting

Cardiff: Wales Millennium Centre, 2000–04, by Jonathan Adams and Arup Acoustics.

projects of the 21st century so far is the regeneration of the port of Cardiff, which was once the greatest coal-exporting port in the world. With the decline in the Welsh coal industry the docks gradually closed during the 1970s and 80s, leaving thousands of acres of derelict land. Where possible historical buildings have been saved and restored, including the terracotta brick Pier Head Building (1896), and nearby timber-clad Norwegian sailors' chapel (1868). With perhaps the vision of Sydney Harbour, New South Wales in the minds of the City Corporation, the harbour was to become a centre of culture and home of the Welsh Assembly. Alos in the City a world-class sports stadium was erected to commemorate the Millennium.

At the entrance to the former oval Bute basin is the Wales Millennium Centre designed by Jonathan Adams, with Arup Acoustics providing the acoustic design. Opened in 2004 it is the home of Welsh Opera and a number of other arts bodies. It is dominated by a domical roof of stainless steel impregnated with copper oxide to give it the appearance of bronze. The shape of the roof is designed to withstand the harsh winds sweeping in from the sea. The steel-clad face above the entrance is inset with glazed letters of poetic lines in Welsh and English, formed by windows in the upstairs bar area, which looks spectacular at night reflected in neighbouring water. Large areas of wall are clad in layers of multi-coloured slate from North Wales. The

Cardiff: Welsh National Assembly, 2004–06, by Richard Rogers Partnership.

ground floor of the building is lit by panels of glass incorporating sketches of the Welsh mountains. The interior foyer, clad in different Welsh woods, is so spacious there is room for informal concerts and entertainment between cafés, bars and booking area. The main chamber is the Donald Gordon Theatre, one of the largest in Europe with space for an audience of 1,900 people. Outside, the Bute Dock has been filled in to provide a sunken area for al-fresco entertainments.

The Welsh National Assembly or Senned, designed by Richard Rogers Partnership, looks directly over the bay and is very different in feeling from its counterpart in Edinburgh. In Scotland surface materials are exploited, whereas here the emphasis is on transparency or 'open democracy'. It is basically a shell of glass reinforced by a frame of Welsh steel, and raised on a slate-clad podium. At its heart is the circular chamber or Siambr which again exploits Welsh wooden panels round a two-metre-wide circular glass abstract pattern design set into the oak floor and representing the 'Assembly at the heart of Wales'. Surrounding the Siambr are committee rooms and a public viewing gallery. The building was created with the idea of energy saving with a geothermal heat pump system. Air is drawn out of the building through the circular funnel leading to a vent above the Siambr. This is topped by a cowl which turns in the wind to draw the stale air out and keep it cool in summer. Perhaps most striking of all is the curving steel-stressed roof which seems to float over the structure and project out over the entrance steps and ramps, supported only by thin steel struts. Its underside is covered by a thin timber soffit incorporating shallow oval domes. Even the roof contributes to the energy saving policy behind the design with the collection of water for flushing the WCs.

The sight of the floodlit Welsh Assembly and Millennium Centre reflected in the harbour is a truly memorable experience. Equally spectacular, the design for the Evelina Children's Hospital, Southwark, London, could hardly seem further from the image of the 19th-century hospital. It was designed by Hopkins Architects (2005), who in 1999 won a Royal Institute of British Architects (RIBA) competition, and whose brief had been to produce something which did not feel like a hospital. Throughout the building the emphasis is on openness, with the wards set within a huge structure that is rather like a huge, transparent aircraft hangar. Light enters from all directions, including a huge atrium which incorporates the lift (elevator) shafts. Occasional entertainments for patients take place in this atrium, which also houses a café; the original plan was to have also included an avenue of lemon trees.

Although modern buildings do not necessarily have a long lifespan, especially in cities where there is often pressure to redevelop in favour of more economic structures, one building—created after considerable controversy—is probably set to last: in the heart of the City of London the Swiss Re insurance building, known more affectionately as 'the Gherkin', occupies the former site of the Baltic Exchange, which was severely damaged by a terrorist bomb in 1992. Designed by Norman Foster and Partners, and completed in 2004, the building is an egg-shaped block of 41 storeys, set within a structure of diagonal aluminium-clad steel braces that form a geodesic pattern—much influenced by the geodesic domes of the visionary American architect and designer, R Buckminster Fuller (1895–1983). Although from a distance it appears curved and gherkin-shaped, the only piece of curved glass in the building is the 2-metre (8-foot) lens-shaped cap at the summit, some 183 metres (600 feet) above the ground; the apparently curved glass surface is made up of thousands of triangular

panes, divided into diagonal tinted bands which twist round the body. The Gherkin is set within a public piazza with about one quarter of its circumference embedded in the ground. Internally each floor receives maximum daylight, and in this green-conscious era, the temperature is controlled and modified by solar-controlled panels, and natural ventilation reduces energy costs to half those of a conventional office block of the same size. Few can fail to be moved by the ever-changing play of sunlight and cloud on the building's surface by day and the magical effect created by the internal lighting at night—it was fitting that it should have won the RIBA Stirling Prize in 2004. This building and many other buildings of the past decade discussed here surely demonstrate that British architecture is alive and vibrant, interestingly both fraught with controversy and enriched by competing styles.

Above left: Southwark, London. Evelina Children's Hospital, 2005, by Hopkins Architects. If only all modern hospitals could be as exciting as this; it is designed to make a stay seem like going from one home to another.

Above: Bishopsgate, London. The Swiss Re Insurance Building, 2002–04, by Norman Foster and Partners. Although a newcomer to the city skyline, it has already taken its place as one of its most memorable icons.

Index

Further Reading

For specialist text but generous and high-quality illustrations, the volumes of the Royal Commission on Historic Monuments published by HMSO are outstanding. The earliest ones published in the 1920s and 1930s survey buildings up to 1715, but recent volumes include the 19th century. The volumes may be consulted in good reference libraries.

The volumes of the Buildings of England series are admirable and indispensable for the study of the architectural heritage of a specific county. Started by the late Nikolaus Pevsner in the 1950s, most have been substantially revised. Similar volumes have been published on Wales, Edinburgh and Glasgow, ands Ireland.

Picture credits

THE NATIONAL TRUST

Working to save and protect our coast, countryside, historic buildings and gardens for ever, for everyone.

Established in 1895, the Trust protects an estate of more than 248,000 hectares of land, some 20,000 vernacular buildings (including almost 200 houses of historical interest), over 200 gardens and landscape parks, and over 700 miles of coastline.

The National Trust aims to sustain local traditions and provide education, enjoyment and a warm welcome to an ever-widening community. Whether you are a member of the Trust, or not, you can contribute directly to the funding of vital conservation work. Please help the National Trust by becoming one of its much valued supporters. There are many ways to support the National Trust, from volunteering and visiting to becoming a member or remembering the Trust in your will.

For more information, please visit www.nationaltrust.org.uk or phone: 0870 458 4000